LANGUAGE AND
PHILOSOPHICAL PROBLEMS

LANGUAGE AND PHILOSOPHICAL PROBLEMS

Sören Stenlund

Routledge
Taylor & Francis Group

LONDON AND NEW YORK

First published 1990
by Routledge
2 Park Square, Milton Park, Abingdon, Oxfordshire OX14 4RN

Transferred to Digital Printing 2005

Simultaneously published in the USA and Canada
by Routledge
711 Third Avenue, New York, NY 10017

Routledge is an imprint of the Taylor & Francis Group, an informa business

First issued in paperback 2013

© 1990 Sören Stenlund

Phototypeset in 10/12pt Baskerville by
Input Typesetting Ltd, London

British Library Cataloguing in Publication Data
Stenlund, Sören
Language and philosophical problems.
1. Language
I. Title
400

Library of Congress Cataloging in Publication Data
Stenlund, Sören.
Language and philosophical problems / Sören Stenlund.
p.   cm.
Includes bibliographical references.
1. Languages Philosophy. I. Title.
P106.S776 1990
121'.68–dc20   90–34968

ISBN 978-0-415-04221-5 (hbk)
ISBN 978-0-415-86204-2 (pbk)

CONTENTS

CONTENTS

PREFACE

This book consists of three parts. Each part is not a chapter in a systematic exposition, but is rather an essay which can be read independently. The three parts treat of common problems in different guises however, and in that way they complement one another. A theme common to all three is our tendency to be misled by certain prevalent views and preconceptions about language. Another aspect shared by the essays is that their way of dealing with the respective issues they treat is the same.

What I am presenting in this book is not only the results of philosophical investigations but also a way of thinking in approaching and resolving conceptual and philosophical problems, in particular problems that arise through the transgression of the limits of the use of various technical notions and methods. As is shown by many examples throughout the book, it turns out that more problems are of this kind than we are at first inclined to expect.

This common source of several, *prima facie* different, kinds of problems is concealed by some of the traditional ways in which philosophical problems have been classified, and by the received ways of subdividing the subject matter of philosophy. In order to show this, a good number of issues from different areas of philosophy have been treated, including issues from the philosophy of language, mind, logic, and mathematics, even though this has meant that some of them could only be discussed briefly.

I have benefited from many sources in the work which has resulted in the thoughts presented here, not least from the writings of the philosophers whose ideas I subject to criticism. But my one most important source of inspiration has been the work of Ludwig Wittgenstein. It is perhaps correct to say that most of what I have written consists of applications or elaborations of thoughts that can

vii

be found, in one form or another, in Wittgenstein. But I am making no exegetical claims. The question of whether, and to what extent, my results find support in Wittgenstein's work is not important for what I have to say in this book. What is important are the problems discussed and the ways suggested for resolving them.

Earlier drafts of this work were read by Pär Segerdahl, Peder Thalén, and Sven Öhman, all of whom offered valuable comments. The English has been considerably improved by the efforts of Craig Dilworth and John Swedenmark. I am especially indebted to Stuart Shanker for encouraging me to write the book and for making valuable comments on parts of the manuscript. Work on the book was financially supported by the Swedish Council for Research in the Humanities and Social Sciences.

1

LANGUAGE, MIND, AND MACHINES

1 INTRODUCTION

There is a prevailing tendency in current philosophy and linguistic theory to forget the difference between a theoretical representation and what it represents, to conflate the rules that govern technical notions and methods in current theorizing about language with the rules of our language as they are manifest in our use of language in ordinary situations. The more established certain technical notions and methods tend to become, the more instinctive this tendency becomes and, as a consequence, questions of the correctness and of the limitations of the technical terms and methods are not raised. The limits of the applicability of the technical terms and methods are taken to be the limits of language. Notions of language connected with technical and formal methods are treated as fundamental.

This tendency is most problematic and seductive when the technical notion consists of a *technical use* of a familiar word or phrase (such as 'language', 'sentence', 'name', 'is true', 'refers to', 'interpretation', 'meaning', etc.) which already has an established non-technical use. Formal similarities between the technical and the non-technical uses – which may have inspired the new notion – may then make it appear as though the technical notion were not a construction, not a new concept, but something inherent in the old notion, something which has now 'been made explicit'. The rules defining the technical notion are erroneously treated as principles of the (hidden true) nature of the old notion. And this confusion is reinforced by the employment of the same familiar word in these two conceptually different forms of use.

This is how several problematic concepts and methods of

1

contemporary linguistic theory and philosophy have originated in mathematical logic and meta-mathematics. Crucial for this influence of formal logic on linguistic theory was the adoption of *the linguistic perspective* in meta-mathematics, i.e. the idea of conceiving certain mathematical calculi as formal *languages*. This point of view stimulated the introduction of linguistic terminology into meta-mathematics, for instance the use of the word 'language' in terms like 'meta-language' and 'object-language', and terms like 'expression', 'form', 'meaning', 'interpretation', 'translation', 'syntax', 'semantics', 'denote', 'use', 'mention', 'proposition', 'assertion', etc. These terms were, however, given a new, technical use in meta-mathematics, a use which was governed for the most part by the efforts of mathematical logic, and these efforts consisted essentially in the construction and study of various *mathematical* calculi, such as the predicate calculus, by means of *mathematical* methods, and employed the 'idealizations' characteristic of mathematical work.

As a result of having uncritically brought this technical use of traditional linguistic terminology back into the study of real languages, modern linguistic theory and philosophy of language is dominated by a view of language that one might call the *calculus conception*, i.e. the view of language in general as a calculus or formal system similar to the systems of formal logic. It is in the context of this view that the new technical uses of linguistic terms appear to be unproblematic and even justified when applied to ordinary languages.[1] The important and difficult thing to understand about this calculus conception is how it manifests itself as a fundamental conception in the use of familiar words from traditional linguistic prose and ordinary discourse, and not so much in the explicit use, which also occurs, of mathematical notation and techniques.

It is therefore also important to distinguish between the calculus conception as a paradigm for a technical, scientific methodology (e.g. for so-called model theory and formal semantics), and the same conception as a fundamental conception of language. As a scientific methodology, as a paradigm for constructing models of various linguistic phenomena, it has its limitations (as have all scientific methods), and its applications have to be justified by their success in solving scientific and technical problems. As such it has indeed been successful, not least within the development of computer science and the construction of techniques for 'natural language processing'. But this success in the application of these

2

scientific methods and principles does not justify taking them as general *normative* principles, and that is what is involved in the attitude towards the calculus conception as a *fundamental* conception. The rules determining the technical use of words like 'language', 'expression', 'sentence', 'proposition', 'reference', 'interpretation', etc., which were originally adapted to the study and the description of formal systems, are taken without investigation or justification to be appropriate for the description and study of language in general. In this way the scientific methods, notions, and techniques acquire the role of a 'philosophical methodology' with the claim to being the appropriate tool for answering philosophical questions on the nature and function of language through the construction of theories of meaning, theories of speech-acts, theories of language learning, and so on. But in this way the conceptual confusions are only increased. For instance, on the basis of the notion of a linguistic expression originating in meta-mathematics it becomes a major problem 'how purely physical sounds issuing from the mouth of a speaker can mean something, can express thoughts and intentions', and on the basis of the calculus picture of a language, it becomes something of a mystery, in need of theoretical explanation, how it is possible that people can understand sentences which they have never actually seen or heard before.

The difficulty with philosophical problems of this kind is to resist the temptation to treat them as scientific problems to be dealt with by theory construction and theoretical explanation, because even if such an approach may lead to good and useful technical results (as by-products), it will (for that very reason) conceal the conceptual confusion which is the cause of the *philosophical* problems. What will solve them is *conceptual clarification* of the basic notions and not additional constructions and new technical notions developed on the basis of the ones that are not sufficiently understood.

In this book it will be shown how various manifestations of this calculus conception are at the root of several conceptual and philosophical problems of current interest. It will be seen that many of these conceptual problems have roots crossing the current classification boundaries of a variety of philosophical problems. As a consequence, this study will be devoted to related problems in the philosophies of language, mathematics, and mind, and in the philosophical discussion of Artificial Intelligence.

2 THE NOTION OF NATURAL LANGUAGE

What then is involved, more specifically, in the calculus conception as a *fundamental* conception[2] of language?

1 It manifests itself in a characteristic use of the term 'natural language'. Natural languages are conceived as being 'in principle' formal languages. (This is explicit, for instance, in Davidson's and Montague's writings.)

2 Separation of form and content, expression and meaning. It is supposed to be possible to give (at least in principle) a specification of all the external features of the expressions of a language that are relevant to their meaning without referring to or presupposing the meaning or the use of the expressions in this specification. Considerations of meaning and use may be necessary to *finding* the specification, to isolating the relevant features of an expression, but once they are found the specification can be stated and understood 'in abstraction from content and use'. (I call this the *external* or *mechanical* notion of the form of an expression and its use, and I shall contrast it below with what I call the *logical form* of an expression and its use. This notion of logical form is not to be confused with the form of an expression as represented by means of the methods of *formal* logic, by means of formalization, which is an instance of external form.)

3 The relation between a language and its use in real-life situations is taken to be of the same kind as the relation between a calculus or theory (such as the probability calculus) and its application. Language is exhaustively defined *as language* through its syntactical and semantical rules. The pragmatic rules, the rules for the use of a language in real situations, are determined on the basis of its syntax and semantics, which are therefore supposed to be conceptually prior to and independent of the pragmatic rules.

This could be stated more generally as follows: the logical grammar of the expressions of a language are supposed to be *formally* specifiable (with the notion of 'form' as mechanical form), i.e. the conditions for the use of an expression are supposed to be specifiable uniformly within some systematic framework external to the situations in which the conditions obtain.

4 Molecularity. There is something which constitutes the 'basic semantical units' or the 'molecules' of language (usually it is the sentences of the language). Meaning is determined uniquely by the notion of a certain form of these molecules. (If e.g. the mol-

4

ecules of language are sentences there is supposed to exist a formally specifiable notion of sentencehood, or of the syntactical form of sentences, on the basis of which meaning is determined.)

5 Features depending on the more specific notion of a calculus as a *calculus of functions* (like the predicate calculus).

(i) Compositionality, or more generally: the notions of 'constituent', 'part/whole', 'simple/composite' are used with the functional notation of mathematics as a paradigm. The grammar of these notions is the grammar of the mathematical use of these expressions.

(ii) 'Determination' and 'dependence' as functional, i.e. the notion ' . . . is determined by . . .' used in this theorizing on language is conceptually of the kind that is expressed by a mathematical function (even when it is not explicitly expressed in mathematical notation).

(iii) Logical form is in general represented by means of functions. (This itself is a cause of much conceptual confusion. There is, for instance, no room for internal relationships and logical dependences in contrast to functional relationships. The notions of dependence on situations, context dependence, and so on are construed as functional dependences.)

(iv) The notion of a rule that is used is the mathematical or algebraic notion (as when it is said that by means of the syntactical rules infinitely many sentences can be generated).

(v) The notions of 'finite', 'infinite', 'sequence', 'string', etc. that are used in this theorizing on language are the ones that we normally employ in connection with mathematical calculi.

More generally, the kind of 'idealization' or 'abstraction from physical and practical circumstances' that is typical of mathematical work, is taken for granted as appropriate also in the study and the description of the nature of language, which means of course that such physical and practical circumstances are considered inessential to language as language. So *to the calculus conception as a fundamental conception there belong definite attitudes to and presuppositions about the essence of language in general.*

The term 'natural language' is used in opposition to the terms 'formal language' and 'artificial language', but the important difference is that natural languages are not *actually constructed* as artificial languages and they do not *actually appear* as formal languages. But they are considered and studied as though they were formal languages 'in principle'. Behind the complex and the seemingly chaotic surface of natural languages there are – according to this way of thinking – rules and principles that determine their constitution and functions; and it is assumed that this hidden structure can be presented as a theory similar to the syntactic and semantic theories of formal systems – with the difference that such a theory will be enormously more complicated, so complicated in fact that we can never hope actually to construct one for more than fragments of a natural language.

What this attitude amounts to *in practice*, in the practice of constructing theories of language (where it does mean something specific), is the following: there are no conceptual limitations to the applicability of the methods and concepts adopted in the description of formal systems to the study of languages in general. The limitations that exist concern only technical and empirical matters and differences in degree of complexity.

To use the term 'natural language' as it is employed in current philosophy of language is essentially to commit oneself to this dogma. And to say in this use that 'a natural language is not a calculus or formal system' tends to mean that natural languages do not present themselves as formal systems and they did not originate as artificial languages. To that everybody will of course agree. But the statement will not be understood as questioning the calculus conception as a fundamental conception, precisely because it *is* taken as fundamental.

As regards the current use of the term 'natural language' one could also say that it presupposes a general notion of language under which both natural and artificial languages fall. What then is the common idea of language here? It seems to me that this common idea, in its most general form, is the following: a language is determined (or given) by its vocabulary (its lexicon) and grammar, or – through the influence of meta-mathematics and logical semantics – by its syntax and semantics.

This, however, is an answer to the question: 'What is the general idea of language in traditional linguistic theory?', or 'What, according to traditional linguistic theory, would the common idea of giving a (complete) description of a language amount to?' The essential and common feature of languages in general is identified with the paradigm of traditional theorizing about language. In much current linguistic theory this takes the form of conceiving a language as 'being ultimately' a formal system.

6

3 CONCEPTUAL INVESTIGATION

If we disregard the use (or family of uses) of the word 'language' in traditional and current linguistic theory, and look at languages, not as empirical phenomena to be scientifically explained, but as they present themselves in life, in their use in human affairs in general (i.e. not only in the human activity of theorizing about language), we find features that are much more fundamental. We find, for instance, that language appears as various forms of linguistic communication between human beings. Language is connected to communication and this connection is not just an empirical or historical fact, it is a *conceptual* connection. The ideas of language and communication are inseparable in a sense which makes it misleading to say that the main purpose or the main function of language is communication between human beings – misleading because it invites the view of language in general as an invention, as something that was constructed (like a nomenclature, a technical terminology or a formal system) for a particular purpose; and it suggests that it would have been possible to have the idea of communication (of thoughts, ideas, information, messages, requests, moods, etc.) without having the idea of language. But our concept of communication extends as far as language.

In recent so-called pragmatics and speech-act theory the importance of the 'communicative aspect of language' is in a certain sense recognized, but only as an additional aspect, neglected in traditional linguistic theory. Its conceptual importance is not recognized. The theories of pragmatics attempt to supplement the view of language of traditional grammar and formal logic by accounting for linguistic phenomena where the traditional view deviates from actual linguistic practice. The various features of linguistic communication and of our use of language are considered as empirical phenomena to be explained theoretically and accounted for on the basis of a picture of a language as being fundamentally a complicated (formal) system. The use of linguistic expressions in communication is conceived as being the ('tacit') application of a system of specifiable rules and principles.[3]

In such a theoretical attitude linguistic practice is conceived as an object to be scientifically explained or an empirical phenomenon to be accounted for on the basis of a surveyable system of fundamental principles which acquire a normative (and sometimes metaphysical) role as regards language in general. In the conceptual

7

investigation, as conceived here, the focus of interest lies in language as it is given in our use of it in the various circumstances in human life, and description replaces theoretical explanation and theory construction. This rejection of the absolute, normative role of the principles of a theoretical methodology does not involve denying the existence of a conceptual and logical order of language, but it involves the rejection of the (preconceived) idea of a synoptic view of this logical structure. It therefore also involves the rejection of the idea of a complete formal specification of the logical structure of (parts of) a language.[4]

The logical structure of language of interest in this conceptual investigation exists only to the extent that it is *completely* manifest in linguistic practice, in the forms of use of linguistic expressions in human circumstances. This means that the kind of 'idealizations', simplifications, and generalizations characteristic of theory construction and theoretical explanation have no place in our description of the forms of language. If theoretical notions and techniques are employed, it is only for descriptive or comparative purposes, never for those of explanation.

The confusion of description and explanation is a source of the most common misunderstandings of the results of conceptual investigation. Through the predominance of the theoretical attitude, descriptions of conceptual relationships tend to be read as theoretical generalizations or as ideas and suggestions to be developed into precise theoretical principles. The facts of actual language use are not allowed to speak for themselves. They are conceived in the theoretical attitude either as evidence for, or as counter-examples to, some general thesis about language. The results of the conceptual investigation, as conceived here, can be understood only to the extent that the described features of language can be experienced or recalled as facts of our own linguistic practice, and not as instances of some theoretical thesis about language. The act of reflection, or rather of unprejudiced observation, required here is foreign to the theoretical attitude.

Characteristic of the theoretical attitude is the conception of philosophical investigation as being the most general and the most 'abstract' of intellectual investigations, or as being concerned with some of the most abstract aspects of reality. There is a sense in which it could be said, contrary to this, that philosophical investigation – as conceived here – is the most concrete study, a study of that which is nearest the ground.

8

The present conceptual investigation is not a new philosophical view, but is rather the ordinary non-philosophical 'view' of the facts of our use of language *employed* for philosophical purposes.

4 LANGUAGE AS A 'UNIVERSAL MEDIUM'

Jaakko Hintikka has introduced a notion of 'language as a universal medium', which he contrasts with the idea of 'language as a calculus'.[5] This contrast has some features in common with my contrast between the calculus conception as a fundamental way of viewing language as a whole, and as a particular scientific approach to the study of language, but there are also important differences. According to Hintikka, it is characteristic of the universalist view that 'you are a prisoner . . . of your language. You cannot step outside it, you cannot re-interpret it in large scale, and you cannot even express its semantics in the language itself.' In contrast, 'the possibility of varying in a large scale the interpretation of the language in question, be it natural or formal' is the characteristic feature of the view which Hintikka calls 'language as a calculus'.

Here Hintikka is taking feature (3) in my list of characteristic features of the calculus conception as *the* characteristic one. In order to 'vary the interpretation of a language in large scale' in the sense of model theory, i.e. to conceive the constituents of a language (its words and sentences) as arguments of a function yielding an interpretation, it is clear that one must presuppose that the features of a linguistic entity relevant to its meaning are formally specifiable. It must be made clear on what features the function that assigns interpretations depends. The dependence of content on form is conceived as an external (functional) dependence.

It could also be said that feature (3), the possibility of specifying within an external systematic framework (i.e. by some method for formalizing or paraphrasing) the features of an expression relevant to its meaning, is precisely what is involved here in being able to 'step outside' a language.

Hintikka's contrast is, it seems to me, misleading when he mentions Frege, Russell, the early Wittgenstein, and the early logical empiricists as belonging to the universalist tradition. What one would expect from this distinction as a *contrast* is that language, conceived as a universal medium, is not at the same time conceived as a calculus. But that is precisely what Frege, Russell, and the early Wittgenstein do. The idea of language – from a logical point of view – as one universal calculus is a much more accurate description of the views of these philosophers. The later Wittgenstein even states this explicitly as his main mistake in the *Tractatus*. So it seems to me that the notion of 'the calculus conception as fundamental' is more appropriate in characterizing these philosophers.

As I shall try to show in the present work, this view of language does not belong only to the past, but is still highly alive in modern theorizing about language. The main difference between Frege, Russell, and the early Wittgenstein and later philosophers in the same tradition, is that the former were much more concerned with and conscious about the philosophical and conceptual presuppositions of their own theorizing about language. This conceptual self-consciousness reached such a height in the *Tractatus* that Wittgenstein was subsequently forced to realize the incoherence of the calculus conception as the fundamental conception of language. It was seen to be a confusion of different kinds of problems – philosophical-conceptual problems and technical-scientific ones.

According to Hintikka, the universalist conception of language of Frege and others was a great hindrance to the development of model-theoretic semantics, and it was through the achievements of Hilbert, which led away from the universalist view and towards the calculus conception, that the way was prepared for the later development of model theory. It seems to me that this is correct; nevertheless, I would describe the situation differently. It was certainly true that the idea of the logic of language as a universal calculus (a universal *Begriffsschrift*) was a hindrance both to philosophy and to formal logic as a technical (mathematical) science, being, as it was, a confusion of *these two things*. Hilbert was more of a mathematician, more of a scientist, than he was a philosopher, and his achievment consisted to a great extent in extracting and making explicit the technical, scientific, and mathematical content of the universalist calculus conception (of Frege and Russell). Hilbert was clearly ignorant of many of the philosophical puzzles that deeply worried Frege.[6] This is evident in the published correspondence between the two. So it is beyond doubt that Hilbert's work was decisive for the development not only of model theory, but of mathematical logic in general (with the emphasis on 'mathematical'). This technical-scientific progress had its price, however – a price that philosophy had to pay. Many of the philosophical puzzles and problems that concerned Frege, Russell, and the early Wittgenstein, and which they presented as motivating their work, were forgotten or were misunderstood and given superficial interpretations. And on the basis of such interpretations it was erroneously claimed (and still is) that many of the philosophical problems had been solved and settled *by* the technical innovations. This attribution to the technical and scientific achievements in mathematical logic of that kind of philosophical significance was part of the (mistaken) endeavour to assimilate philosophical and technical-scientific aims. (Perhaps the recent applications of the results of mathematical logic in computer science and computer technology will make the philosophical claims unnecessary, at least for future generations.)

There is indeed an aspect of language that may be called 'language as a universal medium' and which is not a technical-scientific concern but which is essential to philosophy, to conceptual clarification, namely, the aspect in which the bounds of language constitute the demarcation between sense and nonsense. There is a sense in which you 'cannot step outside' language, and this idea is an example of something that was misunderstood and given a superficial interpretation in the 'universalist tradition' – very much due to the fact that the idea was confused with the universalist calculus view of language. Light can perhaps be thrown on this misunderstanding if we consider what is wrong with the prison metaphor. If a person is imprisoned, his freedom is restricted, he is prevented from doing various things for external reasons – things that he *could* do if he were released. But it is not in that external sense that language limits the possibility of communication or expressing sense, as though we could imagine some definite sense or content expressed in no symbolism at all. The mistake is due to the view of the general notion of language as *a* language (a calculus, a system of notation), which, being general, must be thought of as universal. We may say about someone that he is 'imprisoned' in a specific language (form of expression, jargon, etc.) for empirical or historical reasons, but certainly not for conceptual reasons or reasons of principle. There is nothing in principle which prevents people from expressing what *can* be expressed and from doing it in the best possible way. The freedom to transgress the limits of language is the freedom to express nonsense, i.e. nothing.

It is this misleading prison analogy which is behind various ideas about 'improving' language, making it better suited 'to fulfil its functions'.

A distinctive feature of the theoretical attitude towards language is to conceive of human language in general as a construction designed to fulfil certain functions, or rather, as a means to certain ends. This feature is sometimes present, it seems to me, even in theorizing about language in which the poetic and literary aspects are brought into prominence, as in modern hermeneutics and so-called 'post-structuralism', where a conception of language as literature sometimes replaces the calculus conception, and certain concepts and perspectives of literature theory are treated as fundamental.

As an example of how too narrow a conception of language results in philosophical confusions about communication, thinking, psychological notions, and so on, I shall consider some statements about language made by L.E.J. Brouwer, the founder of intuitionism in the philosophy of mathematics. In Brouwer's remarks on language[7] we find a critique of the 'shortcomings of language as a means of expressing and communicating the mental and spiritual life of man'. It is an idealistic counterpart to the neo-positivistic critique of ordinary language as an imperfect means for expressing truth about the world in which we live. In both cases the criticism is presented as a motive and a reason for *reforming* language, for 'improving' it, for making it more effective in fulfilling its function. Not, however, in order to solve any specific problems of communication or description in any specific kind of situation, but in general.

Brouwer was engaged in the 'Significs Circle', founded in 1922. The basic ideas of this 'Significs study of language and philosophy' seem to have had some influence on what was later called *pragmatics*. In the basic programme of the Significs Circle it is maintained that: 'The meaning of a linguistic act for the speaker and for the hearer can but partly be determined from the words or symbols which are employed in it, and it can only approximately be expressed in other words.'[8]

This statement *could* be understood as expressing an important, new, insight about language, about the *conceptual* tie between language and communication, about the meaning of linguistic expressions and their use. It turns out, however, that this is not the way it is understood within the Significs Circle. There one wants to see this feature of language as an empirical phenomenon and as an object of scientific study and explanation. The problems are framed as though they were a question of laying bare some hidden mechanism in language. And through the generality of the claims of the project, it is hoped that 'a significs philosophy is conceivable

12

which is able largely to influence the social and spiritual conditions of mankind in future eras . . .'.

Brouwer adds to the Significs programme:[9]

> Significs consists not so much in criticism of language as:
> 1 in tracing emotional elements by analysing the causation and the effect of words. By this analysis the emotions which are connected with human understanding can be brought better under control by the conscience.
> 2 in creating a new vocabulary which admits also the spiritual tendencies in human life to considerate interchange of views and hence to social organisation.

But Brouwer sometimes speaks as though this project could never be completely realized for *metaphysical* reasons, or reasons of *principle:*

> The immediate companion of the intellect is language. From life in the Intellect follows the impossibility to communicate directly, instinctively, by gesture or looks, or, even more spiritually, through all separation of distance. People then try and train themselves and their offspring in some form of communication by means of crude sounds, laboriously and helplessly, for never has anyone been able to communicate his soul by means of language.[10]

Brouwer is here suggesting that language, even in the broad sense of linguistic behaviour in general, is never suitable for fulfilling one of its main functions! But, nevertheless, he expresses himself as though he knew what it meant to 'communicate one's soul' completely, as though he had an idea of perfect communication of mental content that was somehow independent of language, of some form of communication by means of signs or symbols – an idea that is clear enough to judge language in general as imperfect for communicating one's 'inner life'. This does not make sense.

One of Brouwer's misconceptions here is to think about the general notion of language as though it referred to *a* language. A particular language in the sense of a terminology, a jargon, or a system of conventional forms of expression, can of course be unsuitable for a particular communicative purpose. As when someone said that he could not express his experience of a certain flower in the technical language of botany. But language *in general* is not something conceptually similar to particular languages or symbolisms in that it can be regarded as a means to an end. We acquire

13

the general notion of language from examples of different particular languages and linguistic phenomena, which are called 'language' on the basis of various common features some of which are characteristic of what we call 'communication'. There exists no more general notion of communication of experience or thoughts or ideas or information than this, and it is as clear as what we would normally call 'linguistic communication'. In this sense, language is 'the universal medium of communication'.

5 LINGUISTIC COMMUNICATION AND SOLIPSISM

'Never has anyone been able to communicate his soul by means of language.' If this is supposed to mean that no one has been able to transform his inner experiences literally into external, publicly observable facts, then it is true, but then only as a logical truth, as something which it does not even make sense to attempt to do.

Once it is made clear what it *can* mean to 'communicate one's soul by means of language', it is not at all true that no one has been able to do it. From the fact that we often fail in making ourselves understood in certain respects, it does not follow that successful communication is in principle impossible. It is certainly not due to some principal deficiency in human language.

In making this statement Brouwer does indeed succeed in expressing *his* feeling of solitude and estrangement. But he seems to imply that this feeling of his would not be communicated completely to another person by means of language, unless the other person came to *feel* the solitude, or even, unless the other person were to experience Brouwer's feeling as his own. He would somehow have to *be* emotionally another copy of Brouwer for a while. But the idea of there being something comparable to linguistic communication that would accomplish this is nonsense.

Part of educating children consists in teaching them how to feel about certain things, when not to be afraid, when they should feel content about something, and so on; and sometimes the education is successful and sometimes it fails. It often fails when the educator relies too heavily on what can be accomplished by verbal information, by the giving of verbal explanations and reasons. But the failure then is not to be blamed on some principal defect in language, as though it 'ought to be' possible to learn everything by means of verbal explanation.

We learn about other people's feelings, about 'their souls', by

14

being with them in activities, by living together, by acquiring similar experiences. It is of course true that in order to understand the thought, the feeling, or the idea that a certain linguistic expression is intended to convey, it is necessary to have had certain experiences. But this necessity is not an imperfection of language. That certain experiences cannot be acquired by means of words alone is not a deficiency of language. To think that it is, is to misunderstand how language is related to our ways of living. It is a misconception of 'the relation between language and reality' (to use the philosophical jargon), which is rooted in the superficial conception of a language as a system of forms of expression.

The very idea of communicating thoughts, feelings, etc. is given with language (in the most general sense of the word), and in that sense language sets limits on what can be communicated in principle. ('Communicating with a computer', 'communicating with the dead', 'parapsychological communication', 'communicating with God' are *other uses* of the word 'communication', other concepts of communication.)

Brouwer and the members of the Significs Circle had the idea that the thought, the meaning, or the content of a linguistic expression can exist clearly and distinctly 'in the mind' without being articulated in some language. Against this one would like to say that if you have a clear and distinct thought at all, then it is already expressed in a language (which of course does not mean that it is actually uttered or transcribed somewhere).

About the Significs study it is said[11] that it 'can further the usefulness of language as a means of understanding and of ordering our thoughts'. We find this intellectualistic attitude to human language also in the programmes of modern linguistics. There language is conceived as a tool or an instrument that people invented for particular purposes such as 'understanding each other', 'communication', or 'ordering thoughts', as though it were conceivable that one could have a definite idea of these notions prior to and independently of language.

The general picture behind Brouwer's idealistic version of this programme for improving language seems to be that of humanity as a totality of individual souls or monads originally in a state of solipsism, but who can build bridges between each other by means of language. And the aim of the Significs study then is to improve this bridge-building.

The picture was perhaps correct as a rough description of the

15

spiritual *problems* in the historical situation, in which there had been a cultural decline, where certain values and traditional forms of expression had lost their meaning and importance. But when human thoughts are here spoken of as being in principle only partly or approximately communicable in language, this state of affairs is being presented as an unavoidable condition of human life. What remains then is only the scientific and *technical* problem of improving these 'approximations'. To create 'a new vocabulary which also admits the spiritual tendencies of human life', as Brouwer expresses it. But this way of stating the problem only reinforces the mistaken view of language which it presupposes.

What we have here is an intellectualistic confusion of the conditions of human life in general and the conditions of human *intellectual* life (and a corresponding confusion of human language in general and the language of intellectuals, i.e. calculi among scientists – or literature among those who feel more at home in the study of the poets).

The solipsistic picture shows perhaps the necessary and unavoidable 'primitive state' of intellectual life (in times of cultural disorder), but not of human life in general.

Improving language as a means for expressing 'spiritual tendencies', conceived as a technical problem, presupposes that the 'spiritual values' and the 'social aims' somehow exist clearly and distinctly in people's souls, waiting to be made public. But does one know *what it means* to 'improve' language in these respects? Can this problem of improving language be separated from the general problem of 'improving' social life and human conditions? It seems to me that there is too much well-meant feeling in these aims. The conception of language as a technical means of communication tends to reduce the 'spiritual values' and 'social aims' of this programme to pious hopes.

Brouwer's ideas about linguistic communication are of interest today because the kind of relativism with respect to language, so popular in current 'postmodernism', is based on similar misconceptions.[12] (A difference is perhaps that the latter is less extreme in its individualism: the soul of an intellectual fellowship kept together by the spirit of a 'discourse' replaces Brouwer's individualistic mentalism.)

The important thing here is that these kinds of problems having to do with communicating 'mental contents' are a direct result of the superficial (but very common) view of a language as a system of notation, detached from the forms of its proper use. It is this misconception which gives rise to the dualism involved in conceiving of thinking and language-use as separate realms. There is another, more 'collectivistic' way of being deceived by this view, namely by introducing the myth of a 'mental language' or a 'language of thought'[13] and conceiving of understanding, language-learning, and so on as consisting in a kind of translation into this 'mental language'.

This way of thinking is more in line with the attitudes of modern popular science, where it is claimed that the theories, technical notions, and results of science can be translated and explained in the colloquial language which most people understand. It is sometimes suggested that this must be so, for how could students of physics otherwise be able to learn the technical language of physics and mathematics if not by having it translated for them into a language which they already understand. As though the technical languages of physics and mathematics differed from colloquial language only in being different systems of notation, which are only used because they are more practical. The truth is that they first and foremost constitute different *forms of use* of expressions, involve different concepts, which do not exist in colloquial language (even when the words and expressions of colloquial language are being employed). These forms of use of expressions in science are determined in the doing of science; they are inseparably connected to particular techniques for calculating, measuring, observing, and experimenting; and they are learnt by practice and *training*, not by being translated into a language which we already possess.[14]

6 THE MENTAL AND THE PHYSICAL

About the mathematical words 'equal' and 'triangle', Brouwer says that 'two different people will never think of them in exactly the same way'; and he continues:

> Even in the most restricted sciences, logic and mathematics . . . no two different people will have the same conception of the fundamental notions of which these two sciences are constructed, and yet, they have a common will, and in both there is a small, unimportant part of the brain that forces the attention in a similar way.[15]

This is obviously the basis for Brouwer's idealism or solipsism and for his criticism of formalism in mathematics. He is thinking as though there were an invisible realm of 'mental processes' which

17

accompanies the (visible) activity of operating in the language of mathematics, and that these mental processes are essential to the conceptual content of mathematical expressions. He is led to this confusion by essentially *accepting* the formalistic conception of the language of mathematics as 'a game with signs'. This forces him to the dualism between mental life and observable linguistic phenomena. Thus he is rejecting the formalistic view of mathematics according to which mathematics is nothing more than operating in such games with signs, and he claims that what is important in mathematics are the 'mental processes' which accompany the operating with the signs.

Brouwer would certainly be correct in this criticism if 'a small part of the brain' were the basis for the agreement among mathematicians in the use of the language of mathematics (as some advocates of AI suggest today). But he is wrong because the conceptually important thing is nothing in the mind or the brain of mathematicians, but agreement in the practice of *doing* mathematics. This agreement is simply a *fact* which cannot be explained on the basis of something more fundamental. Brouwer's view of the language of mathematics, as just a family of systems of notation independent of everything involved in the practice of using them, is here reflected in his separating off 'a small, unimportant part of the brain' as the basis for the agreement in the use of mathematical notation. The view of mathematics he offers in place of formalism, by supplementing the language with a psychological realm of 'mental contents and processes', rests on the same misunderstanding of language; and since it supports misunderstandings of mental concepts it makes things even worse.

It is, of course, true that a word like 'triangle' may not evoke the same ideas in two different people, especially when they have different backgrounds, different education and experiences. It might even be true that this word evokes different ideas and associations in one and the same person on two different occasions. But this is what is irrelevant about understanding the word 'triangle' *as signifying a fundamental notion of geometry*. What is important then is that there is agreement in the use of the word when people are doing geometry (and I am of course not talking about some formal agreement in external behaviour, but agreement in a certain kind of *human action*).

Brouwer is confusing the meaning of a word with the effect the word has on us when it is uttered or read in isolation. He is thereby misled into thinking of meaning as something psychological,

18

something 'in our mind', which is somehow causally related to words. This confusion, in its turn, is enforced by his view of a language as a system of forms of expression, as a calculus of words and expressions detached from the circumstances of their normal use.

Brouwer's remarks on language are of interest because he states so explicitly misconceptions about language that are only latent in some later forms of theorizing. There is a *general picture* of 'the mental' which forms the basis of Brouwer's remarks on the problem of 'communicating one's soul', and which also underpins some modern ways of theorizing about the mental. This picture is roughly the following: a thought or a feeling is an (amorphous) entity existing somewhere, in the mind or the soul, is something caused by external events, and is the cause of certain expressions (i.e. facial expressions, gestures, tone of voice, etc.). According to this picture an expression of a feeling in gestures and words can therefore be at most a kind of 'approximation' of the 'feeling itself'. The expression is bound to be only an *indirect* way of communicating the feeling.

But when one thinks of a form of communication as 'indirect', the idea of a 'direct communication of the feeling' suggests itself immediately. And it is clearly against the background of this mistaken idea of 'direct communication' that Brouwer finds language inappropriate to 'communicating one's soul'. The picture misleads one into a kind of mythological solipsism according to which a person can *never* know what another person feels or thinks on the basis of their gestures and what they say. It is as though it would literally make sense to say: 'Only if I could feel *his* headache would I know how he feels'!

But isn't there a difference between a feeling and the expression of the feeling? In a certain sense yes, but not as two externally (or causally) related entities. We do talk about different expressions of the same feeling, and about two people expressing a certain feeling in different ways. But then the 'feeling itself' is not a third invisible entity somewhere behind the different expressions. This way of speaking refers rather to the *way* in which we compare the different expressions, and the way in which we relate the expressions to the rest of people's behaviour, and to the peculiarities of the situation in which they find themselves, as well as perhaps to their personalities and ways of living in general. To be certain about what a person feels is in many cases to be certain about his (human) situation in this sense, and in the case of everyday feelings of pain, of hunger, of surprise, and so on, we are often certain about other people's feelings, to the point where there is no room for doubt.

Consider the way in which a person's feelings are described in a good novel. What is described is not some invisible entity or state of his mind, but it may be facts about his life, his personal history, the present situation, the external circumstances, what has happened, what he is doing, other people in the situation, what they said, and how they behaved. There need not be any comment regarding feelings at all, or any mention of names of feelings; and the description is not, for that reason, a less direct way of communicating about a person's feelings in writing. It is rather the other way round, because the feelings are not something *in addition to* such human circumstances and situations, but are embedded in human practices (and not in the human nervous system).

It is perhaps incorrect to say that feelings and other psychological 'entities' are conceived as wholly amorphous in modern theorizing about the mind. On the causal picture they are spoken of as kinds of phenomena, states, or processes, in as literal a sense as that in which we speak about phenomena, states, and processes in nature,[16] but with the difference that these psychological phenomena are invisible – they are not accessible to direct observation.

This way of speaking is also rooted in superficial aspects of language. Viewing language as a calculus of words and sentences, there of course appear to be many similarities between the ways in which we talk about thinking, feeling, and believing, and about processes and states in nature. These similarities are, in this jargon, considered to be grounded in a common depth-grammar as well. The logical rules for the notions of phenomena, states and processes in nature are transferred into the language of psychological concepts. In such a naturalistic approach to psychology and the philosophy of mind a fundamental role is given to the superficial analogy between sentences like 'Psychology is the study of psychological phenomena' and 'Natural science is the study of natural phenomena.' But this analogy is highly misleading and is the source of many conceptual problems. For instance, on the basis of this analogy, propositions about a person's thoughts, feelings, or intentions are conceived as propositions about some kind of hidden phenomena, which are accessible to direct apprehension only by the person who is having them, and the result is a complex tangle of 'problems about other minds'.

To the family of 'propositions about states and phenomena in nature' are connected notions like 'evidence', 'verification', and 'justification'. Normally it makes sense to ask for evidence or justification for what is expressed in such a proposition. When the rules for propositions of this family are transferred to the language of psychological notions, there result absurd questions about 'our justification of beliefs in other minds' (Kripke). As though it were only a *hypothesis* we had, albeit a well-supported one, that our friends and fellows have feelings, beliefs, and intentions!

Some philosophers of mind, who adopt an empirical-scientific point of view, reject the existence of 'mental entities', or at least refuse to accept the hypothesis of their existence. Others (the 'mentalists') accept their existence but leave it to future research in cognitive science and the brain sciences to investigate their nature more closely. Common to the philosophers of both camps is the misconceiving of *conceptual* problems regarding psychological notions as being *factual* problems about things in some realm of reality, which is difficult of access. Due to superficial linguistic similarities, the problems are posed (even among opponents of 'mentalism') against the background of a vulgar dualism between mind and body, between a psychological realm of things and the physical realm of things. And as this dualism functions today, it is assumed that one of the two realms is primary, namely the physical one. This is evident from the way in which the word 'ascribe' is used in statements such as, 'We *ascribe* mind to certain material systems', or in such AI questions as, 'Are we justified in *ascribing* intelligence to this system?'. And this jargon is meant to be applicable to human beings as well. As though people appear to us, basically and fundamentally, as material objects or mechanical systems to which we afterwards (and in spite of a lack of complete and direct evidence) ascribe consciousness, mind, sensations, and so on!

But what difference does it make whether we conceive of the problems as conceptual rather than factual? What of importance do we gain by recognizing that the difference between the psychological and the physical realms is a conceptual difference rather than as a difference between two kinds of things or entities in reality? One important gain is that we rid ourselves of such nonsensical questions as: 'Do minds exist?', 'Are there mental entities?', 'Are there such entities as feelings, intentions and beliefs?', 'How are such mental entities related to physical things?'.

It is natural to use these *forms* of question in asking about many kinds of thing in the world, and for this reason they may *sound* or look natural and meaningful; but they actually lead us astray. These questions are posed within the causal picture transferred from the language of physical phenomena to the language of psychological notions. And one insight that our conceptual investigation provides is that this picture is incorrect in the psychological context. But since recent theorizing about mind is so deeply immersed in this picture, it may be difficult for some people to shift away from it.

It should be noted that the 'ontological question' of whether 'minds and mental entities exist' makes no sense without the philosophical jargon in which 'mental entities' are spoken of as a kind of invisible thing in some place in the world (perhaps under the tops of people's heads?). You must be trained in this jargon in order not to be just perplexed by the question, 'Are there minds, feelings, intentions?' – especially when it is posed in the objective and serious tone characteristic of some philosophers of mind.[17]

What the question *really* means is something like the following: 'Shall we adopt the notions of mind and mental entities as primitive notions in our *theories* of human language, action, and behaviour?' There of course exists a legitimate and sometimes fruitful study of human behaviour and the human organism which takes the attitude and employs the methods characteristic of the natural sciences; but when the claims and motives are supposed to be philosophical, the situation becomes different. It is when one poses this kind of question that the analogy with explanation of phenomena in the natural sciences is most out of place.

7 THE IDEA OF ARTIFICIAL INTELLIGENCE

There are parallel conceptual problems in cognitive science and AI. If one were to undertake a conceptual investigation of what might be called 'the machine conception of the human mind', one would encounter problems similar to those that arise in the investigation of 'the calculus conception of human language'.

This is perhaps most obvious if we consider the established use of the word 'intelligence' (or 'intelligent') in AI. If we compare the distinctions

natural language–artificial language

and

(human) intelligence–artificial intelligence,

we find that remarks similar to our previous ones about the use of the term 'natural language' apply to the current use of the term 'intelligence' in AI. On the AI view it is admitted that (human) intelligence is not *given* as artificial intelligence and did not originate as such, but is nevertheless machine intelligence *in principle*. Thus, according to Dennett, AI is not only the study 'of all possible *mechanistically realizable* modes of intelligence'[18] (whatever that might mean exactly), but, precisely because the machine conception of the human mind is taken as fundamental, it is claimed that 'AI is the study of all possible modes of intelligence'.[19]

And it is on this line of thinking that AI is considered to be a promising approach for solving problems in the philosophy of mind. Kelly expresses this as follows:

> Most philosophical interest in AI arises in the areas of philosophy of mind and philosophy of psychology. The idea is an attempt at an existence proof for the computational theory of mind. If one can write a computer program that has the input–output behaviour of a being generally agreed to have a mind (e.g. a human), then we have evidence that cognition is somehow nothing more than computation.[20]

This should be compared with the explicit statements of Montague[21] and Davidson[22] that natural languages *are* formal systems, though very complicated formal systems.

The similarities with the situation in the philosophy of language are in fact more than analogies, because the conception of cognitive functions as being capacities for 'symbol manipulation', ultimately representable in formal systems, is an accepted paradigm, and, furthermore, the theories of language which form the basis of the 'natural-language representations' in several AI systems are designed within the calculus conception of language.

The way in which the philosophical puzzles in AI have originated is also similar to the situation in the philosophy of language. In one's enthusiasm over new techniques and formal methods, one tends to forget the difference between a constructed theoretical model and the 'human cognitive processes' which the model is intended to represent. On the level of language this means that ordinary psychological terminology is assimilated with the new, *technical* use of traditional psychological vocabulary in the computer jargon. One speaks, for instance, about 'machine-learning' as though it were the same notion of learning that we employ in

23

connection with human beings.[23] This gives the false impression that the computer and its program is actually a model of 'the mental mechanism' of learning in humans, a model of what 'goes on in the mind' of people when they learn. The term 'machine-learning' has, however, a perfectly good technical use in computer science, signifying an algorithm that is in a certain formally well-defined sense 'self-modifying'. But that is a different notion of learning from the one that we employ in connection with humans, despite *some* formal similarities.

The philosophically crucial thing in AI is not so much the anthropomorphizing of machines and computer systems, the application of psychological notions that we normally apply to humans (or animals) to machines and computer systems, but the converse application of the resulting technical use of psychological vocabulary to humans. It is *this* step that involves treating the machine conception of the human mind as fundamental; and it manifests itself for instance in the claim made by advocates of AI that it aims at explaining all modes of intelligence, that it is meant to resolve basic problems in the philosophy of psychology.

This step is sometimes explicit, as when Dennett declares[24] that 'Whatever else a person might be . . . he is an intentional system', where the notion of an 'intentional system' involves a technical use of words like 'intentional', 'belief', 'desire', a use which is adapted to a certain strategy and methodology for the explanation and prediction of machine behaviour.

The metaphorical use of words such as 'believe', 'learn', 'understand', 'remember', etc. to describe the behaviour of a computer system is harmless and even very efficient *in its proper comunicative function*, for instance, in communication between programmers or between a programmer and a user of the program. This jargon certainly makes manuals for word-processing programs easier to follow. The crucial step, however, is when this manner of speaking is considered in isolation from these forms of linguistic communication. Conceptual problems arise when it is supposed to have some 'deeper significance' in describing an 'intentional aspect' of computer behaviour, when it is supposed to justify a philosophical view of computer systems as being literally 'rational agents'.

8 MACHINE BEHAVIOUR AND HUMAN ACTION

There are various ways in which computers and computer systems enter into human reality, for instance as basic factors in the organization and design of human activities, or as a source of inspiration for mythologies and science fiction. One fundamental role they have is, however, as tools, instruments *within* various human activities. Computers are *useful* for performing certain tasks, such as doing complicated computations, storing information, and word-processing (whether this kind of technical progress is what humanity primarily needs is, of course, another question).

But computers do not literally perform actions; they are not 'rational agents'. It is not as though there is one general notion of 'intentional action' or 'intelligent behaviour' of which human action and machine behaviour are two subspecies. To believe that there is, is to be misled by the figurative ways of speaking in current computer jargon. This metaphorical language is based on certain external or *formal* similarities (e.g. Dennett's notion of an 'intentional system'), which cut across different conceptual categories. The use of such words as 'intentional', 'belief', or 'intelligent' which is based on these formal similarities is a new and technical use of these words, and therefore involves new concepts.

But can we not imagine (as Turing did) that in the near future people will adopt these new concepts as the normal and more appropriate ones even for describing human behaviour?[25] God forbid! People (and not only social engineers) would then lose the capacity to distinguish between the *essential* differences between men and machines! It is likely that these new concepts will become established technical notions alongside traditional notions of 'action', 'intelligence', and so on, which we use in connection with humans; but to claim (and hope) that the new concepts could *replace* the ordinary notions, and be more *appropriate* than they are, is to be mistaken about what is essential in human action.

A human action is not somehow built up of two separate parts, one mechanical (causal or behavioural) part, which is visible, and inside that part another invisible 'intentional part', which requires 'a mind'. (The latter part would perhaps rather be situated on top of the former, because it is customary to speak of higher and lower *levels* of performance.) This is the picture of *human* action or human intelligent behaviour that forms the basis of the machine conception of intelligence. Applied to human beings it is a misconception, and an old one. It was against the background of this picture that the classical mind–body problems started.

Advocates of 'weak AI' – a more modest technical-scientific form of AI – are content to claim that computer systems can in principle completely reproduce the external, mechanical or behavioural part of human intellectual performances, but not the 'intentional part', which requires 'the mind intrinsically' (in Searle's terminology[26]). Advocates of 'strong AI' – the more speculative form of AI which wants to justify a 'computational philosophy of mind' – claim that even the 'intentional part' can be 'built up' on the basis of physical symbol manipulation: 'it may be possible to construct *high*-level semantics from *low*-level syntax'.[27]

What I want to point out is that *both* forms of AI have this mistaken dualist picture of *human* action as a common ground. It is against the background of this picture of human actions and intellectual performances that it is said that 'whether computation is sufficient for cognition is largely an open empirical question'.[28] But as long as this picture is taken as fundamental, no empirical result will refute it. Only a conceptual investigation can show its proper status: a pattern or paradigm for constructing formal models.

'But what *is* then human intelligence and human action?' Well, what is it to be a human being?

How strange that this of all things is something that we should need to remind ourselves about! One might need to be informed about what it is to be a certain kind of human being, what it is to perform certain kinds of human actions. One might need to be reminded about what it was like to be a child (e.g. to play like a child) or to be a teenager, but to be a human being and act as a human being in general (rather than as a machine or a 'system')! .

(AI people speak about 'a system understanding', 'a system knowing', and a human being is considered to be an 'instance' of such a system.)

The difficulty here is to place apparently trivial, everyday experiences in such a light that it will be obvious how the philosophical claims of AI are nonsensical.

Some of the basic features of the AI notion of 'intelligent behaviour' have their origin in the ideas of a finitary proof theory, which were presented by the mathematician, David Hilbert. In order to get a clear idea of what is wrong with the philosophical claims of AI, I shall conclude this section with some remarks on this origin.

Two tendencies in the late nineteenth century were important for Hilbert's idea of a finitary proof theory. One was a general discussion about the relation between form and content (*Inhaltlichkeit und Formalismus*), which had counterparts even in the philosophy of art and the philosophy of law. (Hilbert mentions in his paper 'Axiomatisches Denken'[29] the problem of the relation between form and content as one of the central problems to be dealt with in his *Beweistheorie*.) I think that the problem here, concerning mathematics, was one of accounting for the relation between form and content in such a way as to justify mathematics as *pure* mathematics detached from its empirical applications (very much in Descartes' spirit), and to oppose the traditional idea that mathematics obtains its content through its empirical applications (like Kant's idea that the notion of number is somehow derived from our notion of time). On this point some of the late nineteenth-century formalists may have influenced Hilbert. The mathematician Hermann Grassmann[30] develops a conception of mathematics in which it is the science 'des formalen Seins'; and he defines pure mathematics as *Formenlehre*. What led to this discussion was very much the problems with mechanist thinking, problems which go back to Descartes.

The other tendency from the late nineteenth century that influenced Hilbert strongly was, it seems to me, the empiricist critique of science delivered by thinkers like Mach, Hertz, Helmholtz, and others. This empiricist tendency in Hilbert is obvious, for instance, in 'Über das Unendliche' and in general in his emphasis on the *concrete* (as an epistemologically secure realm) in his various characterizations of the finitist point of view. This late nineteenth-century scientific empiricism forms the roots not only of formalism, but also of behaviourism in psychology (as a reaction against traditional 'introspective psychology', which was accused of not being sufficiently similar to physics in scientific rigour).

I think that these two tendencies forced Hilbert into the same view of the relation between form and content as was later adopted as a paradigm for the relation between the physical and the mental by advocates of AI (as well as by linguists such as Chomsky). Hilbert conceives of the relation as external, with form being separable from content and as something concrete, extralogical, and immediately given and recognizable by our perceptual intuition. This then is the basis for Hilbert's (questionable) way of making the distinctions between mathematics and meta-mathematics, real

27

and ideal propositions, and so on.[31] The contentual (*inhaltliche*) aspect of the ideal propositions of ordinary mathematics is disregarded in the meta-mathematical point of view, but there is no discussion of whether it is possible to do so without a radical reinterpretation of the propositions. It is by thinking in this way that Hilbert comes to characterize what we do in algebra (in opposition to 'contentual number theory') as follows: 'In algebra . . . we consider the expressions formed with letters to be independent objects in themselves . . . . Where we had propositions concerning numerals, we now have formulas, which themselves are concrete objects that in their turn are considered by our perceptual intuition, and the derivation of one formula from another in accordance with certain rules takes the place of the number-theoretic proof based on content';[32] and in this way, says Hilbert, 'contentual inference is replaced by manipulation of signs (*äusseres Handeln*) according to rules.'

It is here, it seems to me, that we have the fundamental mistake in Hilbert (a mistake which has been inherited by modern AI). It is not as concrete objects *qua* concrete and subject to mechanical rules that we deal with expressions and formulas in algebra (any more than in 'contentual number-theory'). That is so only within certain formal *representations* (mechanizations) of the mathematical operations. In meta-mathematics, for instance, we treat a formula as a mathematical construction generated by iterating operations. The particular physical and concrete appearance of the expression for this construction is no more essential here than is the choice of notation in other parts of mathematics.

Hilbert is thinking as though the meaning (or the real content) of an arithmetical equation such as '$2 + 2 = 4$' on his finitary point of view should coincide with its meaning in ordinary 'contentual arithmetic'. But, as will be argued in part 3 of this book, this finitistic meaning is a reinterpretation determined by a method for formal representation in which its ordinary meaning is presupposed. As an instance of the rule of addition the 'ordinary arithmetical meaning' of the equation involves the (unlimited) rule of addition, i.e. a person would not understand this arithmetical equation as an instance of the rule of addition if he did not also understand, say, $1 + 1 = 2, 2 + 3 = 5, . . .$ as such. The generality of the unlimited rule of addition is involved in the content of every single instance. So against Hilbert's distinction between real and ideal mathematical propositions it could be said: If there is 'reference to ideal elements'

28

in what Hilbert calls 'ideal propositions', then the same is true of what he calls 'real propositions'. The form and the content of ordinary mathematical statements are not separable in the way taken for granted by Hilbert. (This kind of mistake in Hilbert was clearly realized by Poincaré, but, unfortunately, his criticism has been largely neglected.)[33]

It might be said that Hilbert adopts a behaviouristic (or causal) view of such human mathematical performances as calculation, substitution, and so on, as though such performances and operations were basically mere causal or mechanical (or mathematically non-contentual) performances, and the 'contentual or non-mechanical' something that enters only at a 'higher level' of mathematical activity. This is the way that certain formal representations of mathematical performances are being constructed, as consisting of a formal part and a contentual part that are conceptually separable from one another. (Note that Frege did not make this mistake. From his criticism of the formalists in his *Grundgesetze* it is clear that he saw this incoherence in the formalist view.)

It seems to me that it was this way of thinking about ordinary (mathematical and non-mathematical) language that was made into a paradigm, not only for the semantics of Tarski and Carnap, but also for Turing's idea of AI. The basic (mistaken) idea is that at a fundamental level human actions and intellectual performances are mere mechanical or causal operations; a human being is basically 'a physical system to which we *ascribe* intelligence, mind and so on'. The attempts of AI to account for the 'higher-level intelligent performances' in terms of the alleged mechanical operations at the 'basic level', are the counterpart to Hilbert's attempt to secure 'ideal mathematics' on the basis of 'real propositions' and finitary methods of proof.

The truth is that even the most elementary human actions, such as simple calculations and even the following of mechanical rules, are 'non-causal, intentional' actions which can be understood as the human actions they are only in relation to human practices. The alleged causal level in human actions and intellectual functions is an imposed reinterpretation or a constructed representation based on external features.

Am I saying then that no human activity can be mechanized? No. It is of course a fact that human activities have been mechanized, that human tasks such as arithmetical computation have been successfully formalized and implemented in computer systems. But this employment of the expression 'can be mechanized', which refers to certain technical results of modern computer technology, provides no justification for the conceptual and philosophical claims of AI (which are my concern here). In particular these results do not justify the claim that the notions of intelligence and thinking, which we normally employ about humans, are (literally) applicable to computer systems. This claim on the part of some AI advocates presupposes a machine conception of the human agent, which is itself based on the dualist view of the relation between the mental and the physical. This dualist view is really a normative principle for a new, technical notion of intelligence within AI.[34]

9 TURING'S TEST

Notice how Turing introduces this 'separation of form and content' in the preparation of his thought experiment in his paper 'Computing machinery and intelligence';[35] and how he thereby prepares the way for the conclusion he wants to reach, that 'machines can think'. The problem 'Can machines think?' has, says Turing, 'the advantage of drawing a fairly sharp line between the physical and the intellectual capacities of a man'. This is realized in his thought experiment by 'the condition which prevents the interrogator from seeing or touching the other competitors, or hearing their voices.' – as though these assumptions were harmless with respect to the problem of what thinking and intelligence is! The features and circumstances of human action (bodily movements, gestures, facial expressions, tones of voice, attitude) that Turing here wants to 'abstract away from' might be just what is *essential* for judging a certain behaviour as intelligent or a certain response as a result of thinking. In other words, Turing can 'draw this sharp line between the physical and intellectual capacities of man' only by presupposing the mechanistic AI conception of intelligent behaviour he wants to arrive at. It is on the basis of this conception that he feels himself justified in 'drawing this sharp line'. But for the ordinary concepts of thinking and intelligence that we employ about humans it is essential that this sharp line does not exist.

Turing does not realize that by this manner of abstracting he deprives himself of the right to use the words 'think', 'intelligent', 'believe', etc., as we normally use them with regard to human beings (and creatures similar to humans); he does not realize that he is actually introducing new (technical) uses for these words, a new grammar of their employment, which cuts across the *categorial difference* between human action and machine behaviour. It is not to prove anything, but to introduce this technical notion of thinking, that is the real purpose of his thought experiment.

About the new use of the word 'think', Turing is quite right: machines can think, but this statement loses its sensational ring when it is realized that it is a new technical notion of thinking based only on formal and external similarities between human action and machine behaviour. For what is characteristic of the 'intentional notions' we use with regard to humans is that they cannot be formally specified; their employment cannot be characterized by the external criteria of an empirical test. They are inseparable from the human practices and conditions to which they belong, and that is what makes them intentional.

As regards the ordinary notions of 'thinking', 'intelligence', 'belief', etc., there exist certain (very complicated) *logical* or a *priori* conditions for the use of these words. Unless these conditions are fulfilled, a proposition of the form 'X is thinking' is not false, but *does not make sense*. If these conditions are not met (as when 'X' refers to a machine or a physical system), the sentence may sound like or have the ring of a meaningful proposition (and on this basis it may be used in a game with words, in a figurative way of speaking, or in a fictitious story); but as an employment of the ordinary notion of thinking it is nonsensical. One of the mistakes of Turing's and the AI approach is to conceive of these *logical* conditions as empirical, as the criteria of an empirical test. One is trying to conceive of the *conceptual* problem 'Can machines think?' as though it were an empirical problem to be settled by experiment and observation.

When certain empirical criteria about something turn out *not* to be satisfied, the result is a false (but meaningful) proposition or hypothesis. But when the logical conditions for the use of a certain expression are violated, the result is not false propositions, but sentences without (the alleged intended) meaning. And it is only on the basis of the logical conditions for the employment of expressions that one can mean or intend something (or express thoughts, intentions and beliefs). So when the conditions for the use of the expression 'X can think' are construed as the criteria of an empirical test, the alleged, intended meaning is out of the question. If the sentence then has any meaning at all, the empirical or factual possibility expressed by the 'can' in it must be determined by a new (technical) use of the expression 'to think'. This is the

31

reason why Turing's test fails, not because 'thinking is an inner, unobservable or hidden process'.

What will solve the problem 'Can machines think?' as a conceptual problem, is a clarification of the logical conditions for the use of the word 'to think', i.e. we must remind ourselves of the details of its use and of the features therein that are *essential*. But these features are not, as *logical* conditions, formally specifiable or specifiable as criteria of a test. They can be described and understood only within a mode of description which presupposes that the conditions obtain.

As already remarked, the conception of human action and of human beings occurring in AI philosophy is roughly this: an action is basically a physical process and the human agent is a physical system to which we 'ascribe mind, intentionality, belief, purpose, etc.' when such a physical system has reached a certain degree of sophistication and complexity in 'behaviour'. But as with Turing's notion of 'thinking', this is a technical use of the notion of action, based on a certain schema for constructing theoretical models and programs according to which the relation between a purpose (an intention, an expectation) and the action fulfilling it is seen as an external relation. It is seen as being conceptually of the same kind as the relation between a mechanism (in nature) and the function or plan it fulfils according to some theory (as for instance the theory of evolution). So there is always the problem of realizing or judging whether a particular instance of causal behaviour fulfils a certain purpose or is in accordance with some rule in order to recognize it as the action it is.

This is not the way we use concepts of action in connection with human beings, and the difference is conceptual. We identify (describe) human behaviour in terms of people's intentions and in terms of activities, practices, customs, and institutions characteristic of human life (such as calculating, talking, reading, walking, eating, crying, observing something, waiting for someone, etc.). Human behaviour makes its appearance, presents itself to us, as instances of such practices and activities, even when there may be a problem about understanding what someone is actually doing. (Is she crying or only pretending to?) It almost never shows up as a purely causal process which we have to interpret according to some theory. Human action as a purely causal behaviour – *that* is an imposed interpretation.

So there is not one basic form of practice or behaviour which one would call 'behaving causally or mechanically' (i.e. following rules mechanically like a machine or physical system) on the basis of which other actions are somehow built up. Such 'causal behaviour' is precisely what is not human behaviour. The 'basic level' of 'intelligent behaviour' consists of human practices and institutions, and lacking an acquaintance and familiarity with them, the ordinary sense of the expression 'intelligent behaviour' is lost.

According to the AI picture of (human) action, if it were possible for me to see human actions as being what they really are, then, in observing someone doing something, for instance reading aloud from a book, I would see and hear a certain causal behaviour or an ongoing physical process which I *understand or interpret as the person's reading*. But if this picture gave the truth of what an action like reading really is, how would I know what reading is at all? On the basis of external criteria of what it should *look like* and *sound like* when someone is reading aloud? And is it then on the basis of these criteria that I know when I am reading myself? 'Now I must be reading, because someone observing me would find that I am behaving just like someone who is reading.' And how would I distinguish between a good imitation of reading and someone's actually reading? It is only through my familiarity and acquaintance with the activity of reading, as performed by human beings, that I know what reading is.

This is not to deny that certain physical processes are going on in my body when I am performing an action, for instance when I am reading. There are certain characteristic movements of my eyes when I am reading a book. But when I am reading, *the action* I am performing is not that of moving my eyes back and forth. It might be said that moving the eyes, looking at the pages of a book, etc. are parts of what people do when they read a book, but they are not parts that fulfil a function in a mechanism called 'reading' (like the mechanism of a text scanner). The bodily movements, facial expressions, etc. are internally related to *what I am doing*, i.e. reading.

'He moved his eyes as though he were reading', 'He moved his head like someone who is . . .'. We tend to identify even bodily movements by the (intentional) activities and practices in human life of which they are characteristic. When would we take a purely causal attitude to the behaviour of a human being? In the case of a reflex movement? But a reflex movement, like many other processes in our bodies, is something that happens to us, something that we *undergo*, not something that we *do*. Or do we take a causal attitude when we observe someone in a pathological state, such as when he is experiencing heart failure or an epileptic fit? But then, would our attitude be like our attitude towards a mechanism that is malfunctioning, rather than towards a human being who is suffering from a disease and perhaps needs help? It is clear that a strictly causal attitude to the behaviour of a human being belongs to some imposed theoretical perspective on human behaviour, as in physiology, anatomy, behavioural psychology, or acoustic phonetics, or generally in the study of human behaviour and the human organism using the methods of the natural sciences. And such a study may of course be useful, but in the end only for technical and practical purposes.

It may be objected to the above that there is a sense in which the causal activities in the human organism are essential to human action and even to the higher intellectual capacities of humans. Without the physical possibility of moving my legs I would be unable to walk; and if the physiological processes in my brain were destroyed I would be unable to think or calculate. This is certainly true, but it does not mean that the causal processes of the human organism are basic in a metaphysical sense, i.e. in the sense that the human mind is in some way *embodied* in these causal processes. This misconception arises when the point of view of the natural sciences is confused with philosophy and is given a metaphysical role, such as when one claims in neurophysiology to reveal 'the nature of the human mind', rather than simply to solve certain technical and scientific problems.

The physical constitution of the human organism is necessary for human action and mental life in a sense comparable to the sense in which the physical signs and expressions of language are necessary for expressing meaning. Without the perceptible signs and expressions there would be no linguistic meaning, no language. But this is not the only essential thing about language. It does not mean that 'syntax is sufficient'[36] or that meaning is somehow embodied in the expressions *qua* physical phenomena. Nor does it mean that the expressions as physical phenomena are what we endow with meaning through semantical explanations or interpretations. The idea that neurophysiology will one day 'crack the cerebral code and read our minds' is no less absurd than the idea that linguists will be able to derive the meaning of linguistic expressions from a deeper investigation of the physical structure of words and sentences.

This means of course that computers are not literally acting, computing, or thinking; they are not agents (rational or otherwise). They are (among other things) tools, instruments, means of expression and representation *within various human activities*. If a computer is used to perform a complicated computation, then a complicated physical process is going on in the computer; but this process is not an act that the computer is performing, it is a process that is externally caused (by the programmer, or the user, or some other agent). What a computer 'can do' means what we can do by means of it: those defined tasks we can perform by using it, for instance that of simulating some aspect of human behaviour.

The activity of 'simulating human behaviour' on a computer is thus an activity that computer scientists are engaged in; it is something that 'a computer is doing' only in a figurative sense. This would be no less the case even if it were possible to construct computer programs for chess-playing which the World Chess Champion could not defeat, because 'computer chess' is a *different game*, a different (and rather new) human activity with several *formal* similarities to traditional chess-playing. To take the potential existence of such a chess-playing program as evidence for the possibility of constructing 'artificial intelligence', or as evidence for the thesis that 'machines can think' in the same sense as people can think, is to make a mistaken comparison with traditional chess-playing. The mistakenness comes from thinking as though it were the physical mechanism of the human body (or brain) that is the human agent in traditional chess-playing. The existence of such a chess-playing computer would only be evidence however for the existence of an intelligent human programmer.

Would it make sense to say of a chess-playing computer that 'it is playing with enthusiasm and affection'? Or that 'it is proud of its last move'? Or that 'it was astonished by its opponent's move'? Or that 'it is playing carelessly and negligently'? Or that 'it is making a hopeless move as though it did not want to win'? Or that 'this computer is a good chess player but it is no longer interested in playing'? That these things can be said truly or falsely about a human chess-player using already established forms of language marks something essential about playing chess.

The following could be said with regard to a human being: 'He is speaking like a machine', or 'You are talking like a robot', as a kind of *accusation* or *reproach*, for instance. Now, if there were a common notion of action, e.g. of speaking or talking, in which people as well as computer systems could be agents, then this sense would be lost. Then these statements would be just like factual descriptions or classifications of someone's accent, as when we say, 'He speaks like a southerner.'

When one says with indignation to an adult: 'Don't act like a child', one is not just making a kind of request that the person should change some details regarding his external behaviour, such as when we say, 'Take this chair instead of that, which is for the children!' Could an intelligent machine literally be *reproached* for acting like an unintelligent machine? We do of course say things about machines that may *sound like* statements of reproach, e.g. when the car does not work as expected; but we do this in a way that is much more similar to the way in which we express disappointment over an unexpected storm.

It may be objected that 'it is after all on the basis of observable features of people's behaviour that we make judgements about their attitudes and conduct, and it should therefore be possible, at least in principle, to simulate the features of human behaviour that are criteria for certain attitudes, feelings, and so on.' Of course, something like this is thinkable for some limited kind of human behaviour, since it is possible to make a painting of a face expressing a certain feeling; but in such a case this machine behaviour would be a *representation* of a particular human behaviour. The machine behaviour would be governed by formal rules which are *not* rules people follow when they behave in a way characteristic of an attitude. There is not some 'abstract pain behaviour', for instance, which a human being is 'implementing' when he or she shows pain behaviour and of which it might be possible to construct a 'computer-realization'.

There are features of human behaviour characteristic of certain attitudes and feelings, but *as such* they are inseparable from the human activities, social situations, and actual circumstances in which they occur. Suppose that someone constantly showed expressions of joy and pleasure in all kinds of situations. Then we would say that this is not an expression of pleasure in this particular person. It is also in relation to the surrounding circumstances that we decide whether someone is or is not pretending to be, say, in pain. Features characteristic of feelings and attitudes are not representable as formal criteria like bodily temperature or length – but not because feelings and attitudes are some sort of hidden data about people.

10 CALCULATION VERSUS MECHANICAL SYMBOL MANIPULATION

The causal or behaviouristic view of the activity of calculation in mathematics is evident in Hilbert's ideas about a finitistic meta-mathematics. Recall Hilbert's statement, quoted above, that 'In algebra . . . we consider the expressions formed with letters to be independent objects in themselves . . . . Where we had propositions concerning numerals, we now have formulas, which themselves are concrete objects that in their turn are considered by our perceptual intuition, and the derivation of one formula from another in accordance with certain rules takes the place of the number-theoretic proof based on content,' and 'contentual inference is replaced by manipulation of signs [äusseres Handeln] according to rules.' In this statement about 'what we do in algebra', Hilbert confuses the ordinary (intentional) action of calculation in algebra with the action of operating within a certain mechanical representation of ordinary calculation (i.e. with the action of manipulating written symbols according to rules for their recognition, introduction, replacement, transformation, etc. as concrete spatial configurations). Hilbert is thinking as though, on some elementary level of mathematics, calculation *is* mechanical symbol manipulation in that sense, or at least that it can, on this level, completely replace the ordinary *inhaltliche* (contentual) sense of calculation. But this is a mistake comparable to the view of the human activity of walking as being an act of moving one's legs in a certain way, or of speaking as being an act of producing acoustic patterns. The physical manipulation of symbols is certainly a part of the activity of calculating in mathematics, it is even an essential part, but it is a part which is internally related to the human *practice* of calculation. Part of what I am doing when I am adding by means of paper and pencil is sign manipulation; but that is not in some way a *separate* part of my adding, as though I were really doing *two* things, one physical act (the sign manipulation) and the other 'mental' (understanding, interpreting, or 'endowing the signs with meaning'). Viewing what I am doing as only physical sign manipulation is, one might say, a 'non-intended interpretation' of my activity, or a case of someone not understanding what I am doing: 'He appears to be producing some strange signs and moving them about.'

Consider for instance the calculation which proves the equation:

$$(a + b)^2 = a^2 + b^2 + 2ab$$

37

In that calculation there occurs of course physical symbol manipulation, but, as an arithmetical (or algebraic) proof of this algebraic rule, the calculation and its result have a kind of generality which they would not have considered merely as a manipulation of spatial configurations. We could replace the letters 'a' and 'b' by the letters 'x' and 'y', and we would have (as we say in algebra) the *same* calculation proving the *same* algebraic rule. It would only be, as we say, a 'notational variant'. One could think of a more drastic change in the notation of this calculation and we would still say that it is the same algebraic calculation, but not the same manipulation of spatial configurations. And the important thing is that we can only recognize the different cases as isomorphic or as notational variants if we assume this ordinary, mathematical, sense of *the* calculation as expressed in *some* notation.[37]

So, as an ordinary algebraic calculation, there is a kind of generality or *arbitrariness* about its expression, and the limits of this arbitrariness are determined *by the practice of calculation in mathematics*, by the way in which we actually operate with symbols in mathematical practice, and which is ultimately learned through practice and training. There is no way in which familiarity with this human activity could be 'made explicit' and be replaced by formal or mechanical rules, because one would not know how to follow and apply such formal rules correctly other than on the basis of this familiarity. The various features of this human practice, as a practice, are, one might say, what is 'intentional' or the *inhaltlich* about the language of mathematics, and it is involved even in the most elementary forms of calculation.

We could also describe the calculation proving the equation as a *transformation* of the expression on the left-hand side into the expression on the right-hand side according to algebraic laws. But as an algebraic calculation (or proof) the *form* that has been transformed is not just a typographical or physical or spatial form (of a concrete figure); it is the algebraic form, i.e. the physical form in a particular use in the language of mathematics, where certain features of the expression are essential and others are inessential. And then again, it is only *in relation to* this use that there exists a boundary between these essential and inessential features. This does not mean merely that the boundary can be *drawn* only by reference to the use; more important, it means that the boundary cannot be *respected* but against the background of this use. This is true even of simple notational and abbreviational conventions in mathematics. I cannot simply verbally inform someone ignorant of algebra about the notational conventions of, say, Boolean algebra. Even if he learned to state them correctly he would not know what to do with them. To abbreviate, to define, to introduce a new sign for a constant, a variable, an operation, etc. are institutions in the language of mathematics that we must learn through practice. The final form of explanations which all the 'semantical explanations' must presuppose is like this: 'This . . . is how it must be done, not like that . . . !'[38]

The confusion of calculation and mechanical symbol manipulation seems to be an important source of the misconceptions in AI. According to Shapiro,[39] for instance, 'addition, as humans perform it, is an operation on numerals, not numbers.' And Rapaport claims[40] that 'the abstract operation of adding is an operation on numbers . . . but our *human implementation* of this operation is an operation on [physical] *implementations* of numbers.'

'Our human implementation'! The technical computer jargon is here transported to the description of human action. And not just as a joke or an experiment. The objective tone in which this is said is meant to assure us of the correctness of the machine conception of man!

Here one might also ask: who is then performing the *abstract* operation of adding numbers? 'The arithmetical operation "addition" operates on numbers', 'the operator operates', 'the Turing machine M operates on . . .'.

Do mathematical objects perform operations or actions? Is it not only people and more particularly mathematicians who perform mathematical operations? There is indeed a conceptual confusion here due to the ambiguity of the word 'operation'. In the mathematical sense of an operation, according to which we talk of the binary operation of a semi-group or of the Boolean operations of the propositional calculus, an operation is a symbol with a certain 'arity' which we (humans) use to build other expressions and manipulate (calculate) with according to certain rules. But these rules are in general not mechanical rules, in the sense that they govern signs and expressions as physical objects.

The physical object

$$x + y$$

on the one hand, and this mathematical expression on the other, are categorially different things. For many of us the latter is mere spatial configuration, to disregard its normal context. We tend spontaneously to see an arithmetical expression, and we would perhaps remember it as such. It might even be said that this expression has a kind of physiognomy which is connected with its normal use in mathematics. It definitely 'looks like' a mathematical expression.

The idea that we see and deal with the expressions of mathematics as physical objects in calculating (and thereafter interpret them as signifying mathematical objects) is not in agreement with these observations. But what is then the physical object in this case? The expression has a certain size, colour, location, composition, etc. But note that this composition is not necessarily in agreement with the composition it has as an arithmetical expression (built up by a binary operation). What is then its composition as a physical object? Is it built up of the three parts 'x', '+', 'y'? Well, that is one way of seeing it, but certainly not the only one. And that we are likely to regard it as composed in this way has of course to do with the role the expression has in arithmetic. But as a spatial configuration? What is a 'mere spatial configuration'? Where on earth do we find things that are 'only spatial configurations'? Nowhere, it might be said. Being a spatial configuration is an aspect of physical objects. The notion is designed in such a way that irrelevant features of the expression (such as its colour) are disregarded (besides its form as a mathematical expression). And *now* we are definitely concerned with (an imposed) interpretation!

In the theory of syntax developed in meta-mathematics a systematic method for interpretations of this kind was constructed by means of mathematical notions (like the notion of a finite sequence). It is a schema for the mechanical representation of linguistic expressions, propositions and proofs which has turned out to be useful, but not for describing the true nature, or 'the hidden mechanism' of human calculating and proving, but *for the construction of mechanical models of human activities such as calculating.*

11 DECEPTIVE CRITICISM OF AI

There are of course critics of the philosophical aims and claims of AI, but some of the criticism is even more misleading than the ideas it opposes, because it is based on the same conceptual confusions. Here I am thinking about criticism intended to prove that the claims are false rather than nonsensical, i.e. criticism which is framed as if it were somehow a matter of (empirical or factual) truth or falsity whether 'machines can think' or whether 'the mind is mechanical'.

Note for instance how misleading it is to say: 'the machine is . . . restricted to operations on the symbols and representations themselves. It has no access . . . to the meanings of these symbols, to things the representations represent, to the numbers'[41] (Dretske). And according to the same author, 'having access to the meanings of the symbols' is what is required of someone who can actually be said to calculate, and on this ground the author wants to conclude that 'machines cannot calculate'.

In this statement it is somehow understood that 'the machine is so restricted because it has no mind and therefore cannot understand the meaning of the symbols it manipulates'. But the truth is that neither is the machine literally 'manipulating symbols' in the sense in which this can be said about a human being who is operating in a formal system.

It might also be asked whether anyone, on this requirement, really 'can calculate'. Do schoolchildren who have learnt to add and multiply 'have access to some *things* that the numerals represent'? Isn't this a very strange way of describing the ability they have acquired? Philosophers 'have access to' a jargon in which numerals are spoken of as though they represented some kind of objects, but it is certainly not necessary to be familiar with that jargon in order to be able to calculate.

Dretske also says that 'To understand what a system is doing when it manipulates symbols, it is necessary to know, not just what these symbols mean, what interpretation they have been *assigned*, but what they mean to the system performing the operations.' A *system* doing things! What symbols mean to a system! What kind of use of the words 'doing', 'mean', 'understand' is this? It is clear that it is the transference of computer jargon to the description of human activities that creates the absurd idea that an invisible process of interpretation is going on parallel to an external process of symbol manipulation when someone is calculating.

Why isn't there also an additional process of interpreting the external behaviour as 'physical symbol manipulation'? When someone is performing ordinary calculations with the usual notation there may be a problem of interpretation, for instance when his handwriting has been careless, but normally there is no interpretation. So his 'understanding what he is doing' means something quite different.

Searle objects to the claims of AI in a similarly misleading way. He says that 'The reason that no computer program can ever be a mind is simply that a computer program is only syntactical, and minds are more than syntactical. Minds are semantical, in the sense that they have more than a formal structure, they have a content.'[42]

This may sound similar to some of the things I have been saying about such human actions as calculating being 'something more than' mere physical symbol manipulation. But I have certainly not wanted to say that it is 'something more' in the sense that it involves something *in addition to* symbol manipulation. *It is not something more but something else.* It is not a question of more or less, but of something categorially *different* – even at the level of following syntactical rules.

According to another argument against some of the claims of AI, 'not all human problem-solving mechanisms can be explained as rule-governed behaviour, i.e. implemented in a computer' because 'Some human problem-solving activities, at their highest levels, require intuition. Intuition is necessarily not describable as rule governed' (a view Buchanan[43] attributes to Dreyfus).

This may *sound* very good to someone who finds the idea of 'intelligent machines' repulsive or frightening but who is nevertheless unable to deny that computers are 'clever in solving certain problems'. For this reason, these kinds of arguments are, it seems to me, more misleading than the boldest claims of AI philosophers. What one would like to say here is that the logical sense in which *advanced* human problem-solving cannot be taken over by a computer program, is the sense in which computer programs cannot 'take over' the most *elementary* human problem-solving either. The above argument presupposes the idea that a human being or the human mind is *partly* a machine, a machine plus something in addition to that (a capacity for intuitive reasoning). Some advocates of AI deny that there is something more and claim that the machine part 'is sufficient'. In both cases the mistake lies in the underlying machine conception *of the human mind*, the mythology of 'the mechanisms underlying human performances'.[44]

On this way of arguing against the claims of AI it also appears as though intuition is some kind of mystical, occult capacity, a 'ghost in the machine'. It appears as though we have something factual, a real phenomenon which is for *a priori* reasons excluded from being a domain for the application of computer technology.

The advocates of AI are certainly correct in the sense that there are no *a priori* reasons preventing us from constructing something that we can agree to call a computer simulation or a mechanical model of the role and the effects of intuitive reasoning within some limited problem area. But if one succeeds in constructing such a (useful) model, one has not thereby constructed artificial *human* intelligence – one has not thereby constructed a model which, for *that* reason, could replace ordinary human problem-solving. If ordinary problem-solving is 'taken over by' or is replaced by computer problem-solving, it is because *we decide to replace it*; we engage in a new practice, a *different* human activity. And we do that (presumably) because we find it useful, practical, or interesting, but not because we have constructed a machine that can perform 'intuitive reasoning'.[45]

Ordinary chess and computer chess are different games. It is *essential* to ordinary chess that it be played between human beings. The error on both sides in the discussion about the possibility of implementing intuition in a computer is that one thinks as though the truth about what ordinary human chess playing really is should be presented in the form of an explanation of ordinary chess *as a species of computer chess*.[46] According to advocates of AI this will give the whole truth, while according to some of their opponents it can give only half of the truth. 'A hidden mental mechanism' is assumed to be at work in the minds of people playing ordinary chess, and this mechanism may or may not be mechanistically explainable. But there is no such hidden mechanism.[47]

It is this view of the human mind as being (at least) partly a machine (for symbol manipulation) that lies behind the idea that there is a meaningful problem about whether 'Church's thesis is true about the human mind'. The 'mental processes' of the human mind are conceived as symbol manipulation processes, and via Church's thesis they become 'effective processes that can be carried out by a Turing machine'. Dennett, and Nelson,[48] among others, assure us that this is so, and in particular that this way of speaking makes sense!

According to Dennett:

> program designers work backwards on the same task behaviourists work forwards on . . . . The AI researcher starts with an intentionally characterized problem (e.g., how can I get a computer to understand questions of English?), breaks it down

into subproblems that are also intentionally characterized (e.g., how do I get the computer to recognize questions, distinguish subjects from predicates, ignore relevant parsings?) and finally he reaches problem or task descriptions that are obviously mechanistic.[49]

The idea is then that when this mechanistic level has been reached, the tasks are so 'elementary' that they 'can be taken over by a machine'. And that which guarantees that this procedure will work in principle, that it comprises the study of 'all modes of intelligence', is the 'truth of Church's thesis'.[50]

It should be noted here that the methodology for 'natural-language processing' suggested by Dennett is based on a calculus representation of ordinary language. It is (erroneously) taken for granted that what we do when we understand questions in English is to apply some (formal) grammatical theory. The kind of 'intentionality' that is spoken of here is not the one that belongs to understanding English in the ordinary sense, but to the understanding that belongs to the practice of applying and using theoretical notions and formal methods of linguistic theory. The practices of 'distinguishing subjects from predicates' or of 'ignoring irrelevant parsings' are not part of what people are doing when using language in the ordinary sense. But more importantly, the activity of using language in the ordinary sense is not *composed* of separate parts or levels of performance, one of which is mechanical symbol manipulation. This mechanical level belongs to the activity of formal representation only.

There need not be anything wrong about the *general* idea that human thinking is symbol manipulation. But problems arise when this notion of symbol manipulation is oversimplified, when it is understood as a very *special* form of symbol manipulation, and when there is supposed to be *one* form of symbol manipulation that is fundamental and on the basis of which all other forms are built up. The general idea makes sense when 'symbol manipulation' is understood as comprising the various forms and practices of human language and symbol systems in general. But in this sense, symbol manipulation is as complex and unsurveyable as human reality itself, because it is unseparable from the forms of human life. The various forms of use of signs and symbols cannot be understood as what they are (as 'intentional linguistic actions') in isolation from the activities and practices where they belong. (Only in relation to the *practice* of arithmetic is it determined what is essential about the sign 'x + y' and its use as an arithmetical expression.)

When the application of theoretical representations and calculations in formal systems are taken as the paradigms and the fundamental forms of symbol manipulation, the result is a primitive philosophy of mind.

12 DIFFERENT SENSES OF 'ACTION'

In sum, behind the philosophical claims of AI discussed above there seems to lie a conceptual confusion of (at least) the following kinds of things:

1 *Ordinary human action in general*, i.e. cases of established human practices and activities such as reading, walking, speaking, and calculating.

2 *External behaviour* and the effects characteristic of human actions in sense (1) (for instance, the characteristic arm-motion of someone who is walking, the production of strokes on a paper when someone is calculating, etc.) and which we can imitate or reproduce without actually performing the actions of which the behaviour is characteristic. Such imitation of external behaviour is of course also a human activity (or 'intentional action') even if it is not a common, established practice (though it does occur, for instance with children, on the stage, in learning something). We tend to describe behaviour in this sense by reference to the activities of which it is characteristic. 'He moved his arm as if he were . . .', 'He was standing like someone who is . . .'.

3 *The activities of applying formal models and of operating within theoretical representations* of ordinary human activities, such as mechanical models of symbol recognition or sentence parsing, phonetic models of speech production, representations within formal systems of assertion, calculation, and deduction, and so on. To apply and work with formal models in this sense is of course also (intentional) human action, and it is an essential aspect of scientific work.

4 *Operating or using a machine*, a mechanism or an instrument, such as a car, an electronic computer, or a knife. This is still human action and it can mean 'using a machine *in* doing something' or simply operating a machine 'for its own sake'.

5 *The operation (or behaviour or working or functioning) of a machine*, a

45

mechanism, a physical system. For instance, the operation of the carburettor in a car, or the lock mechanism of a door, or the circulatory system of the human body. And here we have something essentially different from human action.

This is of course a very rough classification, and it is intended only to be of help in describing some of the confusions discussed.

What has been lost sight of is ordinary human actions and practices as we perform them as agents, not necessarily as they appear to us when we *reflect* upon them, but as *we normally do them*. As we have seen, the most common mistake about how *we do* ordinary things like calculating, understanding a sentence, or asking a question is to think as though our actions involved the application of a formal or theoretical representation, although in general this application is said to be only tacit or implicit (we have, it is sometimes said, 'only implicit knowledge of the rules governing the use of language'). This mistaken idea comes from taking the formal models and theoretical representations in sense (3) as the fundamental thing. As though all kinds of 'action' were basically of kind (3), but in most cases only 'implicitly'. The 'implicit rules of language' or the 'hidden mechanism of thinking' are metaphysical correlates of the formal models and the theoretical representation.[51]

Human actions in general, i.e. in sense (1), are, according to this way of thinking, considered as being basically of kind (3). Linguists will have solved their problem when they find the formal models of which our ordinary linguistic practices are (tacit) applications. (This seems to be a correct description of the spirit in which much of the research in linguistics and cognitive science is done today.)

However, it is a fact that only some of the *existing* formal models and methods are taken to be fundamental, and, strictly speaking, what is taken to be fundamental is not the formal models as such, but the way they are operated and applied, i.e. what is *done* with them. Is *this* 'doing' then, as a form of human activity, an application of another (implicit) representation? The idea that ordinary acts and linguistic practices are manifestations of hidden mechanisms or applications of implicit rules is even incoherent.

There is a confusion of (5) and (1), and in particular of (5) and (4), when it is claimed that computers are agents, that they literally calculate and understand questions. But the more serious confusion goes in the opposite direction, when sense (3) of 'operating' is taken to be a case of sense (5). This confusion is the source of the idea

46

that 'human acts are at some basic level mere mechanical symbol-manipulation that can be taken over by a machine'. When it is said that 'a Turing machine operates on the symbols on a tape', we have something conceptually different from the operating of a machine in sense (5), as when we say that 'this machine operates on symbols in the form of electric impulses'. And it is also something different from operating in sense (4), because Turing machines are a kind of formal system, and it is human beings who operate and calculate with them and apply them. So it is sense (3) of operating that applies to the Turing machine. The mechanical rules of a Turing machine are rules that *a human being is following* in calculating,[52] and they are 'mechanical rules' in a different sense from the mechanical rules that describe and explain the working of a mechanism. The machine does not 'follow rules' (even partly) in the sense in which a human agent does. The one thing cannot therefore 'be replaced' by the other.[53]

The operation of a mechanism is something different from a human act even if it is described by means of 'teleological' notions like purpose or function. The so-called functionalism in cognitive psychology is based on the rejection of this difference. The forms of explanation which belong to phenomena of kind (5) are transferred to the description and explanation of human behaviour and cognitive acts, together with the claim that this step is in some way metaphysically justified.

In Dennett's description of the working procedure in AI quoted above, there is clearly implied a view of human acts as being *composed* of separate sub-acts, as though an ordinary action consisted of the totality of sub-acts or external behaviour (in sense (2)) characteristic of the action in question. As though walking consisted of doing several sub-acts, such as moving one's legs in a certain way, holding one's body upright, and moving one's arms. Perhaps the totality of this external behaviour is bound together by 'something mental', an intention or a belief, but this is not considered to be a serious complication on this view, because it is on the basis of observable features that we are supposed to recognize people as doing what they do, including intending, believing, understanding, and so on.

This view is, however, an idea for the construction of (systematic) representations or models of human actions that may perhaps be useful for some technical purpose, but which are not useful for the philosophical purpose of making clear what it is to act as a human.

It is not a description of what *we do* when we are engaged in ordinary actions. I am not necessarily performing several sub-actions when I walk; and when I see my friend walking or speaking to someone, I do not infer or interpret what he is doing on the basis of his external behaviour. There may sometimes be such inference and interpretation, but normally there is none, and this is very important. I simply see directly what a person is doing. 'I see that you are eating', 'I see that you are reading a book', 'I see that you can swim'. I do not have to *think* 'I see . . .'.

'But if we want to develop a theory about recognizing actions like these!' And why should we want to do that? With a view to some technical applications or to solving some practical problems? If not, we are presumably misled by the idea of a 'hidden mechanism' (or internal representation) which is involved in our recognizing people's actions. We somehow have the idea that these judgements must be construed as the results of some kind of derivation before we know what is really involved. But this is a prejudice cultivated in a philosophical and scientific tradition.

13 LOGICAL RULES AND CONDITIONS

Certain features of the expressions of a language or of the signs of a system of symbols are essential and others are inessential. For instance, in the usual notation in mathematics, an essential property of the expression

$$(5,9)$$

for the ordered pair consisting of the numbers 5 and 9 is that the sign '5' occurs to the left of the sign '9'; but it is not an essential feature, for instance, that the distance between these signs is 3 millimetres. It is also essential for the expression of the ordered pair of 5 and 9 that it be composed in a certain way in which the sign '5' is a part of the expression but ')' is not – a notation such as [5,9] or 5/9 could do just as well. The essential features of an expression in this sense I call its *logical form*.

Note however that the logical form of this expression is not something purely physical. It is only *in relation to* the existing *use* of this notation that certain of its physical features are essential. We could very well imagine a notation where for instance the expression (9,5) was used for the ordered pair of 5 and 9 as we now use (5,9). In this expression the physical feature that '9' is to the left of '5' corresponds to the converse feature of the ordinary notation. We could imagine finding a more radically different notation for ordered pairs that was actually used by someone, and in order to translate from the new notation to the ordinary one, it would be necessary – lacking a translation manual – to determine how the essential features are expressed in the new notation. And this we would have to do *on the basis of its use*.

But what do different notations for the ordered pair of 5 and 9 have in common? Well, they are all expressions for the ordered pair of 5 and 9.

Here it is easy to see how the idea arises of mathematical expressions being representations of or 'standing for' some kind of invisible things, 'abstract objects or entities', being hypostases of 'what is common to' the different notations. The ordered pair of 5 and 9 as an abstract object is in some way pictured as a copy of the various notations all of whose arbitrary physical features and differences have been done away with. It consists, so to speak, only of the essential features themselves, as though essential features of the use of expressions could in some way exist without being expressed in any notation at all. As though the possibilities for using the expressions as notations for ordered pairs were already in existence somewhere before they were actualized as mathematical practices.

Prior to the invention of the calculus of ordered pairs, the expression 'the ordered pair consisting of the numbers 5 and 9' did not in ordinary language have the precise meaning it has now. The verbal expression today refers to the symbol (5,9) in its use in this calculus. What is common to the different notations for an ordered pair of numbers is not that they 'stand for' some invisible thing (object or entity); it is the way we operate with them, relate them, replace them and translate them, into one another on the basis of their use. This is the 'common thing' about them.

The use of an expression or a sentence may also involve certain kinds of factual circumstances, some of which may be essential to this use while others are accidental. For instance, the sentence 'There is a horseshoe on the road' makes sense as an empirical sentence only against certain facts about the practice of horse management. Consider, on the other hand, the sentence: 'There is a catshoe on the road.' Cats do not have shoes. There is no corresponding fact about keeping cats that would make this sentence a meaningful empirical sentence, but we could very well imagine that this sentence occurred in a story or fable, i.e., in a *different form of use*.

It would make sense to say about a dog that 'he believes that his master is in the next room', but not that 'he believes that the price of food will rise' in the sense that this could be said about the dog's master. The latter sentence applies only to a human who is familiar with the complex human practice of buying and selling food. The difference here could not be explained by saying that *this particular* dog did not *happen* to know anything about the food trade, which the dog's master did happen to know. The difference is therefore an essential (conceptual) one.

Imagine someone, a human being, standing in the bright sunshine and the sky being free of clouds. Would it make sense to say in this situation 'he believes that it is raining'? I mean, could we believe that the person believes that it is raining in the normal sense in which we say this about people in various situations? A remark like the following is more likely: 'He must be mad or drunk because he behaves as if he believed that it is raining.' And this is an understandable reaction, because the normal conditions for using the sentence 'he believes that it is raining' *do not prevail* in this situation. (And 'normal' does not here refer to some statistical regularity but to a conceptual rule about our use of belief sentences. That this belief statement would be nonsensical is not simply a result of the fact that we so seldom say such things in such situations.)

Sentences of the (linguistic) form '. . . believes that . . .', like other expressions of language, do not have meaning in some uniform way regardless of the circumstances of their use. The rules and conditions that are essential about a form of use I call the logical rules and conditions for that use.

As is evident from the discussion of Turing's test and about so-called 'empirical theories of meaning', it is important to be clear about the difference between the logical conditions (rules) for the use of an expression on the one hand, and the empirical criteria and formal conditions (of a theory) on the other. There is no such thing as a verification or an empirical test of whether certain conditions are the logical conditions for the use of an expression. The outcome of a verification or the results of a test or an experiment may exist as 'well-defined' possibilities prior to the actual verification (or test); but logical conditions are the *logical* conditions for a particular use of an expression only when they prevail. What is essential about a particular use of an expression cannot be otherwise for *that* use (even if it is only a fabricated use). There can be no such thing as a counter-example to a logical rule for the use of an expression – in such a case the 'counter-example' must be *another* use of the expression, subject to other logical rules.

Logical rules and conditions concern the conceptual or internal relationships, the relationships that determine the possibilities that can be tested or verified. These relationships do not in their turn exist as mere possibilities regarding something's being the case.

There can be a problem about the validity or the correctness of the logical rules for the use of expressions in a certain situation only in the sense that it is unclear what the logical rules *are* for that use, but as soon as they are made clear there is no additional problem about whether they are satisfied or valid or correct. (Logical rules are not general hypotheses like the laws of nature.)

It should be obvious that logical rules (conditions and relationships) – as we use the term here – are something other than the rules of formal logic. The latter are formal rules and conditions of a theoretical representation. And our logical investigation is something quite different from the application of the machinery of formal logic. We are interested in getting clear about existing conceptual relationships in existing forms of use of expressions in order to sort out conceptual confusions, not in inventing or constructing new forms of language.

If theory construction and theoretical explanation are essential to scientific work, then logical investigation cannot be scientific investigation.

Logical rules and conditions can be an inspiration to the construction of a formal representation or formalization (as in traditional formal logic), but *formalization is something essentially different from describing the essential features of our forms of language.* A formalization has, and is meant to have, so to speak, a life of its own as a calculus, which the sentences of logical grammar have not. Logical conditions can only be described within a system of description or a way of describing which presupposes that the conditions obtain. In this sense it could be said that the sentences of logical grammar are circular – and that would be a problem if our logical investigation aimed at some form of theoretical explanation or justification as in formal logic, rather than at describing and *reminding* ourselves about essential features of our practice of using language.

For this reason, a statement of logical conditions can only be understood by someone who is familiar with the kinds of circumstances in real life where they exist and who can be reminded about them or about similar ones. This could perhaps also be expressed by saying that logical conditions for a certain use of expressions (like belief sentences or expressions for ordered pairs of numbers), can only be described from *within* this use. It is only in this perspective that the difference between essential and inessential features exists.

It should therefore be clear that a formal (or deductive) system, or a calculus, is a representation of *essential* features of the use of certain expressions only when this use actually is an application of the formal system, i.e. when the rules of the calculus are taken as norms. Such forms of use of expressions do of course exist, for instance in mathematics and in (applications of) formal logic and formal grammar (e.g. in the exercises involving typical examples); but inspection of actual language use shows that these cases are exceptions. Most forms of language use are not (either tacit or implicit) applications of (perhaps not yet explicitly formulated) formal rules.

With the traditional philosophical claims of formal logic and formal grammar, as well as in the attempts to solve 'the frame problem' in AI, one must ignore these facts of our linguistic practice, and conceive any linguistic practice as being (in principle) an application of a (tacit or implicit) system of formal rules.

The incoherence of this way of thinking can be seen in another way, namely if we consider the difference between the formal rules (the rules of formal representation) on the one hand, and 'the following of the formal rules' on the other. Formal rules for the use of expressions determine that use only through a human practice where agreement *in action* is the ultimate criterion of correct and incorrect rule-following. In general there is not first a stipulation of the logical rules and *then* their application, but the other way round. And in cases where a practice is defined and initiated by the stipulation of rules, this is done on the basis of what it means to apply the stipulations correctly as determined by an existing practice. The mere formulation or wording of a general rule does not include what it means to follow or apply the rule.

In a certain sense it could be said that not even the explicit, formal, rules of a rigid formal system 'determine completely' what it means to follow them. It depends in the end upon an agreement in the human practice of following them. A stated rule (instruction, program) can always be misunderstood in a systematic way. And every attempt to improve the formulation and block one kind of misunderstanding will introduce new possibilities of misunderstanding (even if it might be less probable that people with certain experiences and abilities will make these mistakes, and that it therefore might still be useful in practice to improve the formulation).

For this conceptual sense of 'depends upon agreement in practice' it is important that it be a question of agreement *in action*, in a living practice, and not in opinion, reasons, or justification. There is no question whether this agreement is correct or justified in relation to something else.

The failure to see this is a great source of philosophical puzzlement, for instance in theories about 'rationality', in speech-act theory (where logical conditions are considered as empirical criteria to be justified or verified), and in the rule-scepticism of Kripke.[54] Kripke is thinking as though there were something else, beyond this kind of agreement in practices, which is in principle inaccessible to us (like the extension of the rule of addition) and on the basis of which our ways of following rules are correct or incorrect, and he is led to an absurd scepticism: 'I can never know for sure if someone is following a certain rule rather than some other one.'

Kripke's argument for 'rule-scepticism' can be seen as a *reductio ad absurdum* argument, showing that the logical criteria for correctly following a rule cannot be captured by formal or external criteria, but are internally related to a human practice. Another argument that could be seen as showing this is Quine's argument for 'the principle of indeterminacy of translation', which can be said to show that the forms of use of sentences of a foreign language cannot be captured in causally conceived criteria for the verbal behaviour of native speakers. The various forms of language are inseparable from the whole way of living of the speakers of the language.

'But are you not expounding some kind of linguistic or cultural relativism?' No, the 'dependence on agreement in linguistic practices' is not meant as an idea on which to base a theory or a thesis concerning a general view of language; it is meant to oppose certain general views and to point to certain simple (and in a certain sense trivial) *facts* about our practice of using language, which nevertheless are fundamental and on which we do as a matter of fact agree – *in practice*, relativists as well as non-relativists. Without *this* agreement there would be no disagreement either. Without the normal agreement in judgements like 'This is a case of that rule' there would not be such a thing as disagreement in views and opinions (e.g. in the philosophy of language) either.

To interpret what I have been saying here as a kind of 'linguistic relativism' is to think as though there might after all be something else, perhaps inaccessible to us, on the basis of which our forms of language and rule-following are correct or incorrect. It is to admit the possibility that this would at least make sense. But since this 'ultimate dependence on agreement in practices' is a conceptual dependence, it does *not* make sense. You cannot admit that a certain possibility makes sense and at the same time withdraw, so to speak, the foundation for expressing sense.

2

NOTIONS OF LANGUAGE AND THEORIES OF MEANING

1 *A PRIORI* THEORIES OF MEANING VERSUS NATURALISTIC THEORIES OF LANGUAGE

Due to the 'linguistic turn' of several traditional philosophical problems that was initiated by Frege and Wittgenstein, the development of theories of meaning has become a central concern of current philosophy, and several theories have been proposed. Frege himself is considered to have made a first contribution. Husserl's philosophy is said to involve a theory of meaning, or even to be one, and there is also said to be a theory of meaning in Wittgenstein's *Tractatus* and another in Quine's philosophy of language. The semantic theories in the traditions initiated by Tarski, Carnap, and others are considered by some to be the proper way of dealing with the problems of meaning, even in the case of 'natural languages'.

These attempts to extend the applicability of the methods of meta-mathematics and formal semantics to the study of ordinary language have also attracted linguists, and this has caused a certain confusion of linguistic and philosophical interests in language. This development seems to be part of the background for the discussion of 'What form a theory of meaning should take', as initiated by Davidson and Dummett, and this discussion has in turn led to a renewed interest in the subject matter of theories of meaning.

What we have here are not only different theories of meaning in the sense of different approaches to the same problems, but there exists a more fundamental (but neglected and misunderstood) difference which makes it questionable whether we can talk about, for instance, Frege's and Davidson's theories of meaning as being theories of meaning in the same sense. It seems clear to me that there is an important sense in which the problems of how the expressions of our languages have meaning, problems which Frege and the early Wittgenstein wanted to solve, are not even touched upon in formal semantics or in such a theory of meaning as Davidson's. And these problems *cannot* be handled in formal semantics, the reason being that Frege and Wittgenstein meant to concern themselves with *the a priori conditions* of expressing sense by means of language. They were interested in the structure of sentences that is *essential* to their conceptual content, while most recent theories of language are developed within a more or less naturalistic perspective.[1]

In the naturalistic attitude of the Warsaw school, and in connection with the various approaches to the study of language within logical empiricism, there was no room for '*a priori* conditions' or 'essential structure' in this sense. The sense of the term *a priori* that Kant used in talking about 'the *a priori* conditions of empirical knowledge' was incompatible with the naturalistic viewpoint. Only what could be conceived as though it belonged to Nature (or as being a mathematical entity) was admissible. The *a priori* was understood as that which is prior to or independent of experience in the sense in which formal or purely mathematical relationships are so. It could not be understood as signifying conceptual relationships. The unifying attitude of the naturalistic traditions was (and still is) that the philosophical study of language (in Quine's words) 'is not to be distinguished in essential points of purpose and method from good or bad science'.[2] A semantic theory or a theory of meaning in this naturalistic attitude is a theory in essentially the same sense, with the same kinds of methods and on the same level as the theories of natural science and mathematics, with primitive terms, axioms, and theorems, which are verified, derived, or proved in the same sense as in other scientific theories. There are differences between various trends within this naturalistic philosophy, for instance in the different attitudes to 'intensional contexts' and in whether one wants the theories to be strictly empirical or to 'admit abstract entities' and be more like mathematical theories; but the basic naturalistic attitude is the same. In order to separate this kind of study from linguistic science, one would perhaps say that these theories, in that they are to be *philosophical* theories, are concerned with more general and abstract aspects of language than are the theories of linguistics. However, this difference is then conceived of as being only a matter of degree.

Such naturalistic theories of language are also meant to be correct or incorrect in the same sense as other scientific theories. They have to be justified on the basis of empirical evidence, applicability, coherence in formal structure, simplicity, and so on. This means that these theories, like other scientific theories, are not immune from revision. They have a *hypothetical* character. In spite of being theories that are meant to solve *fundamental* problems about language and logic, they have a hypothetical character!

The sceptical and relativistic consequences lurking nearby have their precise counterparts in the scepticism and relativism of the late nineteenth-century psychologism and empiricism, which Husserl and Frege criticized. *The wish to overcome these philosophical problems were the motive and the starting points for Frege's, Husserl's, and the early Wittgenstein's work on problems of meaning.* So it seems fair to say that these problems of meaning are not touched upon at all in formal semantics or in theories of meaning such as Davidson's. Hypothetical solutions to philosophical problems are not recognized as being problematic at all, due to the dogmatic, naturalistic attitude that elects a certain scientific method and technique as being 'the last arbiter of truth' (to use Quine's words again).

Considered as theories of meaning, these naturalistic theories of language are attempts to capture meaning in an indirect way. They are extensional in the sense that they attempt to characterize the meaning of expressions and sentences in terms of the extensions (denotations, references, truth-values) of expressions in a 'meta-language'. The meaning of an expression in the meta-language, the language that is used in the construction of the theory, is in general not a matter for investigation, but is taken for granted. In the *a priori* theories of meaning of Frege, Husserl, and the early Wittgenstein, the investigation of categorial differences and the difference between the essential and inessential features of an expression given a certain use, was *intended* to be a main topic. But even such an *intention* is incompatible with the naturalistic attitude, since it involves transcending the naturalistic perspective.[3] By the extensional procedure, categorial differences, and the difference between essential and inessential features of expressions in a given use, are obliterated (as Tarski and Quine explicitly admit). An imposed formal structure of propositions determined by a pre-established technique for paraphrase or formalization is instead what is taken to be the fundamental feature of expressions in the 'meaning specifications' of these naturalistic theories of meaning. Formal reconstruction replaces the articulation of essential features of given notions.

This difference between *a priori* theories of meaning and naturalistic theories of language is reflected in the different ways in which the sense/reference distinction is used in Frege's writings and in later naturalistic theorizing on language. Frege belonged to the Kantian tradition,[4] at least in so far as he recognized the difference between a conceptual component and an empirical component of thoughts and judgements. He realized that knowledge of objects of experience has its own *a priori* conditions and that these conditions are what the subject matter of the logical investigation are. Since these *a priori* conditions are logically (internally) related to the objects of experience, it makes no sense to talk about objects of experience as though they were detached from our conceptual systems (as '*bare* objects' in Dummett's words). Frege's notion of a *Sinn*, being the way in which an object is given or presented or conceived through the name it has, was meant to explain the conceptual link between a name and the object named (the 'reference').

On this point it becomes clear that the sense/reference distinction (as well as the intension/extension distinction) in recent formal semantics is a radically different notion. On Frege's view it would not make sense to speak about a 'theory of reference' as a theory which is separable from the 'theory of sense', as though 'senses' and 'references' were distinct (but perhaps overlapping) realms of *things* or objects externally related to one another and to the names of our language. According to Frege, to give an account of the way in which a name has reference (and the way in which a sentence has a truth-value) is to account for the sense of the name. This involves attending, not to the object referred to or any object at all, but to the way the object is conceived, as it manifests itself in language, in the name of the object. And Frege's account is logical – it is concerned with that in language which renders referring *possible*. This attending to the 'ways objects are given in language' is, however, not a transitive intellectual operation conducted on a higher level, in a 'meta-language', where the ways objects are given in an 'object-language' are considered objects of investigation. This way of thinking – which is characteristic of the meta-mathematical tradition – will wind up in the familiar way in an infinite regress of object-languages and meta-languages, or in an endless hierarchy of 'senses' and 'references'. Within the naturalistic attitude one is quite happy with this infinite hierarchy. It is considered as something natural and unavoidable (Russell, Church), and it *is* unavoidable in the naturalistic perspective. For Frege, Husserl, and the early Wittgenstein this was a *problem* because, according to them, to regard this infinite regress as something that we have to live with would be to regard the project of giving an ultimate and absolute conceptual justification of the laws of logic and the principles of science as an impossible enterprise. Any conceptual justification and meaning explanation would be bound to be only hypothetical or relative (to the notions and methods used in some meta-language), as though we could only have an indirect or mediated relation to our own concepts. So they sided with the Kantian view that the conceptual investigation must be a kind of investigation essentially different from ordinary scientific investigations; it must be an *a priori* investigation of meaning in which we pay attention to the unmediated relationship that we have to our concepts and to the language we use.

In formal semantics, the capacity of referring or denoting is taken to be the basic feature of linguistic expressions, and this denotation relation is conceived as a functional relationship (i.e., an 'interpretation' in model theory assigns a reference to a name, or a class of models to a sentence, in the same sense of 'assigning' as when we say that a function assigns that value to this argument in mathematics). One does not, like Frege, recognize 'expressing a sense' as an essentially *different* aspect of expressions of language, which is conceptually prior to and in a certain sense a precondition for denoting or referring. Linguistic expressions' having *sense*, is rather explained or accounted for *in terms of* denotation in formal semantics. Such explanations will not work, however, as accounts of how the expressions used in the meta-language have meaning.

It may be correct to say that Frege's theory about sense and reference was an important source of inspiration for the later work in formal semantics (e.g. for Carnap and Church), but it is very misleading to describe this work as a continuation and development of Frege's ideas and intentions. In the way the notion of a 'theory' is used in formal semantics, a 'semantic theory' or 'meaning theory' would be inconceivable for Frege (as well as for Husserl and the early Wittgenstein), or rather, such a theory would leave Frege's most fundamental problems unsolved.

2 THEORY OF MEANING VERSUS CONCEPTUAL INVESTIGATION

Another instance of the failure to see the difference between the *a priori* and the naturalistic theories of meaning occurs when recent theories in formal semantics and theory of meaning (such as Davidson's) are classified, together with Frege's theory and the theory in the *Tractatus*, as being all of them *truth-conditional* theories of meaning. The idea that 'the meaning of a sentence consists in its truth-conditions' was understood by Frege and in the *Tractatus* as a principle for the conceptual (or logical) analysis of individual forms of sentences. It was not intended as an answer to the question 'what form a theory of meaning should take' or how to build a formal semantic theory, because these questions as discussed today are framed within the naturalistic conception of a theory, and Frege and Wittgenstein were not concerned with giving 'theories of meaning' in that sense.

There is a parallel difference between two senses of the verifiability principle, that 'the meaning of a sentence consists in the method of its verification'. Within the naturalistic framework it is understood as a principle for the shaping of meaning explanations within a systematic theory of meaning or the construction of a verificationist formal semantics. It was, however, as a principle for conceptual analysis, as a guide to the discovery of meaning whenever there occurs a problem about the meaning of a statement, that this principle was stated and successfully used by Einstein, Bridgman, Wittgenstein, Schlick, and others. It is as such a principle that Arthur Pap states it: 'to find the meaning of a statement, find out how one would go about verifying it, or what sort of evidence one would accept as establishing its truth.'[5] Understood in this way, the 'verifiability principle of meaning' and the principle that the meaning of a sentence consists in its truth-conditions are not opposed to one another; the former principle can be seen rather as a more specific form of the latter. The understanding of these principles as guides in conceptual investigation was lost however in the logical empiricism of Carnap, Hempel, and others, where naturalistic theory-construction replaced conceptual investigation as the main task of philosophy. The problem with the verifiability principle then became one of 'making it precise' as a principle dealing with the form of a naturalistic theory of empirical meaning.

The investigation of the meaning of propositions (in mathematics, for instance) that Frege and the early Wittgenstein were concerned with was conceptual investigation. As they conceived it, the aim was to lay bare the logical *content* of propositions in order to *justify* a certain formalization of a proposition as an articulation of its logical form (in the sense of the features that are essential to it as a true or a false proposition). They realized that such a 'contentual justification' could not consist merely in the application of a *scientific* method, theory or technique (as in Boole's logic or in the psychologism and empiricism of the late nineteenth century), but that it is a *philosophical* task, different from scientific tasks. To give such a contentual justification would be nothing less than to give a philosophical and conceptual *foundation*. The justification had to be conclusive or *absolute*. It had to be based – to use Husserl's notion – on 'apodictic evidence'. There could be nothing hypothetical about it as with scientific explanation. It could not depend on the presuppositions of some scientific theory or method, for then it would not constitute the ultimate foundation. And the ultimate foundation was what one seemed to need in order to overcome the various forms of relativism, subjectivism, and scepticism.[6]

This means that *a priori* theories of meaning are much better described as methods for conceptual investigation or methods for philosophical analysis, rather than as theories about some kind of entities or phenomena (in nature), this being the prevailing notion of a theory in the current naturalistic traditions, where even mathematics is conceived as being a natural science about mathematical phenomena. The task of explaining how arithmetical statements have meaning, as Frege conceived it, and the philosophical task of conceptually clarifying the notion of number, the notion of truth of arithmetical statements, etc., were seen to be inseparable. The same is true of the 'theory of meaning' in the *Tractatus* – it is inseparable from the account of the structure of states of affairs, of thoughts, of the world, and so on.

In the Davidson tradition a distinction has been made between two different senses of 'theory of meaning'. On the one hand, the notion is meant to signify a theory of meaning for a specific language. As such it is said to be a 'non-philosophical' and empirical theory. On the other hand, 'theory of meaning' signifies a system of ideas, principles, and conditions which a theory of meaning in the first sense should satisfy. The philosophical accounts are said to belong to theories in this sense. It should be obvious that neither Frege's theory of meaning nor the *Tractatus'* theory fits into this

61

classification. It would be ridiculous to describe Frege's *Grundgetsetze* – where he applies his sense-reference principles – as presenting an 'empirical theory of meaning for the language of arithmetic' (whatever that would mean). It was meant as the result of a conceptual investigation of the language of arithmetic, and as giving the logical foundation for arithmetic. It is also very misleading to present Frege's *Über Sinn und Bedeutung* as providing principles and conditions that certain empirical theories should satisfy. And it is even more misleading to describe it as a general theory *about* some kind of entities or things (e.g. as a theory about 'intensional entities'). It was rather meant as a presentation of general notions and principles for the *a priori* investigation of the meaning of certain forms of our language. If it has to be called a theory *about* anything at all, then it is a theory about how to deal with conceptual problems connected with the way in which certain expressions of our language have meaning.

According to Davidson's idea of theory of meaning, on the contrary, to give a theory of meaning and to perform a conceptual investigation seem to be different and unrelated tasks, in the sense that the former can be done without involving the latter. In the construction of a theory of meaning for a language, it would not be necessary to worry even about ambiguous expressions because – according to Davidson – as long as they do not affect the grammatical form, they are translated into the meta-language and 'a truth definition will not tell any lies'.[7] In the *a priori* conception of a theory of meaning (such as Frege's), to specify and eliminate ambiguities was rather a prime example of a problem that the investigation of meaning must solve *before* the theory can be given, because this is part of what is involved in making explicit the *logical form* of expressions. Davidson claims instead that we should observe the 'fundamental distinction' between the task of 'uncovering' the logical form of sentences and the analysis of the content of individual forms of sentences!

What we have here are two radically different uses of the term 'logical form' (and hence also of the terms 'meaning' and 'theory of meaning'). To give the 'logical form' of a sentence according to Davidson is simply to find that paraphrase or formalization of the sentence which renders the theory as formally coherent as possible, *by means of a pre-established technique for paraphrase* (usually the predicate calculus).[8] It would thus seem possible to find the logical form of a sentence like 'John believes that the earth is round', without going into the question of the actual content of such a belief-sentence. (To render it as a three-place predicate between a sentence, a person, and a language is considered by Davidson to be a reasonable suggestion!)[9]

Davidson would presumably say, with Quine, that formalization in the predicate calculus makes no 'synonymy claims', its purpose is not to capture a 'hidden meaning'. Therefore, in Davidson's theory, the 'logical form' of a sentence signifies an *imposed* (not 'uncovered') formal structure, while in the *a priori* theories of Frege, Husserl and the early Wittgenstein, it was intended to signify the features of the sentence which are essential to the content it expresses.[10] Finding the logical form of a proposition and getting clear about its content were therefore inseparable tasks. Logical investigation, meaning investigation, conceptual investigation, would be essentially only different names for the same philosophical task. Its aim was to solve *philosophical* problems, not linguistic ones, and not only problems in what is currently called 'philosophy of language'. A reason for calling it an 'investigation of meaning' would be that this lays emphasis on Frege's and Wittgenstein's insight about the advantage of conducting conceptual investigations on the basis of the linguistic manifestations of conceptual relationships, rather than in terms of traditional metaphysical and idealistic philosophical notions, which were becoming obsolete through the rapid change and development of the sciences.

Michael Dummett seems, to some extent, to sympathize with this view of theory of meaning as conceptual investigation and as being the most promising approach to solving philosophical problems in general, even problems which are not normally seen as belonging to the philosophy of language, such as problems in the various disputes over realism in mathematics. What is at the root of these disputes is, according to Dummett, the question of what form a theory of meaning for the language of mathematics should take. Obviously, a theory of meaning must then be understood as being, or as involving, a conceptual foundation or justification. However, in other respects, Dummett is in accord with the ideas of Davidson, and it is therefore not immediately clear where he stands in the opposition between *a priori* theories of meaning and naturalistic theories of language. The correct description seems to me to be that there is a tension or a deep opposition in Dummett's writings between certain incompatible ideas: on the one hand the ideas and purposes that belong to *a priori* investigations of meaning, such as

Frege's, and on the other hand, the notions, methods, and framing of problems as presented in Davidson's naturalistic approach.

In the first part of his two-part essay 'What is a theory of meaning?',[11] Dummett argues that a theory of meaning cannot simply be some form of systematic translation if it is to give a complete account of what it is to understand the expressions of a language. It must be a 'full-blooded' theory in the sense that it should 'explain what it is to have the concepts expressible by means of that language'. Giving a theory of meaning must therefore involve conceptual investigation in order to be able to decide upon and state what is essential about the concepts expressed in a language. Only a full-blooded theory would have the philosophical significance that Dummett wants a theory of meaning to have. The dispute about realism in mathematics, for instance, would not be brought to its roots with anything less than a full-blooded theory of meaning for the language of mathematics. If the conceptual justifications of the basic principles of reasoning in mathematics depended on (what Dummett calls) 'extraneous presuppositions', the justifications would only be hypothetical and relative. The dispute about realism would only be transferred to a dispute about these presuppositions, which may not provide any gain at all.

It is clear that Dummett – in requiring full-blooded theories – shares the philosophical aims of the *a priori* theories of meaning. This requirement is a direct counterpart to Frege's, Husserl's, and the early Wittgenstein's demand that the philosophical justification of the principles of logic must be non-hypothetical and absolute in order to overcome the relativistic and sceptical consequences of psychologism, empiricism and historicism.[12] On the other hand, it is also clear that Dummett accepts several of Davidson's naturalistic notions and presuppositions, for instance the notion of a language as a kind of empirical phenomenon, as a system of expressions to which the 'meaning specifications assign meanings'. He accepts the naturalistic view of these expressions as physical objects in an object-language over which the truth-predicate is defined as a mathematical function. He employs the sense/reference distinction as though theories of reference and of sense were separable theories. And he sometimes speaks about manifestations of knowledge of meaning in behaviouristic terms, as though a practical ability 'manifesting' such knowledge would be specifiable without the employment of 'semantic notions'. These naturalistic presuppositions are, however, incompatible with the requirement of full-bloodedness. By arguments similar to Quine's argument for the indeterminacy of translation or Kripke's argument for his thesis of 'rule-scepticism', it can be shown that a theory of meaning built upon this naturalistic basis is bound to be hypothetical or 'underdetermined'.

The requirement of full-bloodedness is the requirement that the theory not depend on extraneous presuppositions, whereas the essence of the naturalistic conceptions is that certain extraneous presuppositions, in the form of scientific notions and methods, *are to be used and taken for granted* without (absolute) justification. The idea of a full-blooded theory of meaning, or an absolute conceptual foundation, therefore simply does not make sense within Davidson's kind of empirical-linguistic perspective (which is also Dummett's perspective when he conceives of 'a theory of meaning as a theory of understanding'). In this perspective, it is assumed that a theory of meaning should serve to explain concepts to someone who does not already have them! This has nothing to do with the idea of absolute conceptual justification, which Frege, Husserl, and Wittgenstein were aiming at. It is a misconception resulting from a confusion of linguistic and philosophical aims.

3 CONFUSION OF THE PERSPECTIVES OF LINGUISTICS AND PHILOSOPHY

What, then, is the notion of 'meaning' in a naturalistic theory such as Davidson's, if it is something other than conceptual content, i.e. something other than what he would explain by 'an analysis of individual concepts' (in his own words)? Is there a notion of 'linguistic meaning' which is different from that of 'logical content'? – In discussions about Davidson's ideas, people sometimes speak of 'theories of meaning for a natural language like English' or for 'fragments of English'. This is obviously a sense of 'theory of meaning' *essentially different* from the sense in which we talk about 'a theory of meaning for the language of arithmetic' or about 'the verificationist theory of meaning for the language of intuitionistic logic'. And in the discussion of how to handle belief sentences or counterfactual statements in theories of meaning, the discussion is presumably not about belief sentences and counterfactuals *in English*. And Frege was not giving a theory of meaning for the *German* (arithmetical) language.

Someone may think that I am here referring to the current distinction between theory of meaning or semantics for formal (or artificial) languages on the one hand, and for natural languages on the other, but I am not. This distinction, as it is currently employed, involves a misconception of the *a priori* theories of meaning of Frege and the early Wittgenstein, if it is assumed that these theories were only concerned with formal languages, for they were *meant* to be theories of meaning for ordinary language. In the naturalistic conception one overlooks the fact that formalization, in the sense of the articulation of the conceptually essential features of ordinary language expressions, *was seen as part of the conceptual analysis*, as part of explaining how sentences of ordinary language have meaning.[13]

If something was wrong with these *a priori* theories, it was not that they failed to account for a notion of 'linguistic meaning' as something different from *logical* content, because the aims of these theories were philosophical, not linguistic. The failure to see this lies behind a very unfair criticism of Frege by the founders of so-called 'situation semantics'. Frege's theory is judged as a kind of linguistic theory for natural languages. This criticism is particularly unfair since the kind of *logical* or conceptual dependence of statements on the context in which they are used, which one may correctly criticize Frege for having overlooked, is rendered as a kind of functional dependence, and thus as a *non*-logical dependence, in situation semantics. In other words, advocates of situation semantics are making the same mistake as Frege on a point where they claim to have improved upon him.

What we stand before here is *a complicated confusion of linguistic and logical-philosophical aims and interests with regard to language*. As I have tried to indicate, this confusion is unavoidable from a strictly naturalistic viewpoint, in which the philosophical, *a priori* investigation of meaning is something inconceivable, and is therefore a mistaken enterprise. What remains then is only the study of language by the methods of science, but, according to Davidson and others, it is nevertheless somehow meant to be philosophy. This confusion seems to me to be the important common source of problems discussed in recent philosophy of language in several traditions. The attempts to assimilate philosophical and linguistic aims and notions seem to be a basic starting point for Davidson's and Dummett's discussion of theories of meaning, and for the Chomsky tradition, the Montague tradition, situation semantics and in general for what is called 'formal semantics for natural languages'.

This development was prepared for by the naturalistic approach to the study of language. The dividing line between the *a priori* investigation of language and the naturalistic view-point was Hilbert's idea of meta-mathematics. In the methodological programme of meta-mathematics we find the origin of some of the most popular naturalistic views and notions of language in current (analytic) philosophy and linguistic theory. Hilbert's naturalistic attitude is very distinct in his appeal to empirical natural science and to the 'concretely given' as the essence of 'the finitist frame of mind'. His exposition of the idea of *Beweistheorie*[14] as a way of dealing *mathematically* with philosophical problems about mathematics obviously inspired many people to a similar approach to philosophy and to the study of language in general.[15] Hilbert introduced a confusion of philosophical and mathematical aims and perspectives that is a counterpart to (and to a great extent a cause of) the confusion of the linguistic and the philosophical perspectives on language. It is from Hilbert's finitism that we have the naturalistic idea of the expressions of a language as *natural* phenomena, as physical objects, and the forms of linguistic expressions as some kind of merely spatial structures, or temporal structures in the case of spoken language. And this conception forms the basis for technical notions introduced later, such as the distinctions: syntax/ semantics of Tarski and Carnap, object-language/meta-language, type/token, use/mention, and so on, which are commonplace notions in current theorizing on language. Through acquiring and exercising these technical notions and others formed on the basis of them, many linguists and philosophers of language today are acting as supporters of the naturalistic view of language without being aware of it.

The notion of a language which underlies the current distinction between theories of meaning for natural languages and for formal languages is the conception of a language as a *notational system*, a calculus of words and sentences (terms and formulas). The natural languages are taken within this conception to have originated conventionally or naturally in the history of mankind, and are rigorous calculi only implicitly, while the formal languages are explicitly constructed calculi. When Carnap and Davidson speak about a belief sentence as involving an (external) relation between a person, a sentence and *a language*, it is clear that 'a language' is understood as a (conventional) system of notation. And when Dummett says that a theory of meaning for an entire language must give 'a detailed specification of the meanings of all words and sentence-forming operations', he is obviously thinking (like Chomsky) of a natural language as a system of rules for generating sentences. If we adopt this notion of a language as a system of notation, it must then be said that neither Frege nor Wittgenstein were concerned with the theory of meaning of natural or formal languages. In this conception of a language the conceptual or logical perspective is excluded; language is 'separated from reality', from the forms of use of expressions, and it is seen as an empirical or historical phenomenon or as a mathematical structure. In this linguistic perspective, the interest is not in the forms of language as (*a priori*) conceptual or logical relationships. But *this* is precisely what was of central interest for Frege and Wittgenstein.

There is a deep confusion of the linguistic and the logical-philo-sophical perspectives on language. The latter is *conceptual* and not empirical (or historical or psychological or literary or . . .). In the philosophical investigation one's interest is not in language as a conventional system of notation or as a system of conventional forms of expression, i.e. in the sense in which German is one such system and English another as understood by linguists. The logical-philosophical investigation is concerned with the forms of language as manifestations of conceptual systems and relationships. It is therefore conducted on a level of generality where many features of a language, as a system of conventional notations (features which may be of interest to linguists) are irrelevant and are disregarded, as for instance the difference between English and German counter-factual sentences. Linguists treating languages as empirical phenomena or as phenomena in the natural history of cultures may of course be interested in noting ambiguous expressions as empirical linguistic phenomena, without worrying about them as potential sources of conceptual confusion and misunderstanding, because they may not be concerned with any particular form of use of the language. And if they are going to describe the language as the conventional system of forms of expression of a group of people, they will of course describe the language *with* these ambiguities. But it would be misleading to describe a philosophical meaning-theorist (such as Frege) as concerned with something similar to this.

The idea of 'linguistic meaning', as something different from conceptual content, and as something connected with and deter-mined by the mere words and expressions of a system of notation (and which may be studied by way of a systematic observation of the behaviour of the users of these expressions) rests on a confusion of the meaning of expressions and the causes and effects of uttering them (or a conventionalized *reading* of them). The idea seems to come from thinking about a lexicon, a German–English lexicon for instance, as a list of equations, or identities 'X = Y', where 'X' is a German expression and 'Y' an English expression, asserting that 'the meaning connected with 'X' and with 'Y' is one and the same'. It is clear that this idea of a lexicon as a list of identities stating the (absolute) sameness of certain entities called 'linguistic meanings' is again a result of a confusion of the aims of linguistics and those of the logical investigation of conceptual content in traditional philosophy. It is the result of a mistaken view of the linguistic notion of the synonymy of expressions as a logical or *a priori* relationship. A lexicon is concerned with languages, not as manifestations of conceptual relationships, but as conventional systems of notation in an historical situation, and what is asserted in the 'equations' is that two expressions have been observed to be (on the basis of an '*a posteriori* investigation' of readings, not uses) equivalent from some one of *various* aspects, e.g. idiomatic, technical, stylistic, or historical.

The idea of a lexicon as a list of absolute identities is also involved in the superficial notion of translation in Quine's idea of a 'translation manual' as consisting of 'an effective set of rules for mapping sentences' from one language onto sentences of another language. Everyone who has been engaged in translating texts, even stereotyped scientific texts, knows that this is not how it works; translation is, in important respects, dissimilar from the construction of a one-to-one mapping between mathematical structures. Whether a certain English sentence is the correct translation of a particular German sentence depends on the circumstances of the use of the sentence, the communicative situation, and so on. The criterion of correctness is not sameness of an absolute 'linguistic meaning' or 'literal meaning', which would be determined by the sentences as mere expressions. There is no such thing.[16]

Language as a conventional system of notation for communication, of a nation or a group of people, is the basic notion of language in traditional linguistic studies. The idea of a *general* linguistic study concerned, not with particular languages, but with 'the underlying common structure' ('universal grammar', 'the synchronic structure', etc.) of languages-as-systems-of-notation in general, is a misconceived idea. It is the way in which the confusion of the linguistic and the logical-philosophical aims comes out on the part of the linguists (as in Chomsky's work, for instance). It is a misconception because it takes the expressions and their readings, rather than their employment in life, to be the basis for conceptual investigation. Traditional grammar describes, classifies, and compares forms of expressions by means of ancient categories such as 'sentence', 'noun', 'verb', and 'adjective'. On the basis of this grammatical description, the forms of use and the forms of linguistic communication are then explained, derived, and accounted for, as though language were a means to various ends in the 'extra-linguistic' reality. It could be said: 'In the logical-philosophical investigation, language and reality cannot be separated from one another', and this means: the expressions must be considered within their normal forms of use. And these forms of use cut across the traditional linguistic and philosophical categories. The difference between traditional linguistic grammar and logical-philosophical grammar is not just that the latter employs some table of (traditional or modern) logical-philosophical categories, where the former employs the traditional linguistic ones; the essential difference is rather that the former takes (written) forms of expressions as the fundamental thing, while the latter recognizes the normal forms of use of expressions as being the fundamental 'categories'.

4 SOME PHILOSOPHICAL PREJUDICES

It is not my purpose to *defend* the *a priori* theories of meaning as being the correct approach to the problems in the philosophy of language or as being the true method of philosophy. On the contrary, we (should) know through the work of the late Wittgenstein, of Heidegger, and others, that these traditional ways of doing philosophy belong to the past. My purpose has been to point out that these theories involved an investigation of meaning in a sense that differs in important ways from recent naturalistic studies of language – a sense which has been forgotten through the predominance of the naturalistic attitude. If there is anything I would like to defend about the work of Frege, Husserl, and the early Wittgenstein, it is the *need* that motivated their work, it is the attitude to the philosophical problems of relativism and scepticism that was their starting point. As I have tried to show, these problems are no less acute in the naturalistic philosophizing of today than they were in the empiricism, psychologism, and historicism of the late nineteenth century; but for various reasons the need to come to terms with these problems is no longer felt to be urgent among those who call themselves philosophers. They are busy with theory-construction.

The failure of the *a priori* theories of meaning was rooted in three related kinds of traditional philosophical prejudices: (i) the conception of logic as a system of formal rules, (ii) the metaphysical idea of the 'true nature of things' as being something hidden, (iii) the foundationalist idea of certain technical philosophical notions as being fundamental 'super-concepts'.

The features of language of interest in the logical-philosophical investigation are, as already remarked, those expressing conceptual relationships. The first mistake in Frege's work and in the *Tractatus* was to think as though these conceptual relationships coincide with the rules of a formal system, a calculus of functions. This was, of course, a continuation of the traditional conception of logic as formal logic.[17] Second, since language, reality, and reasoning do not in general *appear* to us as the application of a calculus, since language is not *obviously* a construction according to a systematic theory, one is forced to say that the logical and conceptual structure is something *hidden* (or underlying, or implicit). The true nature of things has to be revealed through theoretical explanation. Our language is taken as being the *implicit* application of a system of rules, which it is the task of philosophers to make explicit through explanation. Third, if such explanation is to be possible, the 'hidden logical structure' cannot be too complex and chaotic; it must be simple and surveyable, it must consist of a few basic notions (categories, principles) in terms of which others are defined and derived. Examples of such basic notions are the ones signified by the words 'proposition', 'judgement', 'state of affairs', 'evidence', 'object', 'name', 'sense', 'reference', etc., in their technical philosophical employment.

It is clear that the conception of language and logical structure of traditional logical-philosophical study was a projection of the methods, attitudes, and customs which characterize that tradition, in much the same way as the linguistic conception of language reflects the methods and attitudes of traditional linguistic study. Just as the structure of traditional grammar is seen as the core of language in the linguistic tradition, so the structure and notions of formal logic are seen as the core of language in traditional philosophy. But obviously human language was not invented by these two traditions. Actual language is not a construction or the application of a construction resulting from these two traditions, in which

71

we can somehow discern what each of them has contributed. How do the conceptions of language of these traditions fare in comparison with actual language? What do we find in an observation of language in which its various features are allowed to speak for themselves and not for some position in linguistic and logical theory? It was against the prejudices of the logical-philosophical tradition that Wittgenstein wrote,

> The more narrowly we examine actual language, the sharper becomes the conflict between it and our requirement. (For the crystalline purity of logic was, of course, not a *result of investigation*: it was a requirement.) The conflict becomes intolerable; the requirement is now in danger of becoming empty.[18]

Wittgenstein saw that it was the traditional ways of stating the philosophical problems and dealing with them that constituted the main obstacle to their solution. He saw that the traditional ideas about what would solve them stand in the way of the solutions; the traditional expectations and demands about what their solution should look like are sometimes even the main cause of the problems. He realized that the difficulty of the problems does not consist in logical structure being something deeply hidden, but on the contrary in its being in open view. The most important aspects of language for philosophy are rather hidden because of their familiarity and simplicity. The difficulty is one of recognizing certain everyday facts, on which we all agree in action, as being the logical foundation, as being that which settles philosophical problems absolutely.

I have been emphasizing the difference between the *a priori* theories of meaning and the current naturalistic theories of language. This difference is sharp if we compare the two ways of working from the point of view of the problems that motivated them and with respect to the aims they are meant to have. However, if we compare the two kinds of theories from the point of view of the methods and techniques employed in representing forms and phenomena of language, we find that they have much in common. They are both theories; and explanation is considered a main task of each of them. We find common conceptions of language which are the results of predicating upon language what lies in the methods of representing it. The calculus conception of language and logic, the idea of the logical structure of language as being something hidden, and the foundationalist attitude to certain philosophical notions, are characteristic features not only of *a priori* theories, but of many

recent naturalistic theories as well. It even appears that these traditional philosophical prejudices are what justify the naturalistic
theories as being philosophical. The strict naturalist of course denies
the idea of the 'hidden true nature' of language, as well as any form
of the traditional metaphysical prejudice regarding an ultimate and
absolute truth that is hidden from us; and the naturalist therefore
also denies that some extraordinary kind of intellectual perception is
needed to grasp that truth (idealism). But the naturalist nevertheless
acts and makes philosophical claims about his theory-constructions
as though there were such an absolute truth after all, and as though
its nature were expressed in the presuppositions, principles, and
methods employed. In this sense, the naturalist *has* a conception of
the 'hidden true nature of language', of 'what it is that makes
language *language*'.

In what follows of this study I shall look into some of the details
of this conception as it manifests itself in different ways in some
recent theories of meaning, and I shall show that it involves many
problems of principle when it is confronted with the facts of our
actual language.[19]

5 LANGUAGES WITH 'SPECIFIED STRUCTURE'

The conception of language in theories of meaning reveals itself
perhaps most distinctly if we reflect on the use of the terms
'expression', 'form of expression', and 'sentence' within the discussion of theories of meaning. There is a definite agreement in the
use of these words in the formulation and discussion of the problem
of 'what form a theory of meaning should take', and this use of the
terms points to certain definite but unexpressed answers to the
questions 'What is an expression?', 'What is the form of an
expression?', and 'What is a sentence?'.

One idea that frequently occurs in the literature on theories of
meaning is the requirement of compositionality: the explanation
or description of the meaning of a compound sentence should be
determined in terms of the meaning ascribed to its constituents and
the way they are put together in the compound sentence. This
requirement is considered to be necessary in order to account for the
fact that people who understand a language are able to understand
indefinitely many sentences that are wholly novel to them. Now,
for the requirement of compositionality to make sense for ordinary
languages, there must be a definite way in which a sentence is

composed of constituents, just as, in chemistry, there is a definite way in which a molecule is composed of atoms. And we are supposed to be able to identify the 'atomic sentences', i.e. the sentences that are not composed of other sentences; so this means that a general concept of the form of sentences is presupposed in terms of which each sentence has a unique structure, and the description of the form of a sentence does not refer to anything, so to speak, beyond the sentence as an expression. In particular, it must not refer to the content of the sentence in one of its uses. One would not say, perhaps, that the sentences of our ordinary languages have this structure as they stand, that it is something that we can read off immediately by inspection. But there is supposed to be a general method of paraphrase or formalization of the sentences of a language such that the structure on which their meaning depends can be made explicit. Some people even express themselves as though this structure of sentences exists as a system of formal rules, as a system of 'sentence-forming operations' that 'generates' the sentences of our languages. By reconstructing this system of rules, a formalization of the language under investigation could be given, which would exhibit all features of sentences that are essential to their meaning, not just for some particular use of the language, but in general.

Do we have such a general concept of the form of sentences? Do we have a general framework for the formalization of sentences in this sense? A philosophically more important question in this connection is the following: Do we know what we are asking for here? Does such a general concept of the form of sentences make sense? Is the form and the content of sentences of our actual languages related in such a way that this is possible in principle? There are many facts about language which indicate that this idea is out of touch with reality, that language is not at the mercy of a system of formal rules. For instance, there have been observations regarding ambiguities in the 'surface structure' of sentences, observations about context-dependence, observations about the way in which language and linguistic conventions change in unforeseen ways, not only with respect to vocabulary but also in respect of 'grammaticality'. It is even generally admitted that people do not normally speak in a grammatically correct way, but, nevertheless, often succeed perfectly well in making themselves understood. Whence this idea of articulated sentences which seems to be so important a presupposition in theories of meaning? The answer is that it is a result of projecting upon our languages the notions that belong to the formal methods of representation. The idea is based on the view of a language as being ultimately a formal system like the predicate calculus, though much more complicated. To conceive of language in general as a calculus would perhaps be a normal and acceptable attitude within some limited scientific or technical study of language, for instance in some form of 'natural-language processing' where it can be justified by its success in solving technical problems, but hardly in a project that aims at a philosophy of language.

The formal methods of (some extension of) the predicate calculus are considered by many theorists of meaning to be the appropriate tool for making explicit the structure of sentences which determines their meaning. Each sentence is furnished with such a unique structure through 'regimentation in quantification theory' (to use Quine's expression). This is perhaps the attitude of most writers in meaning theory. It seems to be, for instance, the attitude of most writers in the Evans and McDowell volume, *Truth and Meaning*.[20] It is obviously Davidson's view (following Quine). This seems to be so self-evident to most people that they speak as though this 'regimentation' were already achieved. Thus, people speak about the *truth-functions* 'and', 'or', 'not' and the *quantifiers* 'for all . . .' and 'there exists . . .' in discussions about theory of meaning for fragments of English, as though this were the standard sense of these English terms and not just a particular use of them. This seems also to be the view of Dummett, as is evidenced by the way he speaks about the composition and constituents of sentences in several papers; and in his reply to Dag Prawitz' contribution[21] to the B.M. Taylor volume he says[22] explicitly: 'when it is recalled that the regimentation of the language into quantificational form is presupposed as effected in advance.'

There are perhaps those who would (when asked twice) take a more moderate view and say that by means of the predicate calculus we can handle important fragments of natural languages. And some would perhaps add that promising work is going on to extend the methods of formal logic towards a general framework for the formal regimentation of natural languages. As though our difficulties were only technical! There might perhaps be a still more moderate view. It might be said that we shall never reach a universal framework for the formal regimentation of sentences of natural languages in practice, but such a framework is at least conceivable in principle and therefore it makes sense to strive towards it. What these different attitudes have in common is the general conception of a language as a calculus of words and sentences. It is on the basis of the *picture* of a language as being constructed like a formal system that such a method for formal regimentation 'is conceivable in principle'.

This is sometimes explicitly admitted. Montague,[23] for instance, says that our natural languages *are* formal systems like the predicate calculus, but much more complicated formal systems. And Davidson,[24] commenting on certain philosophers' reservations towards the treatment of natural languages as formal systems, says: 'It would be misleading, however, to conclude that there are two kinds of language, natural and artificial.'

Perhaps these views are extreme. One thing is clear, however: the notion of 'language' that is used in the discussion of theories of meaning (as well as in formal semantics and formal grammar) is what Tarski[25] calls a *language with a specified structure*. Such a 'language' must fulfil essentially three conditions according to Tarski:

1 There must be an unambiguous specification of the expressions 'that are to be considered meaningful.'
2 There must be 'criteria for distinguishing within the class of expressions those which we call "sentences" '.
3 'We must formulate the conditions under which a sentence of the language can be *asserted*.'

A 'formalized language' is, according to Tarski, a special case of a language with a specified structure, so this is meant to be a more general notion; and it is for languages with a specified structure that Tarski's 'semantic definition of truth' obtains a precise meaning.

The same thing is true, it seems to me, as regards the various theories of meaning proposed. They apply only to languages with a specified structure, or at least to languages that can be represented or 'regimented' in such a form. At the same time these theories of meaning are meant to apply to (fragments of) our natural languages. So within this philosophy of language one does indeed share something similar to Tarski's 'hope that languages with specified structure could finally replace everyday language in scientific discourse.'[26]

If we disregard differences in technical details, it is clear that not only Davidson's theory of meaning but also those of Dummett, Prawitz, and Martin-Löf fall within the Tarski tradition of semantics in the sense that they all presuppose a general conception of language as a 'language with a specified structure' (or at least 'with an in principle specifiable structure'). But these modern theorists of meaning go further than Tarski, who explicitly denied the possibility of a systematic semantic theory for ordinary language.[27]

Martin-Löf gives explanations of meaning for expressions of a calculus or formal system, namely intuitionistic type theory. His explanations do not apply directly to expressions and sentences of our so-called informal mathematical language that we find in most textbooks of mathematics, and that most mathematicians, and others, who do mathematics actually use. His explanations apply to certain formalizations or representations within an intuitionistic type theory of propositions of our 'everyday mathematical language'. But the theory is proposed as an *a priori* theory of meaning. The formalization is part of the investigation of the meaning of ordinary mathematical notions, and it is intended to make explicit the features of expressions that are essential to their meaning. The theory is thus meant to provide a conceptual and logical foundation for (a large part of) our ordinary mathematical language, and therefore it involves the claim that (this part of) our ordinary mathematical language *is* a language with a specifiable structure; and what the formalization of it in intuitionistic type theory actually does, is to specify that structure.

The view of 'natural language' as a formal system reveals itself also in other ways in the theory of meaning. If we look at the attempts made to develop such a theory we find, on the whole, that it is the aspect concerning the logical constants that has been developed in the greatest detail. Now, if this fact were pointed out to them, I think that some meaning theorists would react in more or less the following way: 'Giving a theory of meaning for a formal language such as the predicate calculus is an important step towards giving such a theory for more complicated languages such as fragments of natural languages. How could we hope to do the latter if we cannot manage to do the former?' But here it may be asked, why should a theory of meaning for a formal (or artificial) language like the predicate calculus be of any great help in, or even be a part of, explaining how natural languages work? The latter may be something completely different. (This would, it seems to me, be a good question in a discussion about what form a theory of meaning should take.)

There is *some* similarity in the following situation: suppose that someone said that since we can see from physics what form a satisfactory theory of phenomena has to take, those theories therefore provide the first steps in accounting also for psychological phenomena of the human mind. This was roughly the way in which certain materialists and behaviourists were thinking. We would of course say that accounting for mental phenomena, as such, is something wholly different for which the methods of physics might even be misleading.

There is a parallel situation in modern so-called artificial intelligence research. Some people think that the formal theories of problem-solving and decision-making developed in artificial intelligence might be of help in understanding human intelligence as well, namely by extending them to the 'more complicated' phenomena of human decision-making and problem-solving. But it may very well turn out that they will be more helpful in the negative sense that they will show us what human intelligence definitely is not.

The presupposition in theories of meaning is that a natural language is somehow a complicated extension of the predicate calculus, or that the latter displays the *basic* structure of natural languages. One could agree that, in certain aspects of the use of words such as 'and', 'or', 'not', 'for all' in reasoning, the predicate calculus does indeed describe a formal structure that often occurs in ordinary language. But why is it the basic or the fundamental structure? The answer is that this is an assumption (or dogma) made within a certain tradition in the philosophy of language.

6 FORM AND CONTENT OF SENTENCES

Note that I am not saying that the various authors mentioned share some basic common *opinion* on the nature of language. That there are conflicting opinions in the discussion about theories of meaning is obvious. On the other hand, there is a common conceptual framework within which the various views and opinions are formulated and discussed, and *that* is my concern in this study. I am not talking about agreement in opinions on the nature of language, but about agreement in the use of certain notions and terms from linguistic theory – an agreement in the use of terms that is based on a common *picture* of a language. This picture comes out perhaps most clearly in the use of the terms 'expression', 'form of an expression', and 'sentence' (the 'sentences' to which meaning explanations and the truth-predicate apply); and the most characteristic feature of this picture is that it presents languages in general as having a structure which is specifiable in terms of notions that do not refer to the meaning or the use of the expressions.

According to Dummett, a theory of meaning is a theory of understanding. Understanding an expression of a language is said to consist in the possession of a certain 'practical ability' to use the expression. The theory is called *atomistic* if it specifies such a practical ability for any word. It is said to be *molecular* if it specifies such a practical ability for any sentence. Following Frege's distinction between *sense* and *force*, it is said that the meaning of a sentence (its sense) does not comprise all features of its use. It does not comprise the features which express the force of the sentence (i.e. whether it is used to express an assertion, a command, a question, etc.). The sense is said to consist in one *central feature* on the basis of which other features of the use of the sentence can be derived uniformly. There will be different types of theories of meaning depending upon the choice of the notion used in specifying the central feature of sentences. Dummett and Prawitz prefer a molecular theory based on the notion of verification of a sentence as the 'central notion', rather than a theory based on the notion of the truth-conditions of a sentence. In either case, the principle of molecularity entails that the sentence as an expression is 'the carrier of meaning': for any sentence, there is something which is *the* meaning (sense or individual content) of the sentence, regardless of the setting in which the sentence may occur and regardless of the circumstances of its use. Its meaning is one and the same thing in different uses; and it is conceived to be something conceptually prior to the various kinds of significance the sentence may have in different uses.

As it stands, the principle of molecularity clearly does not apply without further ado to what we normally call sentences of ordinary language, because these sentences are often ambiguous in various ways. Consider, for instance, the sentence 'I have plans to leave'. It has at least two different readings. It can mean that I am thinking about leaving. But it can also be understood as saying that I have made up and written out some plans and that I want to hand them over to someone. On the first reading, the sentence may be true about someone in a certain situation, while on the second reading it may be false (or conversely). Regardless of whether truth or verification is taken to be the central notion of a theory of meaning, the principle of molecularity does not apply to this sentence as it stands.

For the principle of molecularity to be applicable to ordinary language, the sentences of ordinary language have to be articulated or paraphrased in such a way that ambiguities of this and other kinds are removed or made explicit. In Dummett's and Prawitz' discussion about problems of principle in developing theories of meaning for ordinary languages, it is obviously assumed that the language under investigation has been prepared in such a way that the principle of molecularity does apply. But what is involved in this assumption? Is this just a problem of detail, a technical problem which does not belong to the difficulties of principle in giving theories of meaning?

It might be said that the principle of molecularity is meant, not as a kind of general, empirical fact about our everyday notion of a sentence of ordinary language, but as a kind of methodological principle whose justification would consist in the success of the project of giving, on its basis, a coherent theory of meaning. This would mean that the principle is the expression of a new and more precise notion of a sentence – in the way the principles of classical mechanics once expressed basic properties of a new and precise notion of a material particle. For a sentence in this new sense, the structure of the sentence that determines its meaning has been identified and made explicit, ambiguities have been resolved, and so on. Someone would perhaps like to call this an 'idealized notion of a sentence'. However, what we are worried about is this: how is this idealized notion of a sentence going to be applied to ordinary language? After all the main problem is meant to be how the expressions of our ordinary languages (including our ordinary scientific languages) have meaning. How is this idealized notion of a sentence related to the things we call sentences of our actual language and which may be ambiguous in various ways? The answer is this: *The notion is meant to apply to ordinary language through the presupposed method for paraphrasing or formalization of the ordinary sentences into such a form that the principle of molecularity applies.* So this method would then involve a general and systematic technique for resolving sentence ambiguities of various kinds, and here we have a problem of principle. Can there be such a systematic method at all? According to what conception of our languages does the idea of such a method make sense? It is clear that the idea has its roots in the naturalistic notion of formalization (or syntactical analysis), according to which there could be a preconceived, systematic method for rendering explicit the structure of sentences that determine their content (or truth-values). The method would be 'preconceived' in the sense of not being adapted to and dependent on a specific kind of use of the sentence in certain kinds of circumstances, but to apply uniformly in different kinds of use. But this *is* the idea of a language with a structure that is specifiable, so to speak, from the outside, i.e. in terms that do not involve the meaning and the forms of use of its expressions.

Even Tarski, the grandfather of model-theoretic semantics, seems to have felt that this idea of a language is not applicable to ordinary language. But it is not applicable to ordinary scientific languages either; it applies only to 'languages' which are *constructed* as systems of forms of expressions, i.e. to non-natural or artificial languages. But this is a different sense of the word 'language'; it is the conception of a language as a calculus of words and expressions, whose structure as a calculus is finished and complete before it is applied, before it is 'connected with an independent reality through interpretation'. The notions of syntax and semantics introduced by Tarski, Carnap, and others in the 1930s were founded on this conception of language and of its relation to reality. But the actual languages that people use in communication (in everyday discourse as well as in science) are not like this. *Neither the form nor the content of a sentence of actual language is specifiable within some framework external to the conditions for using the sentence.* Only through an acquaintance or familiarity with these conditions is it possible to recognize the meaning of sentences and the structure that is essential to them. This is perhaps most obvious if we reflect on how ambiguities are recognized and resolved. In order to recognize the ambiguity of the sentence 'I have plans to leave' it is clearly necessary to be familiar with what we call 'leaving from somewhere' and 'leaving a thing to someone', and with the difference between these human practices. It is necessary to be familiar with what it is like or what it looks like when someone is about to leave rather than when he is about to leave something to someone. The conditions for using a sentence may thus involve facts about human practices and about the world in which we live. Even if we disregard ambiguities which are connected with conceptual problems and which most speakers of a language are unable to recognize or resolve at all, and confine ourselves to what linguists call 'semantic ambiguities', it is clear that for someone to recognize and resolve even these, considerations of meaning and use are necessary; and this in turn presupposes familiarity with human practices and certain facts about the world in which we live. A theory of meaning based on the principle of molecularity would be no more systematic than is the method of formalization and of resolving ambiguities. It would not be sufficient that ambiguities could be resolved in each individual case; there would have to be a uniform and systematic way of going about it. But this means that the method of resolving ambiguities must be based on a systematic account of how the sentences of language have meaning (i.e. a theory of meaning!), which in turn would have to involve a systematic account of human practices and circumstances. And if we were to accept the philosophical claims of Dummett about what questions a theory of meaning is meant to answer, we would have to accept that the idea that such a systematic account could be *complete* makes sense. But this idea would make sense only if human language and human reality involved the ('implicit') application of a systematic theory. But that this should be the case is not just mistaken, but involves a kind of superstition.

It is tempting to express the principal difficulty here by saying that the knowledge we have of our languages is inseparable from our knowledge of the world. This employment of the word 'knowledge' is, however, misleading if it is taken to suggest that this 'knowledge of the world' is something that could be represented in a 'system for knowledge representation', on the basis of which a systematic method of resolving ambiguities could, after all, be developed. This might be a good idea for developing strategies for 'natural-language processing', for solving specific technical problems, but as a picture of how our language works it is misleading because the conceptual problems I am pointing to would only be transferred to the language used in constructing the representation. It is not as objects of knowledge that facts about the world are part of the conditions for using expressions of our language, it is as the characteristic circumstances of our forms of life.

What are the conditions for the correct use of a simple, everyday expression like 'Good morning!'? Imagine a conversation between beings from 'another world' in which it were said: 'In the world in which humans live there is what they call "time", and there are parts of time called "days", "nights", "weeks". They also talk about "beginnings" of various things. A condition for the correct use of the expression "Good morning!" is that it is uttered in the beginning of a day.' 'But what sort of thing is a day? and what is a "beginning of a day" like?' What would it be like to give a *complete* account of the conditions for the correct use of the expression 'Good morning!' as representable knowledge of facts about the world and about the behaviour of humans to someone who is not familiar as a human with these human conditions? It is clear that the familiarity with conditions like these is part of our language.[28] Without it, language is lost. When you misconceive it as representable knowledge, as though our ordinary use of language were the implicit application of a theory of meaning, then it becomes a mystery, for instance, how even small children are able to learn so 'enormously complicated a thing' as the conditions for the correct use of 'Good morning!'. As though the child came into the world and began to form hypotheses about the world and about how our language is related to it.

Consider the sentence

There is water in the refrigerator.

What would be *the* 'sense' or 'individual meaning' of this sentence? Is there some feature of an 'objective reality' that makes this sentence true or false *as a mere syntactical sentence*? Is there some 'canonical' way of verifying or falsifying it regardless of the specific circumstances and purposes for using the sentence? Imagine the following situation:

A friend walks into the kitchen where person A and person B are sitting and asks, 'Is there any water in the refrigerator?' A says, 'Yes', and B says, 'No'. The friend looks in and says, 'I don't see any.' A responds, 'In the cells of all the vegetables'.

The point of this example[29] is that the correctness of the answer (or the truth-value of the assertion 'There is water in the refrigerator') cannot be judged in terms of some *one* objective reality about water or by means of some 'canonical' method of verification that is independent of the circumstances, of the understanding of the relevant background, purposes, and expectations of the persons involved. In different circumstances the opposite answer might count as the correct one:

The friend says, 'I want to store some chemicals that are supposed to be kept away from water.' A says, 'Keep them out of the refrigerator, there's lots of water there – in the cells of all the vegetables.'

It is clear that we have to do with (conceptually) different forms of use of the sentence here. Someone could understand the everyday uses of this sentence, but not the more technical use connected with cells of vegetables. And there is nothing special about this example. Other surroundings to this sentence could be invented where the 'truth-conditions' for the sentence were different again, i.e. where the conditions for using the sentence were different from the ones in the two situations described. There would presumably be similarities between the different situations, but would there have to be some *one* 'central feature' of the use of the sentence from which the significance of the different assertions of the sentence derives – apart from the fact that the same sequence of words is used? Someone who is inclined to say 'yes' has, it seems to me, taken too few concrete linguistic situations into consideration. On the basis of the principle of molecularity it would seem that one is forced to invent such a central feature, or to assume that the different uses of the sentence have already been distinguished syntactically – as though the different forms of use of even this simple sentence could somehow be surveyed and listed, or be described in one systematic way.

Someone may object to my criticism of the presuppositions of meaning theorists on the grounds that no one has claimed that the process of formalization or paraphrasing sentences is just the application of a routine technique; no one has claimed that the preparation of the language so that the molecularity principle applies could be carried out and be completed without taking the meaning and the uses of the sentences into consideration. It would rather be said that the syntactic and the semantic investigations cannot be separated in this way; they are mutually dependent, there is a circular interaction between syntactic and semantic considerations as in any process of interpretation. But what I have been talking about is not the actual *working process* in developing theories of meaning, but rather the *conception* of what one is doing and of the final result one wants to arrive at. Even if there are considerations regarding the meaning and the use of a sentence, so to speak, on the way towards fixing the syntactic structure that determines its sense, it is taken for granted that this structure *can finally be formally specified*. Just as there is supposed to be a sense, an individual meaning, which the sentence has as a sentence and which is the same in different forms of its use, so there is supposed to be a structure of the sentence which determines this sense and which is specifiable independently of any specific use of it, i.e. which refers only to the sentence as an expression of a syntactic category. If this notion of the sense (in contrast to the force) of a sentence is – as Dummett seems to mean – a prerequisite for any systematic theory of meaning, then so is the formally specifiable structure of sentences that determines this sense. But this prerequisite is fulfilled only for

84

a constructed language, or for a language 'reconstructed' as a calculus, where the specification of forms of expressions and the rules for operating with them is completed prior to the application of the calculus.[30] That the rules *can* be so completed in a calculus is a requirement; it is in the essence of a calculus that its rules refer only to the forms of the expressions, regardless of possible applications or intended interpretation. Unless this has been achieved, it is not complete as a calculus. The rules of our actual languages, however, are not formal rules in this sense because familiarity with certain conditions and circumstances of human reality constitutes part of these rules, as in the case of the rules for the correct use of the expression 'Good morning!'. The structure of an expression that is essential in a certain use can only be expressed and understood in a way which presupposes that the conditions of this use obtain. This is, one might say, why explanations of the form and meaning of expressions of actual languages 'are bound to be circular'.

In current theories of meaning one tries to reconstruct what is not a calculus *as* a calculus in the belief that a 'natural language' is only natural on the surface. This strategy for the construction of theories might be useful for practical or technical purposes, in the way this strategy for theory construction has been useful in natural science, but for the philosophical purpose of explaining 'what it is that makes language *language*', the project can only be successful through its failures, i.e. by giving rise to difficulties that show what human language is not.

7 THE NOTION OF LITERAL MEANING

It might be thought that what I am advocating here is some kind of 'pragmatic notion of meaning', but that would be a misunderstanding. I am not proposing any theory about language. I am rather questioning certain common presuppositions of several current theories of language, and in particular the presupposed distinction between the semantic and pragmatic aspects of language, or, in Dummett's terminology, the difference between the central feature of the use of a sentence and other features of its use. What are the grounds for making this distinction? Is it based upon facts about actual language? Certainly not, the motive for this distinction is methodological; it belongs to the demands on 'what form a theory of meaning should have'. On this point Dummett is almost explicit. He maintains that it is (in Prawitz' words) 'a prerequisite for any reasonable hopes of constructing a systematic theory of meaning . . . that the significance of a specific utterance is uniquely determined by the force of the utterance and . . . the individual content or meaning of the sentence used . . .'.[31]

What prompts these distinctions between the 'individual meaning' of a sentence and other aspects of its use, which are derived from or added to its individual meaning in a conversation, is the picture of a language as *a system of forms of expression*, separated from the forms of their use. It is in this picture that sentences are, as one says, 'purely linguistic entities' that have a syntactical form and a literal meaning. It is this picture that constitutes the foundation for the distinction between the syntax, the semantics, and the pragmatics of a language. A language in the sense of a purely linguistic mechanism is meant to be completely accounted for by its syntax and semantics, prior to the pragmatic accounts of language use. There may be disagreement about how and where the boundaries go between the syntactic, the semantic, and the pragmatic aspects, but apart from such disagreement on details, this is the picture of language which is at the bottom of most of the work done in modern linguistic theory as it shows itself in the formation and employment of technical concepts and methods. It may therefore be very difficult for a linguist or theorist of meaning to conceive of this picture of language *as a picture* that can be questioned by being confronted with the facts of actual language, because, in their attitude towards this picture, it contains some of the general and fundamental 'truths about language' which form the foundation for their approach (and professional pride).

What, then, is the 'literal meaning' (or the 'individual meaning', or 'informational content') that the expressions and sentences of a language are supposed to have *as mere expressions*? What is the notion of *the* meaning of a sentence which, according to this picture of language, is supposed to be independent of the circumstances of the use of the sentence and which is meant to be one and the same thing in different forms of use? What is, for instance, the literal meaning that the sentence 'There is water in the refrigerator' has, but which (presumably) the sequence of words 'In is water the there refrigerator' does not have? The sentence has a conventional *reading* which the latter sequence of words does not. What remains when a sentence is considered in isolation from the forms of its use is its reading. The idea of the literal meaning that sentences are supposed to have as 'mere linguistic entities' derives from the fact that they have a reading (or several readings when the sentence is 'ambiguous'). But a sentence has a reading only according to an existing, conventional, way of reading it within a group of people at a certain time and place. Readings change and new kinds of readings arise, sometimes in unforeseen and very complicated ways. Some readings are more frequent and common, others are more special. Some readings have appeared in a natural way in the use of language, others have been deliberately imposed. And typically, the readings cultivated within linguistic theory and philosophy of language are imposed on theoretical grounds, rather than for communicative purposes.

That a sentence has a certain reading means – in philosophical jargon – that there is a disposition among the members of a group of people in an historical situation to recognize that reading. But, obviously, the readings of sentences as such empirical and historical phenomena are not what is meant to be the subject-matter of semantics or theory of meaning.[32] These disciplines are meant to be concerned with something more pretentious than the recording and classification of readings of sentences occurring in various linguistic communities at various times. They are trying to get at 'the underlying laws' of these linguistic phenomena – as though there were some kind of natural laws for language. Their primary concern is the study of 'the literal or primary meaning' or 'the individual or propositional content' of a sentence. This propositional content is meant to be manifest in the reading of the sentence which expresses what it asserts 'by itself' (the 'proposition' it expresses) as a sentence of 'the pure language-mechanism', regardless of what it may be used to communicate by someone in some specific kind of situation. As though there were some kind of *a priori*, canonical or standard reading of the sentences of a language (recognizable perhaps by an 'ideal speaker'), and which would be determined somehow by the pure language mechanism, and not by the users of the language. But there is no such thing. In current theories of language *this 'canonical reading' is determined by an imposed method for paraphrasing sentences* which is based on the techniques of paraphrase of traditional grammar and modern formal logic.[33]

We learn about sentences and we learn their readings when we learn to read and write. Elementary education in these practices has in general been based on traditional grammar. Grammatical examples and paraphrases are exercised and presented as norms for the reading of sentences, and this *grammatical reading* also forms the basis for several linguistic theories, although it has been influenced and refined by formal logic, by the reading which is determined by the rules and methods of paraphrase of formal logic.

An important part in the construction of a system of formal grammar or formal logic is the invention of a method for paraphrasing sentences and expressions of some part of ordinary language, whereafter the rules of this method are treated as normative for actual language (and the readings of the paraphrased sentences are considered to express their 'literal' or 'primary' meaning). The attitude to these rules appears to be that they are normative, which is considered to be the main justification for calling the invented system a 'grammar' or a 'logic', with the connotation that these terms traditionally have. This notion of grammar or logic means of course that one has a conception of our actual use of language as being the (implicit) application of a system of formal rules.[34]

This conception is clearly at the root of the false idea that we have a natural, intuitive, capacity to decide about the grammaticality of sentences (an idea maintained for instance within the Chomsky tradition).[35] According to the grammatical reading introduced by Chomsky the sentence 'Colourless green ideas sleep furiously' is grammatically correct, but Chomsky is wrong in maintaining that any English-speaking person could decide that. Most English-speaking people do not know Chomsky's notion of grammaticality, they do not know how to decide such questions. They may even be unfamiliar with the practice of considering sentences as objects of grammatical investigation at all, and it is only within that practice that the question makes sense, as it is only within the practice of applying the theories of physics that it makes sense to ask for the molecular structure of some ordinary physical object. Chomsky's claim is a way of trying to persuade us that the rules of his formal grammar are generally at work implicitly in our ordinary use of language, i.e. that ordinary language is the application of a system of formal rules.

According to the predicate-calculus reading of ordinary sentences it would be correct and true to say, for instance, that 'Some people in this room are smoking' in a situation in which all the people in the room were as a matter of fact smoking. In the normal use of this statement, it would mean that there are also people in the room who were not smoking; but according to certain current linguistic theories this is something that the sentence only suggests. It is considered a 'pragmatic feature' of the statement to be accounted for by pragmatic rules. The important thing here is that this notion of what the statement only 'suggests' is introduced as a contrast to what the statement 'expresses literally'; and the latter is determined, in this case, by the imposed predicate-calculus reading of it.

Similar remarks apply to other 'pragmatic notions' like 'presupposition', 'background assumptions', 'speech-act conventions', 'conversational implicature'. In pragmatic accounts of language use, these notions operate upon a presupposed literal meaning, which is claimed to be determined by words and sentences as mere expressions, but which really is determined by the readings that are cultivated within current linguistic theory. Pragmatics is thus not something opposed to the view of a language as a 'purely linguistic mechanism' which is complete as language prior to its use. On the contrary, pragmatics is *based on* this view; its task is to supplement and complete it, to *add* to the purely linguistic mechanism in order to take care of the cases where this view is most obviously in conflict with our actual use of language.

The dividing line between the semantic and the pragmatic features of a language is the technique for paraphrasing its sentences into the readings which express their 'semantic content'.[36] This dividing-line is sometimes moved forward. When new and more refined techniques for paraphrase and formalization are invented, some pragmatic features can be treated as belonging to semantics, and thus to the pure language mechanism. But this process of reducing the domain of pragmatics will never reach completion. As long as a language is conceived as a mechanism isolated from existing forms of use of its expressions, it will always be necessary to account for those cases where the mechanism is in conflict with actual language.

The conceptually most misleading thing about pragmatic accounts of language use is their claim that certain pragmatic rules and principles should form the basis of our use of language, and that these principles, therefore, have primacy over the existing forms of use they claim to explain.[37] What pragmatists do not realize is that their principles and explanations make sense only against the background of the existing forms of use they want to explain. They turn the conceptual order upside down.

Consider for instance the pragmatic notion of 'cancellable implicatures'.[38] The sentence 'Tom has ten books' is normally used in such way that it is true when Tom has exactly ten books. The pragmatist does not describe this normal use, but starts with what he takes to be the 'literal meaning' of the sentence and according to which it is true when Tom has ten or more books. The normal use of the sentence is then explained as involving, besides this literal meaning, also the implicature 'Tom has ten books and no more than ten books'. But there are cases when the sentence 'Tom has ten books' is used differently, for instance in a statement like 'Tom has ten books, maybe even twelve', which is clearly a use different from the normal one because it contradicts the 'implicature'. But the pragmatist does not recognize this as simply another and different use, but tries to derive it and explain it as a case of the mechanism of 'cancellable implicatures'. The implicature is cancelled by the addition of 'maybe even twelve' to the original sentence. It is clear, however, that this explanation would not explain anything, it would not make sense, to someone who was not familiar with the two uses as existing, different uses. The pragmatic account would make sense only to someone who is familiar with the kind of circumstances that distinguish these uses, with what would count as a verification of the sentences in the different uses, etc. The notion of 'cancellable implicatures' is only a schematic way of *representing* certain formal features of language by means of certain current methods for theory-construction. It does not explain 'what really goes on' in our use of language in conversation, and it does not explain the possibility of certain forms of use. On the contrary, it is the existence of the different forms of use in actual language that makes the representation possible and meaningful.

It would presumably be possible to give an account of the two different senses of the sentence 'There is water in the refrigerator' discussed above using the theory of implicatures. But such an account would similarly make sense and be an acceptable or unacceptable representation only when the different senses of the sentence, as different forms of its use in actual language, are presupposed. The two uses of the sentence are different because someone could know its more common use without knowing its more special technical use. He would have to learn the latter use as a new practice of employing the sentence. The pragmatic account would not show that there is a common 'individual meaning' of the sentence from which the two uses are being derived by means of pragmatic rules. This is just the 'idealized' pattern according to which the pragmatic representation is constructed. It does not describe the way in which the actual language games are being played. There is no explanation of the existing forms of use of the expressions of actual language in terms of something 'more fundamental'; *they* are what is fundamental.

8 INDETERMINACY OF THE FORM OF EXPRESSIONS

It may seem as though my criticism of the presuppositions involved in the principle of molecularity does not apply to Quine's and Davidson's holistic theories of meaning, where molecularity is rejected. Also, as already pointed out, ambiguous expressions are said to be no problem in Davidson's approach. As long as ambiguities do not affect the grammatical form, they will, according to Davidson, be translated into the meta-language; and, through the extensional approach, the presence of ambiguous expressions will not affect the correctness of truth definitions. We do not first have to resolve the ambiguities in order to get ahead with the theory.

The problems about ambiguous expressions that I have been pointing to do not so much concern the difficulties they may cause in the *development* of one or the other formal approach, but rather the difficulties in *applying* the resulting theory-construction to actual language. One of the main difficulties with the principle of molecularity is the 'idealized' notion of a sentence it presupposes, and the problem of how this notion is to be applied to the sentences of our actual language. How are the sentences of actual language to be identified? It is in this phase that the existence of all sorts of ambiguities involves a problem of principle for giving 'a systematic theory of meaning for natural languages'. But meaning theorists, as philosophers, typically concern themselves very little about this step, convinced as they are by a few schematic examples that this is only a problem of detail. This is a serious mistake, because this phase is the crucial point in Davidson's theory of meaning, and in other theories of meaning as well.

What, then, is Davidson's notion of a sentence? Sometimes he speaks as though he were concerned with our everyday notion of a sentence, a notion we would explain to someone by giving typical examples of what we call sentences. On other occasions, he conceives of a sentence as a 'syntactical object', a sequence of concrete expressions generated by formal rules. But this is of course a technical notion, and how is it to be applied to the sentences that people speak and write? When a person utters a sentence, say, as an answer to a question about what he is doing, is he producing a sequence of expressions according to certain rules? In general, no. To describe

91

his utterance as the (implicit) application of rules of syntax is to impose an interpretation; it involves the application of a method for syntactical representation. And this is a crucial step which conceals problems of principle. In an utterance, certain features of accent and intonation may be essential for what someone wants to say. We do, for instance, discriminate between the two different senses of the sentence 'I have plans to leave' discussed above in that way. By putting the stress on the word 'leave' we have one reading, by stressing the word 'plans' we have the other reading. Do we have two different arguments for the truth-predicate in Davidson's theory here, or is the argument just one ambiguous sentence? Obviously, Davidson is assuming that such decisions have been made, that the language has already been syntactically regimented when the axioms and truth definitions of the theory are about to be given and, more important, it is assumed that things can be taken in that order. What the theory will say about the actual language it pretends to be a theory about will depend on how the sentences of actual language are identified; it will depend on a method for syntactical regimentation which is merely assumed to exist.

Davidson is presumably thinking about written sentences, a written sentence being a certain sequence of words, a word a certain sequence of characters, and a character a 'typographical shape'. Sentences differing only in typographical style could presumably be identified, but what about an italicized sentence? Or a sentence in which one word is italicized or printed in bold face? Is 'The **SUN** is shining' the same sentence as 'The sun is shining'? In some contexts, the difference may be significant. But Davidson is presumably interested in an 'idealized notion' of meaning for which differences of this kind are irrelevant. Our everyday notion of a sentence is of course not a sharp notion with well-defined criteria of identity, and more importantly, the criteria are not formal. There may not be an answer to the question of whether an isolated sequence of words is a sentence, or whether it is the same sentence as some other sentence, if nothing is given about its use or communicative purpose. But it is essential for Davidson's approach that a well-defined criterion of sentencehood can be given (in principle), because the truth predicate is literally meant to be a (mathematical) function defined by recursion. The sentences of a language are supposed to form a domain on which a function is defined by recursion, which not only means that the sentences must have formally well-defined criteria of identity, but also a formal structure over which recursive definitions can be given. This is the idealized notion of a language which Davidson's theory is based upon; and it is determined by the notions and techniques of the 'theory of reference' and the formal grammar expounded by Quine.[39] In Quine's *Word and Object* we find explanations of the technical notion of a sentence, of the form and composition of sentences, of the notion of truth of sentences, and so on. And for this notion of the 'truth of a sentence' there are counterparts to the principles of molecularity: sentences as expressions, as formulas, are the carriers of truth. 'Truth' is a property of (syntactical) sentences, i.e. the truth-predicate applies to sentences as 'syntactical objects', and the truth-value of a compound sentence is determined in terms of the truth-values of its constituents.

However, a sentence of actual language is true or false only if it has a meaning, and it has a meaning only in so far as it has a possible use as a sentence in the language. For the ordinary notion of truth, what is true or false is the use of a sentence (i.e. a statement, a judgement, or a proposition), not syntactical objects or formulas of a calculus. This is obvious for sentences like 'It is raining', whose meaning depends on the context of utterance. But even for an 'eternal sentence' (in Quine's terminology) of the form 'It is raining in the place P at time t', the question of its truth arises only against the background of the normal use of sentences of this form in giving weather reports. To master this use involves familiarity with what we call 'a place where it may rain', how the expression 'P' refers to such a place, how the time t is identified, and so on.

A characteristic feature of the discussion of Davidson's theory of meaning is the identification of the notions of 'sentence' and 'truth' in the ordinary sense and the corresponding technical or formal notions of Quine's theory of reference. The discussion is framed as though the technical notions could completely replace and do the job of the ordinary notions. But the technical notions have their use within the formal representation of language, within the 'idealized' notion of language. Their applicability to ordinary language is limited.

Quine's unwillingness to admit theories of meaning such as Frege's, and I think also Dummett's, is connected with his empiricism and his 'principle of indeterminacy of translation'. If there were some entity – so the argument goes – which would be *the* meaning of an individual sentence, then we could talk about a translation of sentences of one language into sentences of another as correct or incorrect in an absolute sense: a translation is correct if it equates sentences that have the same meaning. On the other hand, there seems to be no justification, from a strictly empiricist (or behaviourist) point of view, for talking about a translation of the sentences of a radically different language into our own as absolutely correct. Quine argues that there may be different, mutually incompatible translations that are all compatible with the total verbal behaviour of the speakers of the foreign language.

If we accept Quine's naturalistic perspective, for the sake of argument, it seems to me that one could argue – with a thought-experiment similar to Quine's – for a much stronger form of indeterminacy, an indeterminacy not only of translation, but of identification of expressions. It is presupposed in Quine's argument that the field linguist, engaged in radical translation, is able to identify phonetically the expressions of the foreign language. He is supposed to be able to recognize two different utterances of the same sentence as such. And this is an important point because it is on this basis that he is able to formulate hypotheses of translation and test them empirically. He must be able to identify the sentences in order to make hypotheses about their correct translation. But how can he even do that? By what criteria is he judging two different utterances as utterances of the same expression? That the linguist thinks that two utterances *sound alike* may not be a good criterion if it is a radically foreign language. Can he determine the 'phonetic norms' of the foreign language prior to the investigation of the meaning and the uses of expressions? Quine is obviously presupposing that he can when he says at the beginning of his argument: 'I shall here ignore phonematic analysis, early though it would come in our field linguist's enterprise; for it does not affect the philosophical point I want to make.'

We may suppose that this foreign language differs from the languages we are familiar with in having a way of symbolization in which difference in accent, tone of voice, pitch, rhythm, etc. make a much greater difference than in the languages we are accustomed to. In order to learn this language one would have to acquire a new kind of sensitivity to such features of utterances. Sentences may change meaning radically when uttered with different accents and in different tones of voice. And we may further suppose that this language exists only as a spoken language, so there is no writing on which to base the identification of expressions and sentences. How is the linguist to know what features of two utterances are essential to them *qua* utterances of the same sentence? Two different utterances may never sound *exactly* alike. What features of an utterance are accidental – depending, for instance, only on a certain individual's peculiar way of speaking, and which are essential?

The linguist in Quine's argument is collecting evidence for a tentative translation of the sentence 'Gavagai' as 'Rabbit'. Suppose that it has turned out to be a good guess so far, but that the linguist suddenly encounters a situation where the translation seems to be wrong. Now, the failure may be due, not to an error in the translation of the previously observed utterances of the sentence 'Gavagai', but to a mistake in the identification of the sentence uttered in the new situation. It may have sounded very much like 'Gavagai', but a slight difference in accent of the utterance in the new situation may have made it into an utterance of quite a different sentence with quite a different meaning. It would be said then that the linguist's phonematic analysis of the foreign language is inadequate (and it is assumed in Quine's argument that it is adequate). But my point is that the idea of an adequate phonematic analysis is as problematic as the idea of an adequate translation. It seems to me that one could argue, from the strict empiricist point of view of Quine, for a 'principle of indeterminacy of forms of expressions' to the effect that manuals for identifying utterances of the foreign language as utterances of the same sentence can be set up in different ways, all compatible with the totality of speech dispositions of native speakers, yet incompatible with one another.

This stronger form of indeterminacy will undermine the conceptual and methodological basis of Quine's indeterminacy principle, as this basis comes out in the remark quoted above. Quine is assuming that the 'phonetic norms' can be identified in naturalistic terms independently of the investigation of the use of expressions and possible translations of sentences. He assumes that this is possible at least in principle. But this amounts to assuming that the foreign language is like a formal system in having a structure which is specifiable in isolation from the forms of use of its expressions. The identification of the forms of expression of the foreign language is indeed a crucial philosophical point if we are interested in the nature of actual human languages and not just in certain limited theoretical representations of them. The phonetic norms, the features of utterances that are essential, are determined in the end within the forms of use of the utterances in certain human circumstances (which may be unfamiliar to us if the language is foreign). Familiarity with such circumstances may be necessary to discriminate between essential and inessential features of an expression as well as between a good or a bad translation. This should be obvious to anyone who is familiar even with different dialects or different professional jargons. The notions and techniques of Quine's and Davidson's naturalistic approach cannot do justice to this fundamental feature of actual languages.

Quine's indeterminacy argument could be transformed into a kind of *reductio ad absurdum* which shows precisely the incorrectness of the conception of language it presupposes. If it were asked: 'To what extent does Quine's principle of indeterminacy tell us something about the nature of human languages?', then the answer would be: 'Only to the extent in which we are justified in regarding a human language as a language with an in principle specifiable structure.'

Imagine that the linguist in Quine's argument were presented with a book containing the results of a good phonematic analysis and a good translation manual of the foreign language (we may suppose that the book had been worked out by another linguist who had learned the foreign language as a native speaker). Or, in other words, suppose that the linguist is presented with a (good) theory (involving a dictionary, a grammar, etc.) of the foreign language, a representation of it as a language with a specified structure. The indeterminacy would then take the following form: from the point of view of an empiricist observer there would be different, systematic ways of applying (or interpreting) the theory in translating the actual speech of native speakers, all compatible with the totality of their speech dispositions, but incompatible with one another. In order to apply the theory correctly he would have to learn the language as a speaker.

Knowing a language is not (implicitly) knowing a theory. If a human language is conceived of as a system of rules for using expressions, then *what constitutes following the rules correctly* is determined ultimately within the forms of life where the language belongs.

9 IDEALIZATION IN SCIENCE AND PHILOSOPHY

It will perhaps be said that theory of meaning as a division of philosophy of language is not concerned with the narrow examination of languages and with the details of testing and applying the theories developed within it. Its main interest is in general 'difficulties of principle'; and in order to fix the discussion and make things accessible to a more exact treatment certain *idealizations* have to be made. My criticism will be objected to on the grounds that any theory must make idealizations, such as in physics, where one sometimes disregards friction and air resistance in the construction of models of phenomena in nature.

This parallel with the ways of working of the natural sciences, which has been so influential in analytic philosophy, is misleading for several reasons. First of all, natural science *does* justify its idealizations by looking into the details of their application. Secondly, (modern) physics is not philosophy. It is not concerned with the philosophical question of 'what makes nature *nature*'. But theory of meaning is supposed to be philosophy of language.

It is important to realize that the current, philosophical, employment of the notion of idealization originates in the naturalistic idea that philosophy 'is not to be distinguished in essential points of purpose and method from good or bad science' (Quine). In scientific work, where this notion of idealization has its proper place, an idealization is a notion or principle (like the principles of classical mechanics) that is *imposed* on the subject matter under investigation, and which is defined by the methods of investigation. The 'ideality' of the idealization consists in treating these methods as *normative*, not absolutely, but *within the activity of the scientific investigation* of a certain subject matter. It was through this insight about scientific work that scientists preferred to speak about *models* rather than theories, to emphasize that the concepts involved are constructions whose principles are imposed, and to avoid obsolete, metaphysical, claims of absoluteness. This procedure of imposing a structure on nature was justified by its success in solving empirical-scientific and technical problems. In the absence of any counterpart to this kind of empirical justification in philosophical theorizing, philosophers have been led to invent one. Supported by the dogmatic attitude of popular science, they treat their principles as being normative in an absolute sense, i.e. as being normative not just within the context of the scientific investigation, but for the subject matter under investigation itself, regardless of the scientific context. The methodological principles, the notions and principles that define their idealizations, are treated as descriptions of (hidden) general facts about the subject matter under investigation. By this manoeuvre they are unable to see the difference between the formal model and what it models, and speak about the formal representations of things as if they were the things themselves. In this way many philosophers of language speak about formal representations of phenomena of language, like sentences, propositions, and assertions and their syntactic and semantic structure, as though they were talking about phenomena of language as they present themselves to us in the practice of using language.

But even if the idealizations of the philosophers of language might find technical and empirical applications (e.g. in computer technology or elsewhere), the philosophical claims to absoluteness are not justified, because this scientific notion of 'idealization' is incompatible with the philosophical purpose of getting clear about the nature of actual language. In a philosophical investigation which takes these purposes seriously, we will have to look more closely at the various phenomena of actual language as they present themselves, not in some imposed representation, but in our normal practice of using language, and we have to pay attention to features which are essential to this practice. It is part of the scientific approach, on the contrary, to disregard the difference between essential and accidental features of a certain linguistic phenomenon *as it is given* in its normal context, and to impose (or reconstruct) an order, to be taken as the essential one, in accordance with certain requirements on 'what form the theory should take'. This is part of the procedure of 'idealization' as conceived by naturalists.

I am not suggesting that in the scientific approach a structure is imposed arbitrarily. From an historical and empirical point of view the process of theory construction is of course much more complicated, but I am here interested in the *conceptions* (and misconceptions) of what is done in theory construction. The normal procedure in applying the scientific approach in modern philosophy and linguistics, is to begin with a few examples, fix upon one aspect of the structure of these examples, and then to generalize to other cases. This generalization involves treating these examples as paradigms or models for paraphrasing the new cases, and taking an ideal notion of the formal structure of a theory as the main criterion for the acceptability of the generalization. In the use of the methods of formal logic in linguistic theory we find many examples of this. It is in this way that a structure is in fact imposed, even though the presence of examples might make it look as though the structure is justified by facts about language. The examples are not allowed to speak for themselves in the normal context where they belong, they are reinterpreted to fit the theory construction. It may look as though the examples were 'empirical evidence' for the theory, but they play the role of illustrative paradigm cases for the theory, i.e. for a systematic method of imposing a structure upon language.

In formal and mathematical theory constructions the idealizations are often motivated solely by requirements of simplicity, formal generality, and the formal coherence of the theory. For instance, by introducing 'points at infinity' and 'a line to infinity' in geometry it was possible to generalize and simplify the proposition about the intersection of lines. By introducing complex numbers it was possible to simplify and generalize the theorems on the existence of the roots of an equation. To make idealizations in this sense is what Hilbert called 'the method of ideal elements',[40] and he proposes it as the most promising approach for overcoming the conceptual puzzles connected with the notion of the infinite. 'Let us remember,' says Hilbert apropos of these puzzles, 'that *we are mathematicians* and as such have already often found ourselves in a similar predicament, and let us recall how the method of ideal elements, that creation of genius, then allowed us to find an escape.'[41] The distinction between 'real and ideal propositions', which forms the basis of Hilbert's proof-theoretical programme, was the result of applying 'the method of ideal elements'. So Hilbert was proposing a well-known approach in mathematical theory construction as a way to solve conceptual and philosophical problems. This was a serious mistake, which, unfortunately, has been very influential in creating a confusion of philosophical and scientific aims, and in particular in giving rise to misconceptions as to the role of idealized theory constructions.

What Hilbert calls 'the method of ideal elements' has certainly been a fruitful approach in mathematics. It consists roughly in isolating and fixing upon certain *formal* properties of a given notion and disregarding others, and then constructing a *new* system on the basis of these formal properties (sometimes together with other imposed ones) as defining properties. But the choice of the defining properties is governed, not by what is essential about the given notion in its own right, but by the possibility of reaching formal simplicity, uniformity, and generality. An example of this was Cantor's creation of the theory of transfinite sets and numbers. The defining properties of these concepts were partly inspired by our ordinary notion of a collection of individual things, while other properties, essential as regards collections of individual things, were disregarded or denied. What is misleading about this 'method of ideal elements' is its presentation (by Cantor, Hilbert, and many others) as a method for conceptual analysis, a method for clarifying a notion that we antecedently have, when it really is *a method for the construction of new concepts*. Cantor's notion of a set, according to which there are both finite and infinite sets, is a concept which is *different* from the ordinary notion of a set as a collection of individual things. The two notions are related only through formal similarities. The latter notion is not a special case of the former, which is being 'clarified' by set theory. The truth is rather that the ordinary notion of a collection (as well as the ordinary non-technical notions of a sequence, list, table, etc.) has been considerably confused through the interpretation of Cantor's set theory that I am objecting to here.[42] The method of ideal elements is not, as Hilbert wants us to believe, a method for stretching the boundaries of given notions, as though the logical boundaries were elastic. It is not a method for 'extending old concepts' but for creating new ones. The conceptual problems that concern philosophy arise, however, in connection with notions that we have, notions that are already in use but which we get confused about. Hilbert's method of ideal elements is therefore not a philosophical method.

The philosophical investigation can also be said to be concerned with idealizations, with giving expression to essential properties of language and to disregarding irrelevant and accidental factors, but in a sense of 'idealization' which is diametrically opposed to the scientific notion. To make an idealization is, one might say, to make up one's mind about what is important and essential about something. However, the grounds for the decision in the philosophical or conceptual investigation are not (even partly) methodological requirements and ideals about what form theories or explanations should take. The grounds are the logical order of the phenomena of language themselves, as they are open to view and agreed upon *in the practice of using language*. However, to exhibit essential features of language is no end in itself. The purpose is not just to develop a general view of language, but to obtain clarification where there is confusion – general views or principles are of interest in the philosophical investigation only as guides, as means to finding features of language that eliminate philosophical confusion.

Traditional philosophy and science, and the *a priori* philosophies of Husserl, Frege, and the early Wittgenstein, were built upon the idea that these opposed notions of idealization after all coincide, that the logical structure of actual language coincides with the rules and principles of some systematic, scientific, theory. But this would be so only if human language and reality actually were the (implicit) applications of a system of theories. This kind of intellectualism was recognized as a superstition by some of the best thinkers in the European tradition at least 100 years ago (e.g. by Nietzsche). Through the professionalism of philosophers and the influence of popular science and popular philosophy, this superstition is still alive – in modern philosophy of language, for instance, as the idea that an ordinary speaker of a language is tacitly or implicitly following the rules of a theory of meaning.

10 SENTENCES OF A LANGUAGE VERSUS FORMULAS OF A CALCULUS

One example of the failure to distinguish between a formal representation and what it represents is afforded by the notion of 'meaningfulness'. A sentence of ordinary language is considered to be meaningful if it has an obvious paraphrase in some formal system; its meaning is uniquely determined on the basis of this paraphrase. This has strange consequences. Consider, for instance the sentence

This ball is red all over and blue all over

which, presumably, would be paraphrased as a conjunction of the two sentences 'This ball is red all over' and 'This ball is blue all over'. What is the meaning of the conjunction? Is it determined in terms of the meanings of the 'subsentences'? There is certainly no use of the conjunction as a sentence for (correctly or incorrectly) describing the colour of a ball in the normal sense in which there is such a use of the 'subsentences', for instance, in a toyshop when someone wants to buy a ball for a child. When a certain ball is in fact white, someone could use either one of the subsentences to lie to someone else about its colour, but could the conjunction be used even to tell someone a lie? 'I told him that the ball was red all over and blue all over and he believed me!!' The conjunction is not false; it does not make sense in its alleged literal use. It purports to express a possibility that is excluded for conceptual reasons. And in order to realize that, it is necessary to be acquainted with the forms of use of our colour words.

Consider the sentence: 'The red spot on this wall has the shape of a square and at the same time the shape of a circle.' One could perhaps imagine some special form of use of this sentence in which it made sense, for instance, if the spot was caused by some phenomenon of coloured light that made it change shape constantly or some such thing. But the sentence has no use in the normal sense in which we describe the shape of a colour spot on a wall, for instance, when someone is asked to cut out a piece of wallpaper to cover it. There is no question of verifying this sentence by verifying the two sentences 'The red spot on this wall has the shape of a square' and 'The red spot on this wall has the shape of a circle'. These two sentences are not logically independent. So we have here another example (and thousands could be given) of two sentences of our language with a kind of meaning that is not 'closed under conjunction'. But these examples are 'idealized away' in theories of meaning.

Someone would perhaps say that this shows that these kinds of sentences ought not to be paraphrased as conjunctions but should be formalized in some other way. But will we ever be able to survey systematically the difficulties of this kind? Does it even make sense to assume that it could be done in principle? If language were basically a calculus, separable from various situations of human reality – yes. The assumption about the syntactical preparation of the language which is supposed to precede the meaning explanations in theories of meaning is out of touch with reality.

We could accept the statement that *some* of the formulas of the predicate calculus do represent (real) propositions of our language. In logical semantics and meaning theory (ever since the days of Carnap, Tarski – and even Frege) one works with the much stronger claim that every 'well-formed formula' of the predicate calculus (or some extension of it) expresses a proposition, i.e. has truth-conditions, if the non-logical symbols have been given an interpretation. The basis for this claim is the identification (or confusion) of a formal representation with what it is intended to represent. And one has to make this identification at the cost of several conceptually absurd consequences.

Let P be the sentence '7 is a prime number'. This sentence does express a real arithmetical proposition. We are familiar with forms of use of this simple sentence even at the level of elementary school arithmetic. But what about a formula like

$$P \to P?$$

Does the sentence 'If 7 is a prime number, then 7 is a prime number' express an arithmetical proposition, whose verification in any way makes use of the rules and concepts of the arithmetic of natural numbers? Certainly not. It has no use as an arithmetical proposition. And that is not because it is so trivial – as, for instance, the equation '1 + 2 = 2 + 1' expresses a trivial arithmetical fact that hardly needs verification – but because it has no arithmetical content at all. In teaching children to add one would perhaps point out that adding the number 2 to the number 1 gives the same result as adding 1 to 2, but, in teaching them about prime numbers, would one have to point out that 'if 7 is a prime number, then 7 is a prime number'? This sentence has its role *only as a formula in a certain formal representation of the language of elementary arithmetic*. And therefore, what *does* express a proposition is the sentence

$$P \to P \text{ is derivable in the propositional calculus}$$

or

$$P \to P \text{ is (an instance of) a tautology.}$$

So if someone says that he is 'proving that $P \to P$', it is most likely *these* propositions that he is proving. He is deriving the formula within a formal representation; but the formula represents no proposition.

Similarly, if Q is a sentence such as 'It is raining', no proposition is expressed by the formula

$$Q \vee \sim Q$$

It has no use as a statement about the weather. It has no truth-conditions as an empirical statement. It does not express a truth in any situation, in the sense in which the subsentences 'Q' and '~Q' may do so. On the other hand, it is a 'well-formed sentence' (i.e. formula) of the propositional calculus, as well as being an instance of a (classical) tautology. And *that* is a proposition that we can verify. So the predicate ' . . . is true' means something wholly different when applied to real propositions from what it means as a predicate of formulas of a calculus.

What I am trying to say here is perhaps even more obvious in the case of contradictions. Expressions like

It is raining and it is not raining

or

7 is a prime number and 7 is not a prime number

do not express propositions. Or, rather, one could perhaps imagine some special (perhaps figurative) use of these expressions as propositions; but they do not express propositions in the sense in which each of the subsentences does. The conjunction 'It is raining and it is not raining' is not false in the sense in which one of the subsentences may be false in a certain situation. This is clear from the fact that the conjunction could not be used, in its alleged literal sense, to convey incorrect information or to tell a lie about the weather.

For the same reason it is nonsense to speak about the expressions

(Q & ~Q) is true

and

(P & ~P) is true

as judgements, or even as potential judgements, if the predicate 'is true' is used as we normally use it for ordinary empirical and arithmetical propositions, respectively. Nor does it make sense to talk about 'knowing (Q & ~Q) to be true', even in the sense of 'potential' knowing that will never become 'actual'.

Does it make sense to talk about 'knowing what it means to be a verification of Q & ~Q'? If the formula 'Q & ~Q' expresses a proposition, then it should be possible at least to *try* to verify it; but what would it mean to try to verify that it is raining and not raining? And then I am of course not talking about trying to derive the formula Q & ~Q from certain premises in a calculus. 'Well, it means that you try to find a verification of the statement that it is raining and a verification of the statement that it is not raining. 'But can one even *try* to do something like that? Of course not. In the presence of evidence for the statement that it is raining there cannot be any question even of trying to verify that it is not raining (and vice versa).

Suppose that someone is about to go out for a walk and wonders whether he needs an umbrella. Would it make sense if he said to

104

someone else: 'Will you go to the window and see whether it is raining – and don't forget to check whether it is not raining at the same time!'?

Likewise, in the presence of calculations which show that no two numbers between 1 and 7 have a product equal to 7 there exists no problem of *trying* to find numbers between 1 and 7 whose product is equal to 7 (i.e. trying to show that 7 is not a prime number). Speaking about 'a possible proof of the proposition P & ~P' means nothing (except a possible derivation of the *formula* in a logical calculus). Do not confuse 'trying to prove that 7 is not a prime number in ordinary arithmetic' with 'trying to derive the formula ~P (or P → ⊥) in some formal system'! The latter can of course be done, *even* in the presence of a derivation of the formula P in the same system, i.e. it makes sense to try to prove that a formal system is formally inconsistent. However, in the presence of a (correct) derivation of the formula P, it makes no sense to try to prove that the formula P is not derivable in the same system.

So it seems to me that Wittgenstein in the *Tractatus* had very good reasons for saying that 'A tautology has no truth-conditions. . . . Tautologies and contradictions lack sense.' (4.461). They are, however, not completely nonsensical but 'part of the symbolism, much as "0" is part of the symbolism of arithmetic' (4.4611). That is, they are meaningful only as formulas of the logical calculus, but not as 'pictures of reality' or as 'representing a possible state of affairs'. This shows that the *Tractatus* notion of 'a proposition as an expression of its truth-conditions' means something essentially (and not just technically) different from what it means in logical semantics and meaning theory, contrary to what is often suggested in the literature on meaning theory when it is mentioned together with Frege's and Tarski's notions as an example of a truth-conditional semantics. Contrary to the *Tractatus* notion, Martin-Löf[43] understands the 'being true on no conditions' of a contradiction as a truth-condition for it, queer as this sounds, rather than as its having no truth-conditions. This is in agreement with Tarski's and Carnap's purely formal notion of 'truth-condition', not with the one in the *Tractatus*.

When expressions such as 'proposition', 'is true', 'truth-condition', 'meaning', 'knowing', 'verification', and 'proof' are used as they are in logical semantics and theory of meaning, in connection with tautologies and contradictions, it is clear that this use is a technical or formal one that is not only different from the ordinary use but in conflict with it. On the other hand, it is at the same time clear why these technical notions are preferred, namely, for methodological reasons. Theory construction is the primary aim and formal coherence an ideal. The technical notions are chosen so that the development of the semantical theory should live up to this ideal. One wants to have access to the mathematical methods of definition (or 'explanation') by induction and recursion in the semantical theory. There is, of course, no such thing as an inductive definition of the conditions of truth of actual propositions (not even of ordinary elementary arithmetical propositions). Such inductive definitions make sense only with respect to a formal *representation* of language, where propositions are represented as formulas generated by inductive definitions. Here we encounter again the situation that certain basic concepts of an alleged theory of language are prompted by the requirements of a methodology for constructing theories, rather than by the facts of our ordinary practice of using language.

Due to the strong and widespread tendency to confuse a formal representation with what it is intended to represent, it is not easy to become aware of this important conceptual difference between, on the one hand, the formal or 'idealized' notions of proposition, truth, etc., that belong to the representation of language as a calculus and, on the other hand, the actual notions of a proposition, etc., that have their basis in the language that we use. Take for instance the notion of a sentence. There is an almost systematic confusion between taking a sentence as expressing an actual proposition (i.e. as having a possible use as a sentence in a human language), and taking a sentence as a formula of some formal system or according to rules of some formal grammar. The difference applies even to a simple sentence like 'It is raining'. It expresses a real proposition in so far as it has a form of use in our language in circumstances which we are all familiar with; but as a formula, the circumstances of its normal use are precisely what are disregarded or abstracted away from. Instead, one treats the sentence as an argument for the (formally defined) truth-predicate and as a possible value of propositional variables. Or perhaps one starts by recognizing it as a grammatically well-formed sentence, but this is done on the basis of a conventionalized *reading* of it and not on the basis of its usual forms of use. But, as a formula, it does not express a real proposition or have truth-conditions in the sense of being true on certain kinds of empirical evidence. It expresses an actual (empirical) proposition only when the conditions of its (normal) use obtain, and to know

106

these conditions is – among other things – to know that in the presence of evidence for its truth, there can be no question of even looking for evidence for its negation. Someone who does not understand this has not yet mastered the language-game of describing and reporting about the weather. He does not yet know what proposition the sentence expresses.

In order to see the difference between a formal representation and what it is intended to represent, consider the following comparison: Imagine the practice of measuring distances between points in a geographical area for the purpose of constructing maps. In this situation it may be useful to employ idealizations. The methods and techniques for measuring distances in an area will of course always have physical limitations, so one could surely describe a real number k (for instance, a very small one) such that a sentence of the form 'the distance between the points A and B is k metres' would have no definite empirical or physical meaning in that practice. There would be no method for its verification or falsification. But this fact does not make it less useful to allow *any* positive real number as a value of the variable x in an expression of the form 'the distance between A and B is x yards' in the calculus of measurements of lengths, i.e. in the theory for constructing maps. It only means that not all sentences of this form in the theory represent empirical propositions.

One may ask in a similar fashion: would it make the systems of formal logic and formal grammar less useful if it were admitted that not all formulas represent propositions of some human language? If so, what kinds of use would be challenged? When it is realized that there is not a complete agreement between our language as we actually use it and its representation as a calculus, it may seem as though there were a choice between two alternatives. Either one can say (correctly) that the formal representation has a limited applicability to our language, or make the (nonsensical) claim that human beings have a limited capacity to use and take advantage of the principles of their own languages. In the theory of meaning and formal semantics one chooses the second alternative!

It is the notion of a sentence as a formula of a calculus that leads to the form of 'postulation of meaning-correlates' manifest in the concept of a 'proposition' that is used both in verificationist semantics and truth-conditional semantics: a 'proposition' as the content of a meaningful sentence or as the sentence together with its meaning. The essential thing here is that the proposition is thought of as something determined solely by the syntactical sentence (as required by the principle of molecularity). Due to the picture of a language as being fundamentally a system of forms of expression, one is bound to conceive of a proposition as something independent of the acts of judging, asserting, or commanding – as though a proposition were an entity that is complete as a proposition before it comes to function in judgements or assertions. One is forced into this misconception by the view that a sentence has meaning in isolation from its forms of use.

This notion of a proposition is, of course, firmly rooted in the tradition of formal logic and formal grammar. It is prompted by the conception of language as having a specified structure, more specifically, by the concept of the syntactical (or grammatically well-formed) sentence, i.e. the sentence as determined (or generated) primarily by a system of syntactical rules that are conceived of as independent of and prior to the circumstances of the use of the sentence. A proposition in this sense was what Frege explained by the expression *Vorstellungsverbindung*, as though no 'assertoric force' were involved in a proposition as such, but rather is something that it has to be supplemented with to make it into an assertion (Frege's 'assertion-sign'), as though the essential aspect of a proposition – that it says something, asserts something – were external features that must be added to it in order to obtain a judgement or an assertion.

Here it is instructive to compare the sentence or the 'propositional-sign' with the sign for an arrow. We can say that a proposition asserts that so-and-so is the case in about the same sense as we say that an arrow points in a certain direction. One need not add to the arrow-sign some additional sign to 'activate its pointing force'; similarly one does not predicate some 'assertion-sign' or 'truth-predicate' of a proposition to make an assertion out of it. One just utters it in the appropriate circumstances. One makes use of the 'assertoric force' that is already in it as an expression for a proposition. The sign for an assertion is the propositional sign, and the sign for someone's making an assertion is (usually) that he utters the sentence in a certain way in a certain situation. What makes an expression or a sequence of words a sentence of *our* language is that it has a possible use as a sentence, e.g. for making a judgement, for saying something to someone, for reporting observations, for answering a question, etc. But it is only *within* such a function that it is a sentence or a 'propositional sign'.

It is not because a sentence is syntactically well-formed (and semantically meaningful) that it can have such a function, but the fact that it can have such a function in our language is the reason why it is a 'well-formed' sentence (and a meaningful proposition). This is, one would like to say, the basic concept of a sentence. It is of course not a precise concept, but, on the other hand, the expressions of our languages that we tend to call sentences (or propositions) do not form a homogeneous category in respect to how expressions have meaning. And we do use the word 'sentence' in various ways: sometimes we call a sequence of words a sentence because it *looks* like a sentence or is similar to other sentences, or because it *sounds* like a sentence when it is read, and sometimes we call a sequence of words a sentence because it is built according to the rules of classical grammar or according to formal syntactical rules of modern linguistic theory.

Could, for instance, a sequence of words beginning with fifty alternating occurrences of the phrases 'for all . . .' 'there is a . . .' be a sentence? Could we imagine someone using such a sentence in communication between human beings? It would certainly have to be a very special situation. On the other hand, as a syntactical sentence or formula of a calculus, it might be as well-formed a sentence as any other. The mistake in the conception of language as a calculus that I am objecting to is to take one version of these conceptions of a sentence as the fundamental one and to pretend that the ordinary notion could, on that basis, be reconstructed or 'explained'.

11 LANGUAGE-LEARNING AND RULE-FOLLOWING

It is sometimes said that a satisfactory theory of meaning has to explain the fact that it is possible to learn languages. In order to do that, it is maintained, it must be explained how our languages 'make infinite use of finite means' (in Chomsky's words). It must be explained how the meaning of each sentence is a function of a finite number of features of the sentence, and how the meaning of a compound sentence is a function of the meanings of its constituent sentences. From this point of view there would seem to be good reasons for holding on to the principles of compositionality and molecularity. The specifications of the meanings of the sentences of a language cannot be listed one by one, and therefore (some people argue) some notion of recursion (in the sense of mathematical recursion theory) is needed to account for the learnability of language. Some writers, such as Chomsky, even go so far as to postulate a kind of 'recursive mechanism' in the biological constitution of the human organism in order to account for learnability.

There are substantial problems in this way of thinking. I am inclined to say that the conception of the rules of language as being the rules of a mathematical calculus has here brought us into the territory of science fiction. Due to this misconception, which is caused by a dogmatic attitude towards the methods of theory construction, one is led to invent a mythology to be able to explain our capacity to learn languages. This means that the conceptual problems concerning language-learning are not solved by these methods and idealizations, they are generated by them. To a great extent it may be said that for our actual languages these problems do not exist.

In what sense is there, for instance, something like an 'infinite use' in our languages, where 'infinite' means mathematically infinite? Is it really true that 'the number of compound sentences in a language is usually infinite', as Prawitz[44] expresses it, granting that we have the mathematical notion of the *potentially* infinite? Perhaps what one has in mind here is something like the following: take the simple sentence 'It is raining'; from it we can construct the well-formed sentence, 'It is not the case that it is raining' and likewise the sentence, 'It is not the case that it is not the case that it is raining', and so on *ad infinitum*. But with the exception of the first two or three sentences of this infinite series, we can hardly imagine a realistic linguistic situation where they would be used in the way sentences are normally used. They are sentences, not of a human language, but in the sense of being formulas of a calculus. They are conceived as constructions according to formal rules. So it is true that the number of sentences of a language is (mathematically) infinite if 'language' means idealization defined by the methods of theory construction borrowed from formal logic.

Or perhaps one is thinking of something like the following infinite series of sentences: '0 is a prime number', '1 is a prime number', '2 is a prime number', and so on. A number n could of course be described (in the mathematical language that we use) that was so large that it is impossible that the nth sentence of the series, with the numeral written out in canonical notation, could be used as a sentence, for instance in a mathematical report on prime numbers. That 'sentence' would be described by means of real sentences of our mathematical language, and it would 'exist', not as a concrete object, not as a sentence in the ordinary sense, but only as a term of a mathematical series.

The idea that misleads us here is, it seems to me, the following: 'The (mathematically) finite sequences can, in principle, be physically represented as lists of concrete, individual, things.' This is a false idea. The fastest computers can certainly write out enormous lists of numerals, but can we imagine a day when we will have a computer that can actually write out *any* finite sequence? Of course not. There is an important (and generally neglected) conceptual difference between the 'finite' as the term-for-term physically realizable on one hand, and as the mathematically limited on the other. The concept of a finite sequence in pure mathematics is not essentially limited by the conditions of the physical world in the way the methods and techniques for writing out actual (finite) lists are. We have therefore to do with two *different* concepts of 'the finite'. The mathematically finite is not the 'abstract' or 'idealized' form of the finite as the physically realizable. It is not the 'in principle physically realizable', but belongs to another conceptual realm.[45] The expression 'in principle' could here only mean *fictitiously* in the sense of science fiction. One can make up some kind of hazy picture of a (mathematically) finite sequence as a list, but it is for conceptual reasons bound to be (in general) only a picture – and therefore it misleads.

It is due to this misleading picture that Tarski[46] finds himself in a situation where he has to adopt the hypothesis of 'the existence of infinitely many physical things in the universe' in order to secure himself of a sufficiently large supply of material from which to construct expressions in the syntactical theory! This remarkable situation is due to two incompatible ideas of Tarski's: one is the conception of the expressions of a language as being the constructions of a mathematical calculus such as that of the natural numbers, and the other is the (in a certain sense correct) idea that the expressions and sentences of a language have to be concretely and physically representable. Misled by the 'idealizations' of physics, he is thinking as though the mathematically finite is what can be physically realized in principle.

On the basis of the conception of a language as an applied calculus, it appears as though there were just 'a practical constraint on the length of the sentences a person can send and receive with understanding.'[47] As though it were only an *accidental* feature of our use of language, due to our limitations as human beings, that we tend to use rather short and concretely surveyable expressions! But is it not actual human languages we are interested in? Such features of our practice of using language are of course *essential* to human languages (including the language of mathematics, which is not itself a mathematical calculus). One overlooks the fact that what is essential about the sentences of our languages is that they have their function as sentences in communication between human beings. Human language is limited and conditioned by various features of human life and the human organism, by the aspect of human reality which Heidegger calls '*in-der-Welt-sein*'. In the theory of meaning and formal semantics those essential features of language are treated as mere accidental features to be disregarded for the sake of theoretical efficiency.

It will be said that one is concerned with 'idealizations of human language'. But the nature of these idealizations is misunderstood. What kind of 'ideality' would it be that disregards the essential aspects of the languages we actually use – and in a discussion that is meant to be about the question of what it is that makes language *language*? The idealizations are the result, not of uncovering fundamental truths about language, but of building models and reconstructions that can only be justified as means to certain technical ends.

The question of how language can be learnt becomes even more puzzling when the calculus conception is coupled with the naturalistic view of the expressions of a language as being physical phenomena. 'How can a child ever learn to connect meaning, purpose, and intention with purely physical sounds and dead visual configurations on a paper?' Dummett[48] gets himself entangled in this 'mystery' when he says: 'Consider two speakers engaged in conversation. To immediate inspection, all that is happening is that sounds of a certain kind issue from the mouth of each alternately. But we know that there is a deeper significance: they are expressing thoughts . . .' 'To *immediate* inspection'! This is a good example of a situation where simple facts about actual language use, available to all of us, are forgotten in reflecting on language. The perspective of what goes on in a conversation between two speakers implied by the description 'sounds of a certain kind issue from the mouth of each alternately', is certainly not immediate. On the contrary it is an imposed interpretation; and when it is exercised systematically as in the syntactical viewpoint and in acoustic phonetics, it is an advanced theoretical perspective on human speech that one has to learn through training (and which, of course, has been useful in the various technologies for transmitting speech-signals).

Suppose that you are observing a conversation between two strangers in a foreign country in a language you do not understand at all. There may of course be situations in which you may be uncertain whether they are having a conversation or are doing something else, unfamiliar to you. But if it is not too foreign a country, there are hundreds of ordinary situations in which you do indeed see that they are talking to each other from the circumstances and from their gestures, looks, and general behaviour. Your attitude towards 'the sounds that issue from their mouths' is the attitude towards *parts of human speech* that you do not understand. You may, for instance, ask someone *what* they are saying (not *if* they are saying anything). It is not like the attitude you have towards the sounds produced by two cars in the street. It may even be misleading to say that you are *interpreting* the two persons as talking to each other or that you *conclude* that they are having a conversation. You just see it. It is a fact that we see such things 'immediately'.

And can we say that the small child 'receives' the loving words, looks, and gestures of its mother 'immediately' in the form of bare physical signals, and that it only later discovers that they have a 'deeper significance'? How can very small children react with satisfaction to bare physical signals? The human circumstances that make our language *language* are here forgotten. The philosophical task must be, not to accept these ways of putting the questions about learning and understanding language, but to reveal the disguised nonsense in them.

If language is viewed basically as a system of forms of expressions, determined by its syntactical and semantical rules, then it will certainly be difficult to understand how a particular language can be learnt at all. How can one acquire, for instance, a concept like 'the addition of numbers' from only a finite number of examples of how the rule of addition works? And how can we know with certainty that two persons have the same concept of addition when we can test and compare their understanding only in a finite number of cases? Can we, for similar reasons, be certain about the rules for using any expression of language? Do the concepts of meaning or intending one rule rather than another make sense at all?

Such are the problems that Kripke[49] deals with and his sceptical conclusions are prompted by his conception of the rules of language as the rules of a calculus which are, so conceived, somehow complete and finished *before* they enter into use in communication between human beings, *before* they are applied to a reality that is already there. It is a fact that most of us *can* acquire a concept like addition and, in normal situations, it *can* be determined with certainty whether someone else has acquired the same concept (as every school-teacher knows). And as concerns the usual use of words of our everyday language regarding, say, colours, points of time, the weather, food, etc., the rules for using the words can be learnt 'completely', and it can be determined whether someone has learnt them to a point where *further doubt does not make sense.* So there must be something wrong with a conception of language that comes in conflict with these facts. The philosophical task here is not to 'explain' these indubitable facts, but rather to investigate where things have gone wrong in our conceptions of language so that we are led to such absurd sceptical conclusions.

Let us examine Kripke's 'sceptical argument' more closely.[50] He begins with the idea that to learn to add is to 'grasp the rule for addition' and that the rule determines a person's answers for indefinitely many new sums that he has never previously considered. However, since a person will only have done finitely many sums at a given time, and since the totality of his past and present behaviour and mental states are finite, it is possible to interpret his behaviour in such a way that it accords, not only with the rule of addition, but with other rules. As Kripke puts it, there appears to be no fact about me, neither in my past behaviour nor in my mental history, that constitutes my having meant the rule of addition rather than some other rule. The conclusion seems to be that meaning or intending one rule (or function) rather than another makes no sense.

If Kripke's argument shows anything, it is that a human practice of following a rule cannot be defined or determined or characterized in terms of external criteria. A statement of the form 'He is following the rule "plus" ', or 'I meant to follow the rule of addition' cannot be verified on the basis of external evidence in the sense in which an empirical proposition like 'The movement of this planet is in accordance with rule R' can be so verified. In this respect Kripke's discussion shows the same thing as Quine's argument for the 'indeterminacy of translation': the rule is not determined on the basis of facts external to the practice of following the rule. But Kripke as well as Quine refuses to learn what can be learnt from this, namely, that the existing practice of following the rule is the logically fundamental thing. Kripke tries rather to *reconstruct* these existing practices (of doing mathematics as well as of using language in general) on the basis of what he takes to be fundamental: the extensional picture of rules and functions and the naturalistic conception of language.

Kripke seems to think that his argument differs from Quine's in that he, unlike Quine, is not confining himself to an 'observer, who can observe my overt behaviour but not my internal mental state'. But this is an unimportant difference. Kripke is nevertheless asking for external evidence for 'his meaning plus and not some other rule, in the past'. To observe or recall my mental states while I am computing the sums of numbers is as much to observe features external to the practice of adding as to observe my eye-movements while I am adding. The important sense of 'external' here is not external as opposed to mental, or what someone else can observe about me as opposed to what I can observe about myself, but 'external' in the sense of *being conceptually independent of the practice of following the rule*. The relation between the rule and the practice of following it is internal. Detached from the practices of computing, adding, counting, the rule of addition is just a mathematical expression with a verbal reading, which – in Kripke's case – is inspired by the extensional picture of rules and functions. But understood in this way, it is not determined what it means to follow the rule. Despite the fact that *we do know* what it means to follow this rule to a point where there is no room for doubt, Kripke refuses to question the extensional picture as the fundamental notion of the rule, and he is thereby forced to a 'sceptical solution' of the 'paradox that we follow the rule as we do without reason or justification'. This 'paradox' exists only against the background of the extensional picture of the rule (or function) of addition as being ultimately an 'infinite list' of individual equations (or ordered pairs) such as:

$$1 + 1 = 2$$
$$1 + 2 = 3$$
$$2 + 1 = 3$$
$$2 + 2 = 4$$
$$\cdot$$
$$\cdot$$
$$\cdot$$

This is the basic notion of the rule of addition Kripke uses and takes for granted throughout his discussion, and his attitude towards it is that it is unquestionable despite the paradox and the absurdities it causes. How can I know, Kripke argues, that I meant plus in the past, when 'I gave myself only a finite number of examples instantiating this function'? '*Only* a finite number!' It is understood that *any* doubt as to what function I meant would have been excluded if I had access to '*all* examples instantiating this function'! But this is, according to Kripke's way of thinking, impossible, not nonsensical. It is impossible for factual rather than conceptual reasons: I am a finite being with a finite mind without access to the 'realm of infinite objects', where there are 'infinite lists of individual things'. Kripke is considering the possibility that there may be something in a person's mind that tells him what to do in all future cases when following the rule, but he rejects this alternative on the grounds that

> The infinitely many cases of the table are not in my mind for my future self to consult. To say that there is a general rule in my mind that tells me how to add in the future is only to throw the problem back on the other rules that also seem to be given only in terms of finitely many cases.[51]

We have access 'only' to fragments of the 'infinite list'. The presupposed 'realm of infinite objects, infinite tables' is obvious here. But this 'realm' is only a *picture*, a metaphor that may be a harmless, and sometimes even useful, way of speaking in the practice of calculating and doing arithmetic, but which produces nonsense when it is used as Kripke uses it for philosophical purposes. The best proof of this is of course the 'paradox' and the absurdities that Kripke derives on its basis. There are no infinite lists or infinite tables of individual things. The notion of an infinite list as used within mathematics is a technical notion with a *different* logical grammar and with *some* formal similarities with the ordinary notion of a list, which explain the choice of the term 'list', but it is a different employment of the word. The puzzles that Kripke derives arise at the points where the similarity does not hold, while Kripke takes it for granted that there should be complete similarity, that it is the same concept of a list (or table), since we use the same word.

The extensional notion of rules is the main cause of the problems not only for the mathematical examples but also for the other examples that Kripke deals with, as for instance the rule for using a word like 'green'. He argues as though the rule for using this word were ultimately determined on the basis of the totality of all past, present, and future cases where it is correct to say of an object, at that time, that it is green. Since a person can only be in contact with a few of all these cases, the rule for using 'green' is not determined. These cases may be in agreement with the rule for using some other colour word, 'grue' say.

One problem here is what 'correct' means, another and related problem is what 'rule for using a word' means. In order to be able to state the problem, Kripke must somehow assume that past, present, and future objects have the colours they have regardless of our use of colour words, and therefore regardless of our colour concepts; he must assume that it makes sense to talk about the colour that an object *in fact* has at a certain time – but independently of our language of colours (i.e. of our rules for using colour words)! But it is obviously not independent. Kripke must assume a 'meta-language' in which he can refer to the extensional picture of the rules he is discussing in order to be able to state his problem. He is assuming that he can talk about green as one colour (or rule) and grue as another and with the understanding that their 'ident-ities' are ultimately those of their extensions. The corresponding assumption in the mathematical example is that the mathematical functions themselves, as extensionally conceived 'abstract, infinite objects', are presupposed in the statement of the sceptical problem. It is assumed that he can refer to them in some meta-language that we are using 'in the present'. Now, Kripke seems to mean that this assumption is made only provisionally: when the argument is given, we can throw away this assumption as the ladder we have used in reaching the sceptical conclusion, which then extends to the whole of language, even to our present meta-language. But this is a mistake. The extensional picture and the assumed meta-language *in which this picture exists*, are not just preconditions for *stating* the problem, they are preconditions for there *being* a sceptical problem. Why should the problem and its solution otherwise be called 'sceptical'? Kripke does not see this mistake because he is thinking of a language as a calculus of expressions which can be separated from reality, from the expressions' use in referring to things. Reality, for Kripke, is the extensional picture; but this picture exists only within a calculus of expressions, namely within the philosophical jargon which Kripke uses in stating his problem. When this jargon is removed, what remains is our ordinary language – without the sceptical problem.

What Kripke means by 'a rule for using a word or an expression' is not, strictly speaking, a rule for a certain use of *the word*, but a rule for the word in a system of conventional notation, i.e. a terminological rule. By 'the rule for using the word "green" ' he means a rule that would describe the whole terminological history of the word 'green'. And the colour green 'itself', the extension of green, is simply a postulated objective counterpart of this terminological history. It is the picture accompanying the description of the terminological history of 'green'. The terminological rule for the word 'grue' is stated by Kripke as follows: 'past objects were grue if and only if they were (then) green while present objects are grue if and only if they are (now) blue.' This rule must, however, presuppose the *forms of use* of the words 'green' and 'blue' for attributing colours to objects, i.e. it must presuppose the concepts of green and blue. But Kripke is blind to the non-temporal, conceptual sense of the use of expressions, i.e. the use through which the expressions 'are connected to reality'; he thinks as though all rules for using expressions were terminological rules. This is because a language for him is essentially a system of notation.

Kripke explicitly admits that he can state his 'sceptical paradox' only in the 'metalinguistic sense', i.e. not as a sceptical problem about arithmetic or about colours of objects, but only as a problem about 'linguistic intentions': 'Am I presently conforming to my previous linguistic intentions?' But what are our 'linguistic intentions'? What picture of a language and its use lies behind this (technical) notion? The sceptical problem exists only within a conception of the language under discussion as being a system of notation or a system of expressions (an 'object-language') which stands in an external relation of 'denotation' to the 'non-linguistic reality which it is about' (i.e. as it is conceived within model-theoretic semantics). When I want to use language – according to this conception – in order to say something about an object in reality, I first form the 'linguistic intention' of meaning what I want to mean by the expressions I use. When I want to say that this tree is green, I first form the linguistic intention of meaning this tree by 'this tree' and green by 'green'! Do my past and present linguistic intentions agree? As though there could *always* be a problem of whether I am mistaken about what I mean by the words and expressions I use! The sceptical problem arises only in what Kripke calls the 'metalinguistic sense', i.e. only against the naturalistic calculus-conception which forms the background of notions like 'object-language', 'meta-language', 'use vs. mention', ' "X" denotes

118

X', etc. So what Kripke's discussion could be said to show is that this picture is definitely wrong as a picture of our actual language and how it works.

The generality of the rules for using a colour-word such as 'green' is not extensional. It is not as though we would have to have access to all green things in the past, the present and the future in order to grasp these rules completely in their full generality. We learn to use the word from examples, and we learn to recognize an object as green although it may have a shade of green which we have never encountered before. It might be said: we learn to recognize an object as green 'if it is sufficiently similar in the relevant respect' to the green things we have seen. The generality of the paradigm examples is here expressed by the 'relevant similarity'. There is, however, no way in which this 'similarity' could be defined or characterized in a framework external to the practice of using colour words, i.e. this similarity is inseparable from the human practice of using 'green' in making colour judgements. It might therefore be said that any attempt to explain or define this similarity (i.e. what green things have in common) is bound to be circular. But this 'circularity' constitutes no problem when it is realized that the existing practice of using colour-words is logically the fundamental thing. It is, conceptually, the beginning. The circularity is felt to be a problem only from the misconceived point of view according to which the practice of using colour words could be reconstructed, derived, explained, or justified.

Related to the 'problem' of recognizing new shades of colours is the following question: 'How can we use and understand new sentences, sentences we have never heard or seen before – and so many of them?' Answering this question about the 'productivity of language' is considered to be one of the most important tasks of modern linguistic theory. But how can it be a problem? That it has the form of a question is not sufficient for it to be a problem. It is hardly ever a problem in our practice of using language, in the way that, for instance, it is often a problem for us that we do *not* understand certain new sentences, or sometimes even sentences that we *have* used before. What are the conditions for this question to be a problem? It is a problem within linguistic theory. It is a problem which arises against the background of a conception of language within linguistic theory. And it seems to me that the extensional view is also at work in the way this problem is dealt with in the Chomsky tradition and in recent formal semantics. There a language is conceived of as the totality of its syntactically or grammatically well-formed sentences, and this totality is conceived *as an extension of individual things*, of individual sentences, which in turn are conceived as finite sequences of physical objects and as each having a certain grammatical structure.[52] Obviously we cannot – according to this conception – learn these individual sentences one by one as we learn the items of a finite list or table, because there are too many of them. It must be explained how we 'generate' them and derive our understanding of them 'on a finite basis' (in Chomsky's words) by means of recursive rules and the principle of compositionality. The sentences of a language have to be reconstructed as formulas of a calculus, and 'reconstructed' here is the appropriate word because, according to the extensional view, all present, past, and future sentences of a language already have an individual, time-invariant, existence. It is as though these processes of generation were already completed somewhere in some shadow reality. Expressions that will be used and called sentences in the future are conceived as already being determined as sentences by the rules of formal grammar, despite the fact that forms of expressions change in unforeseen ways, ways that are sometimes in conflict with past and present standards of grammaticality.

What we have here is an unhappy influence on linguistic theory of ideas from mathematical logic and the discussions about the foundations of mathematics. It was on the basis of this misleading extensional picture that Chomsky found a 'justification' for using the calculus conception for 'explaining natural languages'. 'How should we otherwise explain the fact that we can understand new sentences?' The picture is misleading for several reasons, but most of all because there is no such thing as an unlimited extension of *individual* things. The mystery about our understanding new sentences arises because of this extensional view together with the foreign misrepresentation of the sentences of actual language as 'syntactical objects' of a formal system. If a new, ordinary, sentence that I understand were given to me as a sequence of signs of this representation, then there might be a problem of interpreting it, of deriving its meaning from 'the process of its generation', but normally there is no such problem. I just read what the sentence says in the context where it occurs.

That the extensional picture is at the root of the problem is also clear from the way the problem is worded: 'sentences that we have *never seen before*.' As though all sentences nevertheless existed somewhere beforehand, only not here with us! Does the problem not arise for sentences that I *have* seen before? Consider a sentence of the form 'X was born on 14 May, 1367,' which we might imagine in some history book. I may not have seen this sentence because I may never have seen exactly this date before. On the other hand, I may have seen it. If so, I do not remember it. How would it help me if I had seen it before? It makes no difference, I know the rule, the practice of giving people's dates of birth. The wording of the problem suggests that to know this rule completely is somehow to have access to all past and future dates *individually*, rather than mastering a practice of language. I learned expressions of dates from examples of their use, and I learned to recognize new expressions of dates and sentences containing them on the basis of what they 'have in common' with the paradigm examples I once learned. But then again, there is no formal characterization of this 'having in common' within a framework, model, or theory external to the existing practice of expressing dates and communicating people's dates of birth, because the practice, in the everyday sense in which most of us are familiar with it, is logically the fundamental thing. When I have learned the rule, when I master the practice, I no longer need the paradigm examples, I simply immediately see a date when I come across one, just as I immediately see that the tree in front of me is green, when I master the language of colours. There is no question of 'how I understand', which would suggest that I am interpreting or 'implicitly' applying some method or technique or theory.

To learn or to 'grasp' a rule of language is to learn a human practice. There are logical criteria for saying, in specific circumstances and with certainty, that 'now he has learned the rule, now he can follow it', but these criteria are not (even implicitly) formal criteria, external to the practice.

12 THE DISPUTE OVER REALISM IN MATHEMATICS

According to Dummett, the philosophical disputes over realism are at bottom problems about what form a theory of meaning should take, and the philosophical dispute between intuitionists and adherents of other philosophies of mathematics is no exception. Martin-Löf and Prawitz are, to some extent, in agreement with this philosophical motive for expounding a theory of meaning, and the verificationist theories they have proposed are meant to support anti-realist conceptions of mathematics. It seems to me, however, that these anti-realist conceptions are not quite free of realist presuppositions. They still involve a kind of realism in respect of proofs and provability, which is enforced by two mistaken ideas. First is the idea that a sentence has a definite individual content, which is determined by the way it is composed out of its constituent expressions – or rather, that there is a general method for paraphrasing ordinary sentences such that this principle holds. Second is the idea that mathematical and empirical propositions have meaning in the same way, and the meaning explanations are therefore assumed to apply to both kinds of proposition.

Frege realized that much conceptual confusion is caused by considering words as having a definite meaning in isolation from the context of sentences. It leads to the postulation of some kind of meaning-correlates of words, and this causes philosophical problems. But Frege was not free from being misled in this respect himself. Similar problems arise if we take a sentence as having a definite, individual meaning in isolation from the forms of its use. The notions of *the* 'central feature' of a sentence or *the* 'canonical verification' of a sentence are postulated meaning-correlates in this sense. What prompts this postulation in the theories of meaning of Dummett, Martin-Löf, and Prawitz is the principle of molecularity according to which there should be something which is *the* individual meaning of a sentence and which is tied solely to the sentence and its syntactical form. The mistaken idea that sentences have a (definite) meaning in isolation from their forms of use prompts the kind of realism with respect to proofs and provability that we find in these theories. The formalization of a sentence (or proposition) in the predicate calculus or in intuitionistic type theory is taken to be sufficient as syntactical regimentation for the principle of molecularity to apply. This means that the property of a sentence of having a well-formed paraphrase in these formal systems is identified with its being meaningful, or with its having a definite meaning. For such a 'meaningful sentence' or 'proposition' there is postulated a 'central notion' as its meaning in the form of a notion of a possible (direct) verification or proof of the proposition. The meaning of a sentence is taken to be given by 'what counts as a direct verification or proof of the proposition', and the latter is supposed to be completely determined by the formalization of the sentence.

This means that a technical use of the expression 'knowing what counts as a proof of a proposition' is introduced, according to which we know from the semantical explanations what counts as a (direct) proof of a proposition as soon as it has an obvious formalization in the predicate calculus. This, however, has some strange consequences. Sentences expressing Goldbach's theorem and other open mathematical problems are said to have as definite a mathematical meaning as the sentence '7 is a prime number'. One is led to say that 'we know what it means to be a proof of Goldbach's theorem' or that 'we can give the criteria for something to be a proof of Goldbach's theorem', although the mathematical methods and concepts that may settle this problem some day may not even have been dreamed of yet. It is in order to satisfy the requirement that a sentence should have a definite, individual meaning regardless of its specific mathematical surrounding that one is led to postulate a sharply delimited domain of proofs associated with the formalization of a proposition in this way, despite the fact that that domain may be mathematically undetermined.

What makes many open mathematical problems *open* is not just that we lack methods for finding proofs (or disproofs) that actually are out there somewhere waiting to be found. This is a point where the analogy between empirical and mathematical propositions leads one astray. A sentence expressing an open mathematical problem is not like an empirical hypothesis which no one has yet been able to verify (or falsify) but which may nevertheless be a perfectly meaningful, empirical proposition. A mathematical problem is open because its proper mathematical context or surrounding, in which it becomes well-defined and solvable, has not been found, or may not even be invented. It is an openness with respect to its precise mathematical content as much as to its truth. In the history of mathematics we find many examples of solutions of open problems which consist in the old statement of the problem being given a new and precise mathematical sense.

The normal mathematical sense of the expression 'knowing what it means to be a proof of a certain mathematical proposition' is, it seems to me, that of knowing what a proof looks like from having seen one, or having a method for constructing a proof or, perhaps, knowing proofs of other propositions that may for some reasons be expected to have similar proofs. Knowing *what* to do (in proving a mathematical proposition) and knowing *how* to do it are not conceptually independent things in mathematics (in the way that they are for many empirical propositions). There are many examples of how the invention of a new method or technique in mathematics comes to determine *what* it means to be a proof of an old open problem. So, in this sense, one does not yet know (as far as I know) what it means for something to be a proof of Goldbach's theorem.

This difference between mathematical and empirical propositions reflects of course the fact that mathematics is not a science of 'independent mathematical phenomena' in the way that physics is a science of natural phenomena. The postulation of a sharply delimited domain of possible proofs of a proposition in verificationist semantics is, it seems to me, an attempt to furnish mathematics with such 'mathematical phenomena' – the 'objects' explored by mathematicians. This, however, is only a picture, and for the reasons stated I do not think that it is a good picture. It is enforced by a false idea of how the language of mathematics works.

I think that the idea of a perfectly *mathematically* meaningful proposition (or well-defined problem) that is at the same time undecidable (unsolvable) is a misconception. In saying this of course I do not intend to question the famous meta-mathematical results on undecidability and incompleteness. What I am questioning is their interpretation, or more specifically, the notion of mathematical meaningfulness or well-definedness which is involved in this interpretation, and which is roughly the following: If a mathematical sentence has an obvious paraphrase or formalization, with the usual readings of the logical symbols, in some formal system such as first-order arithmetic, then it has a definite mathematical content. There may still be a problem of whether it is true or false, but there is no problem concerning what it means mathematically. This comes from a notion of the 'meaningfulness' of mathematical propositions that belongs to the conception of the language of mathematics as being basically a formal system – the conception that Peano, Frege and Russell tried to work out in detail, and which dates back to Leibniz. What is wrong with this conception is not just that there is no such system that is formally complete and recursively decidable, but that it presupposes that mathematics has its *conceptual* foundation in such a system and not in the existing forms of use of expressions and symbols in mathematical practice. The existing practices of mathematics are seen in this traditional view rather as something conceptually secondary, to be derived, accounted for and justified on the basis of the rules of the formal system. In this view one forgets that the construction, operation, and application of the formal system are parts of the mathematical practice, and that this formalization is therefore a *mathematical* enterprise, a mathematical construction. Instead, it is given a false philosophical status when it is believed to provide a logical foundation for mathematics. Frege shared this mistaken belief in 'the possibility of the formalization of mathematical thought' with Peano and Couturat. It was the basis of their foundationalism in mathematics, and this foundationalism is still alive in the form of the identification of 'having a definite mathematical content' and 'having a well-formed paraphrase in a formal system'.

The mathematical content of an arithmetical proposition is not in general determined by its formalization in some formal system such as first-order arithmetic or intuitionistic-type theory. These formal systems do not have an exceptional position in mathematics. They would have only if mathematics in general consisted in their application (which logicians sometimes pretend is the case). The purely formal-semantical sense of knowing what counts as a proof of a proposition of a certain form in verificationist semantics relies too heavily on general verbal descriptions that are adapted to a particular formalization. That these verbal descriptions are integrated into a coherent system of explanations, into a systematic theory of meaning, does not make them more reliable as explanations of mathematical content, because the systematic structure is bound up with the formalization. The explanations do not go deeper into the conceptual content of propositions than the formalization, and they may therefore leave the mathematical content of a proposition largely undetermined.

An example of this is the paraphrase in first-order arithmetic of Goldbach's theorem: 'For any natural number x such that x is even and greater than 2, there are natural numbers y and z which are prime and whose sum is equal to x.' According to verificationist semantics, a proof of this proposition is, roughly, a method which to any even natural number x greater than 2 assigns two numbers and verifications that they are prime and have a sum equal to x. I do not want to say that the verificationist explanation is wrong, but as long as nothing more is said or known about this 'method', this verbal explanation does not give the proposition a more definite mathematical content than does its original verbal formulation.

If the verificationist explanations express what is meant by 'understanding a mathematical proposition' or 'knowing what counts as a proof of a proposition', then we certainly do understand Fermat's theorem, and we know what it means to be a proof of Goldbach's conjecture. But what is the point of making this weak notion of understanding into *the* understanding of a *mathematical* proposition? That it prompts the postulation of a sharply delimited domain of possible proofs of those propositions, which may actually be mathematically undetermined, is something which speaks eloquently against it.

One can say that I am here objecting to the anti-realist view of mathematics for containing too much realism, for its having failed to get to the roots of the realist misconceptions. Those roots are the underlying conceptions of language that are common in both realist and verificationist semantics, namely everything that depends upon the view of the expressions of a language as having a sense as mere expressions, outside the conditions of their normal use. As another example of this, consider the realist/idealist dispute over whether the notion of truth in mathematics is 'tensed', and whether it is 'knowledge-dependent'. According to the realist view, mathematical truths are 'timelessly true' and 'independent of anyone's knowing them to be true'. The anti-realist, or at least the extreme idealist, denies this. Now, if we look at the use of this notion of 'timelessness' we find the realist view expressed in statements such as 'if a mathematical proposition is true, it is true at each point of time, even before it is (eventually) proved'. This shows that the timelessness of mathematical truths is understood as their being in some sense *time-invariant* rather than non-temporal. The expression 'timeless' is used as though it made sense to relate mathematical truths to time at all, as though it made sense to talk about a mathematical fact as being a fact before, after or simultaneous with something else, which it obviously does not. We do not ask questions like: 'When did $2 + 2 = 4$ become true and who made it true?' Mathematical truths are non-temporal. And this is a *conceptual* and not a metaphysical remark.

When the anti-realist maintains the opposite of the realist thesis about the time-invariance of mathematical truths, *he is committing the same mistake* as the realist. In order to maintain the opposite or the denial of the realist thesis as a positive thesis, the anti-realist has to admit the realist thesis as *making sense* even though he considers it to be false. In that respect he is guilty of the same conceptual confusion as the realist. He is not only implying that it makes sense to relate mathematical truths, as such, to time, but that they are so related. Thus, Heyting writes: 'a mathematical theorem expresses a purely empirical fact, namely the success of a certain construction. "$2 + 2 = 3 + 1$" must be read as an abbreviation for the statement:

I have effected the mental constructions indicated by "2 + 2" and by "3 + 1" and I have found that they lead to the same result'! Here one would like to ask: 'What then if someone else were to obtain a different result, or if you were to find that these "mental constructions" lead to a different result tomorrow?'[53]

The situation would of course have been different if the discussion concerned the truth of statements about the invention of mathematical concepts or about the *event* of someone's establishing the truth of a mathematical proposition by giving a proof of it. Such empirical or historical statements are of course temporal. The dispute I am talking about concerns the truth of strictly mathematical statements; and they are true, roughly, on the basis of the rules of a mathematical system in which there is no temporal reference. This holds *despite* the fact that the system itself and the mathematical constructions made within it were invented by certain people at a certain time. But such truths about mathematical rules and concepts are not mathematical but historical (and therefore temporal).

It is when one thinks of the non-temporality of mathematical statements as time-invariance that there appears to be a conflict here – a conflict which seems to necessitate the postulation of some mathematical 'reality' or realm of facts which is constant and unchanging as time flows along, and which exists prior to the invention of concepts and methods for 'discovering' it; in short: 'an objective realm of mathematical objects waiting to be discovered'. But the mathematical facts, as such, are neither prior to, posterior to or simultaneous with anything in the temporal sense. Whenever there is a temporal reference in the statements, one has left the conceptual sphere of the strictly mathematical content, and is instead, perhaps, in the sphere of (historical or empirical) statements about the activity of doing mathematics. And such statements are of course also used by mathematicians in doing mathematics, but the two kinds of statements must not be confused. They have meaning in different ways.

There seems to be a similar misconception involved in the idealist thesis that 'the notion of truth is knowledge-dependent', advocated for instance by Martin-Löf.[54] What is correct about the *opposite* realist thesis is that there is no causal dependence between the (historical) event that someone gives a proof of a proposition and the proposition's being true. Mathematicians do not *cause* their theorems to become true. It would not make sense to ask questions like 'Who caused or made the number 7 a prime number and when did they do it?' The being true of a true mathematical statement is not an empirical or historical fact, which someone's knowing a statement to be true certainly is. We have here two different conceptual realms, and there is therefore no question of a causal connection between them.

This much is correct about the realist thesis, that mathematical truths do not logically depend, as regards their being true, on someone's knowing them to be true. But it is not as such a purely conceptual statement that realists understand their own thesis; they claim to be expressing a metaphysical truth about 'mathematical reality', which they then conceive 'as existing independently of us'. Now, it is as such a metaphysical or 'ontological' statement that idealists deny the realist thesis and maintain its opposite. Idealists therefore commit themselves to the realist interpretation of the problem and are forced to express their contrary view in a form which invites the mistaken causal interpretation of the relation between 'being true' and 'being known'. They will say something to the effect that it is only as a result of someone's knowing a proposition to be true that it makes sense to talk about the proposition's being true. But to this the realist will respond correctly that we do speak of 'truth waiting to be discovered', and apparently it makes sense to do so, so . . . . But again, the realist does not mean this argument about 'truth waiting to be discovered' in the sense in which we all would agree with it. Realists give the argument a metaphysical interpretation according to which 'there are *actual* truths', i.e. truths that are, somehow, 'true already today' waiting to be discovered. But then, again, realists are talking about mathematical truths as temporal; they are thinking as though mathematical truths were in time, and are confusing the two different conceptual spheres. And in this way the dispute continues without touching the conceptual confusion which is at the heart of the matter.

So, it seems to me that the problem about the notion of truth in the realist/idealist dispute is rooted in a confusion of the logical rules for mathematical and empirical propositions, i.e. in the attempt to bring these conceptually *different* kinds of propositions under *one* notion of meaning and *one* notion of truth. The starting point for this attempt is the conception of language according to which there should be *one* system of formal rules, one calculus, that is the logical basis for both kinds of proposition.

This illustrates what seems to me to be generally at the root of the philosophical positions of realism and idealism: a dogmatic attitude to certain conventional forms of expression; the tendency to give certain linguistic forms (like the forms and laws of traditional formal logic) an exceptional position. This attitude – supported by tradition and by the professionalism of philosophers – is then felt to be in need of metaphysical justification. The realist postulates a kind of independent metaphysical correlate of the linguistic forms, while the idealist justifies his choice of distinguished linguistic forms by what their internal formal coherence means to someone who has this dogmatic attitude towards them. These 'justifications' are not really justifications at all; they have rather the character of philosophical ceremonies. The common conceptual mistake is the idea that language is a hierarchy of systems of forms of expression, detached from their forms of use, and with one distinguished system constituting the foundation. As I have tried to show, this idea manifests itself most concretely in the methods and techniques for the paraphrase and formalization of expressions of ordinary language.

Is the realist/idealist dispute a central philosophical issue? Should every self-respecting philosopher take a stand in this dispute? I think that there is one aspect of the issue which has not been taken into consideration sufficiently, namely that philosophical idealism and realism are primarily two opposite sides in a classical philosophical *battle*. The realist and idealist theses have had an important function as battle-cries, and as is usually the case with battle-cries and ideological statements, they overstate their case and therefore create confusion (and sometimes hard feelings). I do not believe that in the realist/idealist dispute there exists the peace of mind necessary to obtain conceptual clarity about the notion of truth. I believe that if the difficulties in this dispute were sorted out on the purely conceptual level, there would be nothing left on the 'metaphysical level' to dispute about, there would be no metaphysical or ontological standpoint left to take. By 'sorting out difficulties on the conceptual level' I do not mean conceptual clarification in the *mathematical* sense, i.e. the construction of a new conceptual system or the invention of an 'exact' terminology for speaking about mathematical statements and their truth. I am talking about getting clear about some of the basic properties of mathematical concepts, not, however, with respect to a *reconstruction* of mathematical concepts, but with respect to such concepts as they are given in the forms of use of expressions we already have in established (elementary) mathematical practice. In so far as our difficulties are philosophical (and not scientific or ideological), it is only on this level that they can be completely resolved, since the deepest cause of the philosophical problems discussed is forgetfulness of the 'basic principles' in this sense (as for instance the principle of the non-temporality of mathematical truths). And it is also with respect to the 'basic principles' in this sense (i.e. as forms of use of expressions in established mathematical practice) that we can speak of the 'correctness' or the 'validity' of proofs without committing ourselves to some kind of obsolete, metaphysical realism, idealism, or relativism.

3

FORM AND CONTENT IN MATHEMATICS

1 WORD-LANGUAGE AND MATHEMATICAL CONTENT

A rewarding approach to the various problems in the philosophy of mathematics is to ask the question: What is the role of word-language expressions and idioms in mathematics? How does 'mathematical prose' contribute to the conceptual content of mathematical notions? It was one of Wittgenstein's achievements to show that the employment of word-language in mathematics is a main source of conceptual confusion in the philosophy of mathematics.[1] There is an almost irresistible temptation to give certain informal modes of expression, which accompany technical-mathematical notions and results, a conceptual role for which there is no justification in the actual mathematics. And this fact has been most devastating in mathematical logic, meta-mathematics and set-theory.

Informal idioms, in the form of 'intuitive explanations', 'informal readings' of technical-mathematical notions and results have important functions in mathematical *activity*, in communication between mathematicians. We do not want to deny that. It may also be useful from a practical, pedagogical point of view to use a more vivid, summarizing mode of expression. It might be useful in scientific work to give rough, provisional expression to an idea or a problem and to outline the content of established results. But the choice of terminology and expressions from word-language is also made in order to express the 'significance' of notions and results, to give expression to what is considered to be important, interesting, and a sign of progress.[2] And this is achieved by the choice of words that mark connections and similarities with other areas of mathematics, with certain applications and with the 'intuitive idea' in which a certain notion originated. Modes of expression are employed that give prominence to certain lines of development, expressing affinity with a certain tradition and suggesting certain applications. (Cf. 'continuity', 'linear space', 'theorem', 'set', 'one-to-one correspondence', 'extension', 'transfinite number', 'effective procedure'.)

In many cases expressions of word-language have been introduced by being transferred from one mathematical context into another, or from a non-mathematical use into a mathematical one, on the basis of analogies, pictures and partial formal similarities, which may have been stimulating from a mathematical point of view in suggesting constructions of new notions and techniques, but which may nevertheless be conceptually misleading by giving rise to a confusion of readings and conceptual content. The fact that expressions of word-language give familiar readings, which may be natural and appropriate in conceptually different mathematical situations, may lead one to the mistaken idea of there being a common conceptual ground for two essentially different notions (e.g. that there is a common notion of 'list' in 'finite list' and 'infinite list').

There need not be anything wrong with the technical employment of expressions of word-language in mathematics, but the *precise* mathematical content of an expression in a certain form of use may not be transferable into another use (e.g. from actual, finite lists to infinite sequences, or from empirical propositions to arithmetical ones), although *some* features are common and although the reading of the expression may suggest the opposite.

The danger of being misled in this way is perhaps not impending in actual mathematical work, in calculating and proving and applying mathematics, but rather in discussions about the 'justification' of axioms and formal rules, in the statement of the results, in interpretations of what one is doing, and in discussions of the significance of what has been achieved. This justifying and interpreting activity is the place where the tasks of philosophers and mathematicians often get mixed up and the resulting confusions are typically confusions about the conceptual role of mathematical prose. All this is therefore something that the philosopher of mathematics has to be extremely careful about. His primary aim is conceptual clarity rather than mathematical progress. His aim is to get clear about *existing* notions and results that have given rise to philosophical puzzles and not to contribute to the construction of new mathematical notions and methods. In this respect the philosophical and the mathematical interests and efforts are essentially different. It is not just a difference in subject matter or in degree of rigour or generality, but a difference in kind.

The philosophical investigation cannot be governed by the prevailing aims and virtues of mathematical science, because the efforts of mathematical progress according to the ruling standards, on the one hand, and the efforts of getting conceptual clarity on the other, are efforts that may pull in opposite directions. It is a virtue of the mathematician not to be concerned with what is 'trivial' in mathematics and to dismiss as trivial what does not contribute to the progress of some branch of mathematical science. And there is considerable consensus among mathematicians about what is trivial mathematics, just as there is considerable consensus about what constitutes progress. This trivial mathematics is, however, of great importance to the philosopher of mathematics, whose worries are not about the foundation of (some branch of) the *science* of mathematics, but about the existing practices of doing mathematics. In various views about 'trivial' mathematics, views which are crucial in the so-called 'intended interpretations' of set theory and formal logic, the philosopher can find the roots of several conceptual confusions.

That the philosophical and mathematical efforts are essentially different can also be seen from the fact that the tendency to be misled about conceptual connections by mathematical prose is enforced by the characteristic mathematical endeavours towards generality, uniformity and completeness, and by the introduction of 'idealizations' that 'abstract away' from those features of an existing notion that prevent the mathematician from reaching these goals. Such idealizations are often suggested by the employment of suggestive expressions of word-language (e.g. 'points at infinity', 'infinite lists'). By fixing upon similarities suggested by mathematical prose (e.g. in the general definition of a set or a function), the philosophizing mathematician claims to be able to 'take care of' many individual cases by means of some unifying formal generalization. He constructs a mathematical system on the basis of such similarities which is claimed – through this assimilation of philosophical and mathematical aims – to present the common conceptual ground of the different cases, but which is really a *new* mathematical system.

133

In most handbooks of mathematics and mathematical logic we find examples of notions that have been invented in this spirit. They exist, for instance, in the introduction of general mathematical concepts such as 'set', 'function', 'proof', 'object', or the 'logical constants': 'for all x . . .', 'there is an x . . .', 'and', 'not', 'implies', when these concepts are presented as *fundamental* concepts, as belonging to the foundations of mathematics. They are erroneously presented as fundamental concepts of ordinary mathematics, as though it were an established mathematical fact based on proof, that they are in such an exclusive position. The truth is rather that they were *appointed* fundamental concepts within the branch of modern mathematics called 'mathematical logic and the foundations of mathematics', where the concern has been with the *construction* of a foundation for mathematics. This mathematical enterprise was, and still is, mixed up with the philosophical task of clarifying the conceptual foundations of existing mathematical practice. As a consequence thereof, this branch of mathematics is given a distinguished and influential position in the ongoing discussion about the philosophy of mathematics. Many people have been persuaded that the concepts of mathematical logic and set theory are fundamental to ordinary mathematics. Thus, the prevailing view of mathematics in discussions about the foundations of mathematics is still that mathematics is a family of *theories*, conceived as deductive systems of *propositions* (expressing 'necessary truths' or 'knowledge about a mathematical reality'). This conception (which has its roots in the Aristotelian tradition) rests heavily on similarities in conventionalized prose readings of mathematical notions and results. It is an application of the traditional idea of a *formal* logic, and as such it is based on similarities in linguistic forms, similarities which often cut across conceptual boundaries.

This is not to say that there is something wrong with the *mathematical* constructions and results that have been obtained in mathematical logic. The trouble is rather that the strict mathematical content of these constructions and results has been obscured by the erroneous foundational claims, by the way in which the significance of the notions and results have been expressed in mathematical prose. The readings of 'informal' modes of expression, their 'intuitive meanings', are often given a conceptual significance for which there is no justification in the technical/mathematical employment of the expressions. It is of course true that several of these concepts (e.g. the logical constants and the notions of set theory) are mathematically precise as technical notions determined by the rules and the axioms of the calculi or formal systems to which they belong. It is also true that there are techniques for paraphrasing ordinary mathematical notions and results into the concepts of set theory and formal logic. But the further claim that these concepts are *fundamental* to existing mathematics, that they are clear and precise as parts of the conceptual foundation of *ordinary* mathematics, is no mathematical result. It depends on accepting that the methods and techniques for paraphrase and formalization are conceptually adequate *vis-à-vis* the existing concepts of ordinary mathematics, and that the 'intended interpretations' and the results of formal logic therefore apply immediately to ordinary mathematics. This presupposition manifests itself in the fact that when logicians and philosophers speak about, say, arithmetic, what they usually have in mind is 'first-order arithmetic' or some other formal representation of elementary mathematics, as though these formalizations could replace ordinary mathematics, not just for some technical/ mathematical purpose (e.g. in computer science), but in philosophical discussions about the nature of actual mathematics. It is, on the contrary, this passage from ordinary mathematics to the formal representations that is the philosophically crucial step.

It is true that the rules of these techniques of formalization express conceptually essential properties of the resulting formalizations, but the further claim that they display what is conceptually essential about existing notions and practices of ordinary mathematics is in many cases mistaken (as will be shown in the sequel). It is not true in general that the formalizations make explicit what is implicit in the ordinary mathematical practices. What they make explicit are the views and preconceptions with which philosophers of mathematics approach ordinary mathematical practices.

Someone would perhaps say that the foundational claims do not involve the requirement of complete conformity to ordinary mathematical practice. This may not be desirable or even possible to achieve at all, because ordinary practice is incoherent, unsurveyable and in some respects inexact and confused. To give a foundation for some branch of ordinary mathematical practice, it would be said, is also partly to reconstruct it, reform it, and improve it. In order to obtain uniformity and coherence it may be necessary to change a practice partly by imposing, in some respects, a new conceptual structure, which avoids problematic notions and assumptions that have led to philosophical problems . . . In remarks like these we have perhaps the most obvious expression of the *mathematical* character of the enterprise of what has been called 'the foundations of mathematics'. The conceptual foundation of mathematics is conceived as something to be *constructed*. Conceptual clarification is seen as a mathematical, scientific enterprise whose success is to be judged by existing scientific standards. Its results are measured by their usefulness as tools for the progress of the science or some of its applications.

This is perhaps a natural misconception of philosophy in 'the age of technology', where progress is a kind of universal form of being, and where progress means the reconstruction and reformation of activities and practices by the invention of more refined and effective tools and techniques – in the belief that these reformed practices will increase our freedom by being better under our control and command. This belief may, however, turn out to be a great illusion, based as it is on the often mistaken idea that one has captured what was essential and important regarding the original practices in the reconstructions, and that one has at the same time eliminated what was problematic.

In the philosophy of mathematics, as elsewhere, conceptual clarification conceived as reconstruction never gets at the real foundations. In its efforts towards mathematical progress, it passes too quickly over the points where the conceptual problems can be resolved absolutely.

The formalizations of ordinary mathematical notions and the various systems that have been proposed as foundations for (parts of) mathematics are not built upon nothing; they are not developed in a vacuum but within the language of ordinary mathematics and on the basis of the 'trivial mathematics' which is erroneously considered to be conceptually unproblematic (on the grounds that it is mathematically trivial). Many of the original conceptual puzzles which motivated the foundational studies therefore still arise *within* the formalizations as much as in ordinary mathematics. They are present in various misconceptions of the alleged unproblematic 'trivial mathematics' and in mistaken views about how the language of mathematics works, because the techniques of paraphrase and formalization are based upon such views. The choice of terminology and notation reflects these mistaken views. In particular it manifests misconceptions of the conceptual role of word-language in mathematics.[3]

2 THE TRANSFINITE AS AN IDEALIZATION

What is the justification for thinking that we can talk about 'the totality of all natural numbers' as a *set* in the same sense as we say that there is a set consisting of the three numbers 1, 2, and 3 – and to manifest this belief by using the same familiar bracket-notation in the different cases? It would perhaps be answered that 'the general concept of a set' applies in both cases, the general concept of a set which Cantor explained as follows:[4] 'By a "set" we shall understand any collection into a whole M of definite, distinct objects m (which will be called the elements of M) of our intuition or our thought.'

It is clear that the word 'concept' and the expression 'the concept applies' do not have a precise mathematical meaning in this explanation. This is admitted by calling Cantor's concept 'the *intuitive* concept of a set'. It is not a 'concept' in the same sense as 'natural number' or 'prime number' are concepts. The latter have a precise meaning based on the calculus of natural numbers. However, there is a common opinion that we have 'intuitive concepts of a set' which are clear enough to *justify* rules and notational conventions in the calculus of sets. We are supposed to have 'intuitive concepts of a set' on the basis of which certain axioms of set theory are seen to be justified (or evident).

This quasi-psychological talk about the justification of formal rules on the basis of 'intuitive concepts', 'intuitive meanings', 'intuitive evidence' – which has been so influential a model for 'philosophical analysis' in most branches of analytical philosophy – is the point where the confusion of conceptual content and the readings of informal modes of expression is crucial. It is rooted in the same kind of misconception of language as has been discussed several times before in this book: a language is seen as a system of forms of expression detached from the forms of their proper use. The talk of 'intuitive justifications' amounts to the idea that words and expressions of mathematical prose (such as 'all', 'totality', 'collection', 'part', 'whole', 'object', 'larger than', . . .) have a meaning by themselves as mere expressions and independently of some specific technical employment in mathematics. They would therefore be transferable into a new mathematical system where they could be used to 'justify' the choice of technical notation and of axioms and rules. And it is even taken for granted that they can be used in 'general definitions' that are supposed to take care of cases that may not yet be anticipated.

According to Hao Wang: 'An intuitive concept . . . enables us to overview (or look through or run through or collect together), in an *idealized* sense, all the objects in the multitude which make up the extension of the concept.'[5] This is not meant to be just a parenthetical remark made for the purpose of illuminating and dramatizing the exposition of modern set theory, because later it is said: 'Once we adopt the viewpoint that we can in an idealized sense run through all members of a given set, the justification of SAR [a form of the axiom of replacement] is immediate.'[6]

To adopt this idealized viewpoint consists, however, in nothing but taking a (mistaken) attitude of objectivity towards certain pictures and similarities in forms of expression, as though they actually represented some (hidden) objective mathematical reality. But they do not. In most cases these pictures and similarities are just associated with the readings of expressions of mathematical prose. Like the readings, they are detached from the context where they may have proper applications and actual mathematical contents.

The expressions 'overview', 'look through', 'run through', 'collect together' are normally used to signify certain human acts or activities (in this case in doing mathematics). Everyone knows that these acts are performed in time and space whether they are performed 'in our heads' or by means of paper and pencil or on a computer, so the number of steps or objects that can actually be 'run through' will always be limited. Now, this is something conceptually *essential* about the employment of these expressions as signifying human acts or activities, whether in mathematics or elsewhere. We cannot 'idealize' away from this and still claim that we are literally talking about activities performed by mathematicians. The 'idealized sense' of these expressions must be a *new* sense in which they do *not* signify human acts in the way in which their readings suggest, and we do not know what this sense is on the basis of their normal, 'unidealized', employment. Their idealized sense is not something inherent in them as expressions of mathematical prose prior to the invention of the technical details and rules of modern set theory.

So the idea that the 'idealized sense' of these and other expressions of mathematical prose can be used for the purpose of justifying the axioms and rules of set theory is wholly misleading. Instead of the word 'justify', the proper word would be 'inspire' or 'stimulate' or 'illuminate', because what we have here is more a psychology of invention than a justification. Certain intuitive pictures and linguistic similarities have stimulated the introduction of new notation and particular axioms and rules of calculation.

According to the modern 'iterative' idea of a set, a set is a collection of previously given objects. But then it must be added that the word 'given' has to be understood in an 'idealized sense' according to which these objects may be 'given' by a 'transfinite iteration' of set-forming operations! A set is conceived as being generated at a certain stage from objects 'given' at that stage. For each natural number n there is a stage S_n. And at this point in expositions of set theory we often find the bold remark: 'There is no reason to stop here, we continue to the further stage S_ω which collects together all the finite stages.' No reason! What notion of 'stopping' or 'continuing' a process of iterating an operation is this? If we are talking about acts that mathematicians actually perform, we will of course always be at some finite stage whether we decide to stop the iteration or not. Someone may want to reply: 'We are not concerned with the physical realization of this process of iteration, but with the abstract intellectual operation. Human thinking is capable of transfinite iterations of an operation which are physically unrealizable.'[7] But what does this mean? That the human mind can perform 'transfinite iterations'? The mere expression only suggests certain vague pictures. If we look at what is actually done with this expression in the mathematics of set theory we find that it means roughly the following: we can place ourselves *outside* the activity of actually iterating a mathematical operation, of actually working out particular instances of a rule, and instead we fix upon some general description of this process of iteration and form for ourselves a *picture* of its results as a 'completed whole'. We fix upon the mathematical *form* of this process of iteration and conceive of the expression for the form *as though* it literally summarized a 'transfinite number of individual steps'.

Understood as the capacity to form and use general representations and pictures, it might perhaps be said that 'we can perform transfinite operations'. But this capacity is very much *the same thing* as our ability to form and use general and summarizing words and descriptions in language, in particular in mathematical prose. In the interpretation of the concepts of set theory as idealizations they are, however, systematically misused.

In 'stepping outside' the actual activity of iterating an operation in order to 'overview' its results (which means: in order to form for ourselves the extensional picture), we pass the *conceptual* bounds of the original mathematical operation, we place ourselves in another conceptual system. The word 'stop' in this step of 'not stopping at the finite' therefore means something wholly different from what it means when we talk about stopping or not stopping the iteration of an operation within one conceptual system, say, on the natural numbers. If an operation or a rule is *given* as applicable indefinitely, without end, or as incompletable, it does not make sense to speak about the result of completing the operation, of carrying on the application to the limit of applicability it does not have. To postulate such a limit is not just to 'extend' the original concepts a little, it is to introduce a different conceptual system in which *everything* has another sense. So the senses of the prose expressions 'apply or iterate an operation', 'stop', 'continue', 'complete', etc. are essentially *different*, in a context where 'unbounded wholes' are treated as bounded. The traditional interpretation of set theory is, however, based on the mistaken view that these expressions have a common meaning in the sense that the new senses extend the ordinary senses of these expressions. This is a confusion of the origin and the logical content of the concepts.

The 'paradoxical' character of certain features of the theory of transfinite sets and cardinal numbers, for instance that a proper part may be as large as the whole, that the addition of a new element to a set does not make it any larger, and so on, is not due to prejudices obtained from occupying ourselves too much with finite sets, because it is indeed an *essential* property of a finite class or an extension that the whole be larger than its proper parts, that the addition of a new element make it larger, etc. The air of paradox is due to the mistaken belief that the words 'set', 'whole', 'larger than', 'addition', etc. signify the same concepts when applied to finite classes of individual things and to transfinite sets. The common readings of sentences in which these expressions occur do not express a common mathematical meaning. The concept of transfinite cardinal number does not *extend* the ordinary concept of finite cardinal number which we employ in counting actual things.

It might be said that counting a collection of books, say, is to 'establish a one-to-one correspondence' by actually connecting numbers with books. The interpretation of set theory that I am questioning here is based upon the idea that essentially the same notion of 'one-to-one correspondence' is involved in establishing the cardinality of transfinite sets. As though the establishing of a one-to-one correspondence between, say, the natural numbers and the rational numbers were, or could be, a counting or connecting of actual things, which, however, cannot be 'physically realized' (due to our physical and practical limitations) but which can be realized 'in principle' or in an 'idealized sense'. As though we had to do with a kind of counting or an operation of connecting things together that can only be 'carried out in our thoughts or in our minds'.

It should be obvious how this view of the notions of set theory as idealizations is connected to the misconceptions of mental concepts discussed in the first part of this book, in particular to the dualism between the physical and the mental according to which thinking is a kind of 'invisible process' which goes on in our minds and which accompanies the external, physical behaviour. The transfinite operations of set theory are thought of as 'mental processes' of this sort which, as such, are free from the bounds of the physical and finite and can only have incomplete 'physical realizations'. As though there were a kind of 'mental calculating' which is not limited by the practical and physical conditions that limit actual calculation – or more generally, as though there were, besides the ordinary acts of 'calculating', 'iterating an operation', 'running through the items of a list', etc., another 'mental version' of all these acts which we can perform, as it were, *flying* over the ground where we must normally walk step by step.

This talk about transfinite operations that can only be carried out completely in our thoughts refers to *pictures* which are not pictures *of* some reality. These pictures may be useful for communication within mathematics in the same way that mathematical prose and figurative ways of speaking may be useful, but in their philosophical employment they are misapplied.

The word 'transfinite' is misleading if it is taken to suggest that the actual applications of rules and operations performed by mathematicians when they are calculating in set theory would be 'transfinite' (whatever that would mean). The practices of calculation, construction, and proof in set theory are of course as finite (and as real) as in other parts of mathematics.

The 'one-to-one correspondence' of the natural numbers and the rational numbers refers to the construction of a mathematical law or rule or technique for correlating a natural number with a rational number which is applicable indefinitely. The *actual* applications of this rule of correlation, the number of instances actually worked out, will of course always be finite, and there is therefore no such thing as the 'completed extension' of this rule (that is again just a picture). The 'unactualized instances' of the rule signify the possibility of applying the rule again and again. The rule is not determined by its extension (or determined *as* an extension of correlated numbers) but by what it means to follow it. The rule determines 'all' its instances in the sense that what it means to follow it is determined. The rule is determined *as a practice of calculation*.

3 MATHEMATICAL REALITY

Before the technique of the one-to-one correlation of the natural numbers and the rational numbers was invented, the question of the 'denumerability' or 'countability' of the rational numbers did not have a precise mathematical meaning. The problem was not 'well-defined'. In that situation a correct answer to questions like these: 'Can the rational numbers be counted?', 'How many rational numbers are there?', would be: 'Only what is bounded can be counted, only for finite collections of things do these questions make sense.' Through the invention of the technique of correlation a precise meaning was *given* to these questions. To some extent this new, technical sense of correlation may have been suggested or inspired by formal properties of actual counting, but a genuinely new sense of these questions did come into existence with this technique.

Someone may want to object to this on the grounds that 'the objects and the results of set theory are eternal, as are other mathematical truths. The *mathematical fact* that the rational numbers are denumerable was not something that became a truth by the end of the nineteenth century when Cantor invented the method of proving it, it always was and always will be a mathematical truth.' This philosophical statement tends to make the mistake of confusing timelessness and infinite duration, by making illegitimate use of a picture which is taken from the language of empirical events. There is *some* truth in this objection. It is correct in so far as there is no temporality *within* the conceptual system of set theory. There is no question of 'when this or that became a truth' within that system. But neither is there an 'always true' as an answer to that question. It makes no sense to apply the logical grammar of (historical or empirical) *events* to the strict mathematical content. 'Two plus two is equal to four' describes no event, not even one with 'infinite duration'. There is no temporality in this 'is equal to'. So for the questions and statements of 'when' and 'always' to make sense, they must be understood as referring to the activity of doing mathematics and to the historical development of mathematics. By confusing these temporal perspectives with the non-temporal perspective of a mathematician who is working *within* the conceptual system of set theory, there seem to arise questions about the existence and the reality of sets which are neither mathematical nor empirical, but ontological or metaphysical. I am not denying the 'ontological standpoint' that there are actual infinities and transfinite numbers and affirming the opposite ontological standpoint, I am rather denying that the expressions and sentences of set theory have meaning in the way presupposed in these points of view.

The mistaken view of how mathematical expressions have meaning, which underpins these 'ontological standpoints', was enforced by the endeavour to exhibit mathematics as a science similar to the natural sciences, especially to physics. Mathematics was conceived as a natural science about a mathematical reality (pictured either as external and pre-existing or as a 'mental reality'), a reality which is not available to direct observation (except perhaps in our 'intuition'). On this view, the axioms and principles of mathematics become a kind of *hypothesis* about this 'mathematical reality' (cf. the discussions about the continuum hypothesis in set theory), and there arise epistemological questions of the *reliability* and the *justification* of the basic rules and principles. (It was clearly against the background of this view of mathematics that Hilbert's programme was formulated.) And it is by being related to this 'reality' (by 'referring' to it) that the expressions of mathematical prose and the 'intuitive concepts' of mathematics appear to carry a definite mathematical content by themselves as mere expressions, before they have been given content within a technique of proof or calculation.

This view of mathematics also appears in presentations of the intuitionistic critique of classical mathematics. According to Dummett: 'In intuitionistic mathematics, all infinity is potential infinity: there is no completed infinite.'[8] Is this a proposition or hypothesis about how things are in 'mathematical reality'? The correct criticism of the 'classical view' that there exist 'completed infinities' is not that it happens to be false, that it does not accord with the facts in some region of reality, but that it *does not make sense* in the way in which the 'platonist' thinks it does. Platonists think that they are saying that there are completed infinite totalities with the same

143

notion of 'totality' as when we say that all the people in this room together form a totality of people. But then they rely on similarities in forms of expression like 'the totality of all . . .' within conceptually *different* forms of use of the expressions. As the technical form of use of the words 'totality', 'set', 'extension', etc., of the calculus of transfinite sets and numbers, there do of course exist what has (perhaps unhappily) been called 'infinite totalities'. But then, this is no 'ontological statement'.

The intuitionist does not really reject the classical *interpretation* of Cantor's set theory, he rejects essential parts of the *mathematics* of transfinite sets and numbers, assuming that it *must* have this interpretation. The intuitionist critique is therefore (like the classical view) based upon the prejudice that *if* the calculus of transfinite sets and numbers can be made sense of, can be 'justified', it must somehow be understood as extending the ordinary calculus of finite classes and numbers, it must be justified on the basis of some common notion of 'totality', 'set', 'extension', and 'number'. Brouwer realized (correctly) that it cannot be made sense of in this way, and he concluded (incorrectly) that considerable parts of *the mathematics* of transfinite sets and numbers must be revised. However, the theory of transfinite sets and numbers as new practices of calculation, construction, and proof are justified as mathematics by their mere existence. What is needed is a clarification of the conceptual nature of these mathematical practices, what is actually done in them behind the various intuitive interpretations. The task for this conceptual clarification is not to come up with a new interpretation; nor is it to revise actual mathematics.[9]

The prevailing idea that the numbers are 'abstract objects' to which the numerical expressions of the language of arithmetic stand in an external relation of 'denotation', results from the hypostatization of possibilities, namely the possibilities of applying rules anew – as does the jargon of 'abstract objects' in general, which has been so generally and wholeheartedly accepted in modern analytic philosophy. This talk of abstract objects as a manner of speaking may be harmless and even practical in mathematics, where the technical details are what really count, but in philosophy, where this jargon is meant to have a literal 'ontological meaning', it creates nonsense.

The importance for philosophy of Cantor's ideas of transfinite sets is clear from the fact that the 'idealization' which seemed to justify the concept of an infinite extension is also what seems to justify the ontological jargon of abstract objects. The idealization consists in both cases of stepping from the results of actually applying a rule to a *picture* of the results of 'all its applications', and of misinterpreting this picture as another actuality, an 'abstract reality' (or 'immanent reality', as Cantor called it).[10]

Just as there is supposed to be a general notion of set, of which ordinary, finite classes and infinite sets are two subspecies, so there is supposed to be a general notion of 'object', of which concrete, physical objects and abstract objects such as numbers are subspecies. But this is a conceptual mistake caused by mere linguistic similarities. It is caused by similarities in forms of expression imposed by the techniques of paraphrase of set theory and the predicate calculus. It is caused, for instance, by paraphrase into linguistic forms like 'the totality of all objects x such that . . . x . . .' and 'there exists an object x such that . . . x . . .', where the expression ' . . . x . . .' is dealt with as expressing a function in the mathematical sense. The set/element categories and function/argument categories are (erroneously) assigned the role of universal categories of logical grammar. Being an element of a set or an argument of a function (or a value of a variable) is treated as a paradigm for this general notion of an object.

This is of course a new, technical, notion of an object, which is wholly different from the ordinary notion of an object or a thing which we employ when we say, for instance, that there are three objects or things on this table: a book, a pencil, and a piece of paper. To think that the technical notion of an object, which originates in mathematical logic, is involved in a statement like this, amounts to the idea that the everyday language in which we talk about ordinary things around us is the (implicit) application of the calculus of sets or of predicate logic. (Here we see again that the calculus conception of language criticized in the foregoing parts of this book is not just a matter for the 'philosophy of language'. It is the basis for prevailing 'ontological views' of current philosophy as well.)

Are there no abstract objects then? Of course there are abstract objects! Once we make it clear to ourselves what it *can* mean that abstract objects exist, we must admit that there are a lot of them. They exist as well-established forms of use of expressions in various mathematical calculi and in various technical jargons of modern philosophy and linguistic theory (e.g., 'sets', 'numbers', 'propositions', 'possible worlds', . . .). I am not advocating some 'finitistic or nominalistic standpoint' to the effect that 'there are no abstract objects in reality'. I am saying that the ontological interpretation of this talk of abstract objects is a misunderstanding of a picture, of a figurative way of speaking, of the prose in a technical jargon.

4 POTENTIAL INFINITY

On the intuitionistic conception of mathematics there is a kind of 'realism with regard to *potentiality*'. There is an element of realism in the concept of possibility used in notions such as 'prov*able*', 'decid*able*', 'comput*able*', and '*can* be determined'. Intuitionists would say, for instance, that *any* proposition of the form 'n is a prime number' is decidable, or that its truth-value can be determined, even in cases where the number n is so large that we have no method for actually determining the truth-value (i.e. when it *cannot* be determined!). In such a case the truth-value would 'exist only potentially'. They would say, likewise, that the nth digit of the decimal expansion of π exists potentially, even when n is so large that we have no way of determining the digit. I think that some intuitionists would even say that the proof of the four-colour conjecture (said to be proved in 1976) 'existed potentially', say, fifty years ago, and that the proofs of the mathematical propositions that will be proved next year also exist potentially.

Does this notion of 'unactualized possibilities' make sense as a notion of existence in mathematics? I do not think so. I would rather say that *there is no potentiality within the content of mathematical propositions* in the same way that there is no temporality. The distinction 'actual–potential' only makes sense in connection with time, or development, or 'coming into existence', or – in general – in connection with *change*. And this is precisely what we do not have *within* the realm of the strictly mathematical content.[11] In this conceptual sense, what mathematical propositions express is non-temporal, non-developing, unchanging, indestructible, and so on. In *this* sense one could say that mathematical entities are stable, or that they 'are outside time and space'. With what is perhaps too benevolent an interpretation, it could be said that this is what is correct in the platonist conception of mathematics. But then it must be understood, not as a metaphysical statement about some independent mathematical reality, but as a conceptual statement about the logical order of mathematical notions.

Note that the statement 'a mathematical proposition, once proved to be true, always was and always will be true' can be understood as a metaphorical way of expressing precisely that there are no potentialities, no unactualized possibilities expressed by mathematical propositions. In a certain sense it could be said that once something in mathematics is possible, then it is actual. Something *can* be proved (decided, determined), only on the basis of a method for actually doing it. I think that this is the fundamental and the strict notion of possibility in pure mathematics. This is not to deny that there are other senses of possibility in established 'mathematical prose'. One does, for instance, sometimes speak of a conjecture, an idea for investigation, an open problem as (expressing) mathematical possibilities. But then the problem is also a problem of giving the possibility a mathematically precise meaning by finding or inventing a method for solving it. As already remarked, open problems in mathematics are open, not just with regard to their truth-values, but also with regard to their mathematical sense. That a prose sentence of arithmetic has an obvious paraphrase in some system of formal logic does not necessarily mean that its arithmetical sense is obvious.

What I am saying here may sound unacceptable to someone who thinks of mathematics as a (natural) science of mathematical phenomena, i.e. as concerned with establishing the truth of propositions about objects of some invisible mathematical reality (mental or not). This way of thinking relies, however, on the prose of mathematics, on certain verbal forms of expression, and on misleading similarities with non-mathematical language. I think that the description of mathematics as being concerned with the construction and study of methods and techniques of proof, computation and formalization, gives a much more truthful picture of what is *actually done* (if not said) in pure mathematics.

The basic notion of possibility in mathematics must be 'what is actually within our capacity', it must refer to the activity of doing mathematics (where there is temporality, development, and change). And it is with respect to mathematics as such an *activity* that we can sensibly say that 'there are mathematical truths waiting to be discovered' and thus express our conviction regarding how we expect the development of mathematical research to proceed in the future. Such a statement should be compared with an empirical statement like 'there are new books of mathematics waiting to be written', rather than with a strictly mathematical proposition. The statement 'a mathematical proposition, once proved to be true, always was and always will be true' is a *metaphorical* way of expressing

147

the conceptual truth that there is no potentiality in mathematical content. It is metaphorical because of the improper use of the temporal mode of expression in connection with the content of a mathematical proposition. But in the realistic as well as in the intuitionistic conceptions, it is misunderstood as some kind of *literal* statement about the nature of mathematical facts. The misunderstanding is due to the assimilation of the temporal and non-temporal conceptual realms.

This assimilation is most explicit in Brouwer's metaphysics of mathematics. He introduces a notion of temporal development on the basis of which he appears to speak literally about the 'origin', 'stages of development', 'growth', etc. of mathematical entities, not about their invention in the historical sense, but in the conceptual realm of strict mathematical content. He is speaking as though he were referring to some higher, 'mental reality', accessible only in 'intuitionistic thinking', in which there is development and change. The 'classical' picture of the subject matter of mathematics as something static and timeless, a 'reality' where all questions have already been settled, is in Brouwer's intuitionism replaced by the picture of this reality as being 'in the process of growth'. But like the classical picture it is 'painted' by transferring, from the language of empirical events and phenomena, words such as 'growing', 'proceeding', 'complete', and so on, which have a temporal meaning in their normal, non-mathematical use. When such notions are allowed to give sense to the word 'potential' in 'potential infinity', there arises a picture of the subject matter of mathematics which is as misleading as the classical one.

The main function of the distinction 'actual–potential' in Aristotle's philosophy appears to have been in accounting for change. And there seem to me to be elements of Aristotelian realism left in current philosophical uses of the notion of potentiality. It involves an 'entification' of possibilities that leads to problems similar to the ones that occur in connection with the traditional notions of 'power', 'disposition', 'necessary connection'. I think that the use of the notion of 'potentiality' in mathematics, as in the concept of 'potential infinity', belongs to a way of thinking in times when there was no clear separation between pure and applied mathematics; when one could not distinguish the conceptual systems of pure mathematics from their applications in empirical situations; when mathematics was 'the science of quantity', as it is even in Kant's philosophy. (Remember that Kant – who is said to have been one of Brouwer's sources of inspiration – 'derives' the concept of number from our 'intuition of time'.) On this conception, to make sense of mathematical notions was also to give them a concrete, empirical, content, or at least to relate them to their 'natural' application or to the empirical, historical, or psychological origin of their invention. A mathematical notion such as the natural number series, which cannot be physically realized as a list of concrete things, would then exist as a 'totality' only potentially. A notion from pure mathematics is here explained with reference to the concrete or physical notion of a totality, i.e. by means of the *picture* of a list with 'the power to develop or grow in a certain way beyond all limits'.

This way of explaining notions of pure mathematics by relating them to empirical applications and concepts belongs to the past. For instance, the difference between the finite sequences that exist, in this sense, actually, and those that exist only potentially, in that they cannot be realized as concrete lists completely, plays no role at all in the pure *mathematical* theory of finite sequences. A well-defined sequence of the second kind is as good and as actually existing as one of the first kind, and that is because the pure mathematical notion of a finite sequence is a *different concept* from the notion of a finite sequence as a list of actual things. A finite sequence in pure mathematics is an expression $a_1, a_2, \ldots, a_n$, in which the terms may be listed or given by some law, and which we operate with according to certain rules. The size of the number n is irrelevant to it as a finite sequence in the pure mathematical calculus of finite sequences.

The notion of potential infinity is a kind of hybrid between mathematical and non-mathematical concepts. The notion is usually explained by statements such as: 'The series of natural numbers 1, 2, 3, . . . is potentially infinite in the sense that to each natural number, a larger number can be constructed.' But what about the 'can' in this explanation? What notion of possibility is involved here? Obviously, it is not some notion of physical possibility; it does not refer to the possibility of making physical constructions by some technical means. It is not a process of construction that goes on in time. The explanation is obviously not meant in such a way that it would make sense to ask: 'What was the last natural number constructed today at five o'clock, and how soon after that was the next number constructed?' It is then tempting to say: 'We are not concerned here with actual physical constructions but with "mental constructions" that can only be carried out "in our intuition or thoughts". We have to do with an "idealized sense" of the expression "can be constructed" in which we have "abstracted away" from any technical means of physically realizing the constructions.' As though such a notion of *construction* were already in our possession! We have such a notion of construction in about the same sense as we have a notion of the construction of a tower that reaches up to heaven. This talk of 'mental constructions' is a figurative way of speaking, which results in misconceptions and nonsense when it is taken literally, and that is how we tend to take it in philosophizing about mathematics.

The 'can' in the explanation of the notion of potential infinity is a concept determined by the rules of the arithmetic of natural numbers as an autonomous conceptual system. There is a technical, arithmetical employment of the word 'can' in expressions like 'can be constructed', 'can be proved', 'can be given', 'can be found', etc. In this employment there is no temporal reference, and what is being asserted is the existence of an *arithmetical* method, technique or rule for operating with symbols (usually described by giving examples of a possible application of the rule or of the *form* of an instance). It is only with this technical/arithmetical sense of the expression 'can be constructed' that the explanation of 'potential infinity' receives a correct and precise meaning. And the specific arithmetical rule or technique alluded to in this case is of course the operation of iterating a successor operation.

So it is only *within* the language of arithmetic, within this conceptual system, that the explanation of potential infinity has the precise meaning which is intended. But then it does not work as an explanation or definition, since it presupposes the very concept to be defined as an existing form of use of expressions. The definition will not be clearer or more definite than is this practice of operating with symbols. It is rather a verbal *description* of an essential feature of this form of use. But then the word 'potential' is superfluous since it alludes to a picture derived from a non-mathematical context; and it is misleading since the word was presumably chosen with the aim of providing an explanation and definition.

Cantor thought that he could prove that the notion of potential infinity presupposes the notion of actual infinity. *So much* is true in Cantor's argument,[12] that the notion of an unending sequence of applications of an arithmetical rule (or the arithmetical sense of the idea that a new member *can* always be constructed) presupposes the arithmetical concept of a series generated by iterating an operation. It presupposes this concept *as an existing practice of calculation,* which is *complete* as a system of *forms* of use of expressions. It is not as though we *extend* the language and the conceptual system of arithmetic when new applications of the rules are being actualized – any more than *the game* of chess is extended when new *games* are being played. According to Cantor there must be a 'range of change' ('Ein Gebiet der Veränderlichkeit') of an unending sequence within which it is changing (or 'growing' as Brouwer would have said), but that 'range' is not an infinite totality of objects but an existing human practice of calculation, of construction and proof, in the conceptual system of arithmetic.

The idea of potential infinity is derived from the *activity* of doing mathematics, of successively working out actual instances of a rule, considered as a temporal phenomenon which is in a process of development. Like Cantor's idea of the actual infinite, it is an 'idealization' obtained by 'stepping outside of' this activity and forming a picture of the process as 'a whole'. But unlike Cantor's extensional picture (which fixes upon the *results* rather than the activity), the temporal aspect of the series of applications (or constructions) is not abstracted away from, but is preserved within the picture. The result is what one might call a 'dynamic picture'.

Which one of these pictures is the best? That depends on the use made of it. Either picture may be useful for some communicative purpose *within* mathematics, or as a source of inspiration for the invention of new *mathematical* constructions. But, as already pointed out, the *philosophical* employment of *both* pictures is notoriously misleading.

5 THE FINITE AND THE INFINITE

The picture of an extension, determined by the members it contains as individual things, was a leading idea in Cantor's invention of set theory. This picture has its proper application, however, to finite classes or collections whose members *are given as actual things*. But Cantor 'idealized' the picture by 'abstracting away' from this essential feature of actual extensions, i.e. that their elements have to be individuated and therefore that an extension is *given* as finite.

The natural numbers are of course 'definite, distinct objects of our intuition or our thought' in the sense that *the rules* for making statements of the form 'x is a natural number' and for distinguishing one natural number from another are clear and perspicuous on the

151

basis of the existing practices of following and applying these rules. But this does not mean that each number is (or can be) *individuated*, even in our intuition or our thought. It might be said that 'most' natural numbers will not be given as anything other than the *possibility* of applying these rules over and over again, because that is what the natural numbers are, what constitutes their 'totality'.

As a *possible* instance of the rules of arithmetic, each natural number is definite and distinct, but not because the possible instances are already actualized instances of the rules somewhere, but because the practices of applying the rules are actualized, they are 'definite and distinct' as forms of use of expressions. What it means to follow them and what constitutes an instance of them are never problems in normal mathematical situations. Such questions belong to what mathematicians are inclined to call 'the trivial'.

The traditional interpretation of set theory is based upon the assimilation of two different concepts of a set. There is, on the one hand, the idea of a set as determined by a rule for constructing (or 'generating') the set's members by means of some method or technique. On the other hand, there is the concept of a set as an actual extension, i.e. as being determined by actually listing the elements it contains as actualized and individualized things. Cantor's mythology of the 'immanent reality of mathematical objects' was designed for the purpose of concealing the essential difference between these concepts.

A set in the latter sense must be bounded and finite, since its members must be capable of individuation. If the members of a set can be given (for conceptual reasons) *only* as the unactualized instances of a rule or defining property, then it is not a set in the latter sense. But the difference between these senses of 'set' does not coincide with the difference between infinite and finite sets in mathematics. As already pointed out, there is a mathematical notion of 'finite' in the calculus of finite sets (and sequences) which means that a limit or an end to a process of generation is given or stipulated. However, in general it may not be possible to list or 'run through' the members of a finite set in that sense. The defining property may be so complex that the expression 'run through its members' has no literal meaning. The set may not exist as an extension of individual things, so it is a set in the first sense but not in the second.

As an example of these different senses of 'finite', let N be a large natural number and consider the set

$$\{0, 1, 2, \ldots, N-1, N\}.$$

If N is large enough, then the sense in which this is a finite set of numbers is different from the sense in which the written signs between the two brackets (i.e., '0', ',', '1', etc.) form a finite set of signs. The latter set can of course be realized by actually listing its members, but not the former. The expression between the brackets expresses, as a whole, a *rule* for generating the members of the former set. It is not an abbreviation for a list that could be written out in full. Obviously, we could describe an N so large that this impossibility would not just be an empirical fact about the limits of our technical expedients, but would be such that the expression 'written out in full' (by men or machines) would lose its (literal) meaning. Nevertheless, it would be a 'well-defined' finite set in the technical mathematical sense.

In many pure mathematical contexts, the possibility of realizing a finite set as an actual list or extension is an accidental property on which the mathematical results do not depend. It is therefore a different concept of 'finite set'. A finite set in this sense is simply a form of use of expressions, usually written in the form a_1, a_2, . . ., a_n, which is subject to the rules of the calculus of finite sets. It may be tempting to regard this mathematical notion of a finite set as an 'idealization' of the notion of a finite set that can be realized as an extension of individual things – an idealization obtained by abstracting away from any practical and technical means of realization. This is a source of conceptual confusion of the same kind as the one we have encountered several times before: this 'abstraction' takes us into a completely (not just partly) new conceptual situation, because the technical means of realization are what *define* the possibility of realizing a set as an actual extension. There is no precise 'abstract sense' of realizability as an actual extension, regardless of any technique for actually accomplishing it. Or rather, this 'abstract sense' is again just a picture based on external similarities with situations where we have a technique, and it is this picture that leads one to the mistaken idea that we can represent *any* mathematically finite set as an actual extension 'in thought', or, as one also says, 'in principle'.

The prose expression 'being realizable as an extension of individual things' has a precise meaning only on the basis of such a technique. Since the means of representation are essential to the sense of 'realizability as an actual extension', it is clear that we must arrive at a new concept when *any* means of representation are 'abstracted away from'. This new, mathematical, concept of a finite set is determined solely by the rules of the mathematical calculus of finite sets. That some of these rules were inspired by formal properties of concrete, finite sets tells us something about the origin of the new concept and suggests applications for it, but it does not justify the extensional interpretation.

The difference between the notion of a set as a rule for generating its elements and a set as an actual extension is concealed by the usual employment of the same bracket notation in the different cases. In the expressions

$$\{2, 4, 6, \ldots\}$$

and

$$\{a, b, c, \ldots\}$$

for the set of even numbers and for the letters of the alphabet, respectively, the sign '. . .' has different logical functions. In the latter case it is an abbreviation for the letters of the alphabet from the letter 'd' on, but in the former case it is not an abbreviation for something which has been left out: it is a part of the notation for a rule of unlimited applicability, namely the rule for 'generating' the series of even numbers. On the extensional view of traditional set theory, these different logical functions of the sign '. . .' are assimilated into one.

In the sentences

'a, b, c, . . .' denotes the sequence of consecutive letters of the alphabet

and

'2, 4, 6, . . .' denotes the sequence of consecutive even numbers,

the word 'denotes' has different senses. Regarding the first sentence we may say that the expression 'a, b, c, . . .' *stands for* a list of individual things that have an existence independently of this way of abbreviating the list. The list could be given in a way which would not involve this or any other way of abbreviating it at all, while the sequence of even numbers is given only as a rule for constructing the sequence (possibly expressed in terms of the form of an arbitrary member of the sequence). There is no such thing as the 'sequence of even numbers itself' to which the rule (or the notation for the rule) would stand in an external relation. This way of thinking results from confusing the two senses of 'denotes', i.e.

by making the sense of 'denotes' of the first sentence into a paradigm for all employments of the word (as though the mere similarities in prose would justify this generalization).

Here we can also see how misleading it may be to speak about the sequence

$$x_1, x_2, x_3, \ldots$$

(of individual variables of the predicate calculus, say) as an 'infinite list'. It suggests (erroneously) that we have to do with a common notion of list of which finite and infinite lists are special cases, and therefore, that the sequence x_1, x_2, x_3 would be *a part of a whole* in the same sense as the sequence a, b, c is a part of the whole alphabet, or that the infinite sequence of variables contains x_1, x_2, x_3, as an *initial segment* in the same sense as the sequence of letters of the alphabet contains a, b, c as an initial segment.

The ordinary use of the words 'part', 'whole', 'list', 'sequence', 'contains', 'initial segment', etc., in connection with actual, finite extensions and sequences, is in this jargon transferred into the different conceptual system of infinite sets and sequences, where these words only have a figurative meaning, which may be useful in communication within mathematics. But this communicative function is misunderstood as having conceptual, or even metaphysical significance on the extensional view of traditional set theory. The employment of these words is understood as though they retained their ordinary meaning in the new employment. (As though the meaning of the words were connected to them in isolation from their use.)

This amounts to a conception of infinite sets and sequences as being very large finite sets and sequences. The mistaken idea is that the very long finite lists of actual things *are more similar* to the infinite sequences than are the very short finite lists. The difference between the finite extensions and the infinite sets is not just a difference in magnitude, but a conceptual difference. If I were to 'run through' the sequence of natural numbers starting with 0, then I would get further and further from 0, but would I get closer and closer to infinity? No, to say so would be to misapply the figurative way of speaking, because 'infinity' in this case means that there is no end or limit to come closer to.

'Does the "infinite list"

$$x_1, x_2, x_3, \ldots$$

consist of three actual, physical, expressions, and otherwise of unactualized expressions?' Someone would perhaps be inclined to say that there must surely be expressions in this list that have never been written out. It would seem that these 'unactualized expressions' are standing in a row one after the other from left to right. A certain unactualized variable is standing immediately before its successor, the latter immediately to the right of the former. But are there such things as 'before', 'right', 'left' even in the realm of the unactualized? In what sense do these unactualized expressions exist? As abstract objects? But it is supposed to be something essential about expressions that they are *concrete* objects!

There are of course *pictures* representing concrete objects that may not be pictures of *actual* concrete objects, although the pictures are actual. There are plans, paradigms and rules for the construction of expressions which may not have been realized in all instances. In mathematics there are such rules for construction which, by definition, cannot be completely realized, i.e. in the logical sense that the expression 'realized in all instances' has no meaning. The 'unactualized variables' of the list do not exist as objects at all, but as the possibility of applying the rule x_1, x_2, x_3, . . . for constructing expressions again and again.

By inspecting the use of variables in operating and calculating with formulas in the predicate calculus, we see that the *concrete* realizability of the individual variables is not one of their essential properties (any more than the physical possibility of writing out the natural numbers as actual numerals is an essential property of the numbers). The rule x_1, x_2, x_3, . . . for the construction of variables is therefore a *mathematical* rule. The 'can' in the prose expression 'for any given variable, a new one can always be constructed', does not signify physical possibility. It refers to the mathematical concept of a series generated by the unlimited iteration of an operation as an existing, autonomic, form of the use of expressions. It would be wrong to think that the 'infinite list' of variables can be – due to their concreteness – 'at most potentially infinite'. The sequence of variables is infinite *in the same sense* as the sequence of natural numbers. So even at this level of working within formal logic, the conceptual system of arithmetic is presupposed in an essential way.

The expressions 'a, b, c, . . .' and '2, 4, 6, . . .' signify 'totalities of objects' in different senses. What it means to say that something *is true of all objects* in these totalities is also different in the two cases. It seems reasonable to understand a proposition such as the following:

All letters of the alphabet occur in that text,

as a conjunction of the propositions

'a' occurs in that text
'b' occurs in that text

.   .
.   .
.   .

'z' occurs in that text.

We would, presumably, decide whether the proposition is true or false by checking the occurrence of each letter one by one. At least, this is a very clear and straightforward way of understanding the proposition. But this *sense* of generality is out of the question for a mathematical proposition such as this:

Every even number greater than 2 is the sum of two prime numbers.

It is not just that we are unable for practical, technical, and physical reasons to decide whether this proposition is true by 'checking each instance one by one' – it is not just an empirical (or mathematical) fact that we cannot do this, but the expression 'checking each instance one by one' *does not make sense* in this case. To think that it does make sense, to think that this expression can be employed in the same sense in the finite and the infinite cases, is to rely on the false picture of the infinite totality of even numbers as being an immensely large finite sequence (about which it is an empirical fact that we cannot 'run through' all its members).

The usual interpretation of generality as the universal quantifier of the predicate calculus is based on this false picture. There is supposed to be one notion of generality, one sense of the expression 'for all' and 'there exist', which is common to finite extensions and infinite domains. And the paradigm for this sense of generality is the accidental generality exemplified in the above sentence about 'all letters'. In the extensional view this notion of generality is given an 'idealized sense' applicable to infinite domains by disregarding the fact that we cannot literally 'run through' or 'overview' the 'infinite list' of instances of a general proposition about, say, all even numbers – i.e. the 'cannot' is misunderstood as though it signified just a factual and not a conceptual impossibility. This is one point where the method of paraphrase of formal logic is conceptually inadequate. Consider the sentence

Any individual variable occurs in some formula,

which might be found in some textbook in formal logic, and where the 'domain' for this use of 'any' is given by the 'infinite list',

$$x_1, x_2, x_3, \ldots$$

Verifying this sentence by 'verifying each individual case' is of course out of the question here too, and for similar conceptual reasons. The 'any' in this sentence does not express a kind of accidental generality similar to the generality expressed in the sentence about all letters. It is no accident that any individual variable occurs in some formula. The correctness of the proposition is clear from the (mathematical) rules for constructing formulas: If 'x' is a variable and 'P' is a predicate symbol, then 'P(x)' is a formula containing 'x'. The generality of this proposition is the non-accidental one that is connected with the mathematical rules for the construction of formulas in the predicate calculus by unlimited iteration of a number of operations. The 'any' and 'some' that appear in this proposition are therefore of a different logical category from the ones that occur, for instance, in the proposition

Any letter occurs in some word on this page.

Furthermore, the word 'occurs' has conceptually different senses in the two sentences. In this sentence the word has its normal sense of referring to an empirical fact or an event in space and time. But about the sentences or formulas in the predicate calculus it might be said (metaphorically) that 'most occurrences of individual variables will never be in space and time'. The word 'occurrence' has a technical meaning which is determined within the language of mathematics. It refers to the form of mathematical symbols (or constructions) and not to the form of concretely realizable, typographical configurations.

6 FORM, FUNCTION, AND GENERALITY

There are different senses of generality in mathematics (as elsewhere). There is, on the one hand, the notion of generality in the sense of *the general applicability* of a rule or law to some previously given kind of object or mathematical construction. On the other hand, there is the *generality of the* (logical) *form* of a kind of object or construction, which we express by examples such as 'arbitrary instances' or by means of schematic variables. For instance, in the former sense of generality we say that:

(i) Each numerical equation obtained by substituting any numerals for the variables 'a' and 'b' in the expression

$$a + b = b + a$$

is valid.

But in this statement there is also another sense of generality which is not asserted but *shown*, namely in the algebraic equation as the expression for *a form of numerical equations*, the form that equations such as

(*) $1 + 2 = 2 + 1, 5 + 3 = 3 + 5, 4 + 7 = 7 + 4$, etc.

have in common. In the statement about their validity, this form is an *internal* property of these equations. It is the form in which they are *given* (or 'identified') in the statement.

Two essentially different senses of generality are expressed in the sentences:

(1) All the equations (*) have the form $a + b = b + a$
(2) All the equations (*) are valid.

This is clear by the fact that the first statement is in a certain sense circular (or 'impredicative'). In order to understand what is merely *meant* or intended by the description 'the equations (*)', and thus to understand what the statement says, one must recognize the statement as true. The conception of the 'totality' of the equations (*) must not, however, involve their validity.

It might be said that the 'totality' of the equations (*) is determined as all equations of the form of an arbitrary equation belonging to this totality. The expression 'etc.' in (*) involves or presupposes the form by which these equations are constructed or are recognized as belonging to the totality. To understand the 'etc.' is to be able to produce or recognize new equations from the totality, i.e. equations of the form $a + b = b + a$.

Here it is easy to be misled by the extensional picture of this 'totality of equations'. When we say that 'this equation belongs to the totality *because* it has the form $a + b = b + a$' it may sound as though we were making an inference from one proposition to another, but we are not. The expressions 'belonging to the totality' and 'having this form' are just two different prose expressions for one and the same thing. The 'totality' of these equations *is* their common form, and this form is no 'abstract or mental entity', but the (normative) practice of producing or recognizing equations of this form. There is no non-circular way of defining it. The form 'itself', so to speak, is determined as an existing form of use of symbols of arithmetic.

The different senses of generality expressed in the sentences (1) and (2) are confused by the widespread misconception of a (logical) form as a function, and thus, of the generality of a form as the general applicability of a function to some previously given kind of objects. It is clear that the extensional picture of the content of the expression 'All equations of the form a + b = b + a' as an 'infinite set of individual equations' arises from the confusion of the form as a function or a predicate, whose 'extension' is meant to be what the expression refers to.

It is generally admitted that there is something strange in thinking of this set as an *actual* infinity. Its elements are equations, concretely manifested things, and any such set is finite or at most 'potentially infinite'. According to the extensional view, the commutativity of addition, as a mathematical 'fact' is therefore not properly and fully expressed in the statement (i), which refers to 'linguistic or syntactical entities' such as numerals and equations.[13] The correct and full statement of the commutativity of addition would be as follows,

(3) For all natural numbers x and y, x + y = y + x

But even in this proposition there is a generality which is not asserted but shown in the use of the variables x and y *as variables for natural numbers*, or as we also say, in the use of x and y as 'arbitrary natural numbers'. What is involved in understanding 'x' and 'y' as number variables? Or, what amounts to the same thing, what is it to possess the concept of a natural number? It is to know the (logical) *form* of the numbers. The concept of a natural number is a form not a function. The number variable expresses the generality of this form, which in modern pure mathematics is made explicit in the rules,

(4)

0 is a natural number.

If x is a natural number, then Sx is a natural number,

where it is understood that 'Sx' signifies the result of performing the operation of giving an immediate successor of x, the internal relationship between two consecutive numbers. In the *Tractatus* Wittgenstein expressed this rule (or this conception of a number) in the notation:[14]

$$[0, x, x + 1].$$

It could be expressed in other ways, for instance, as follows:

$$0, S0, SS0, \ldots,$$

or in the following way:

$$0, 0', 0'', \text{ etc.}$$

In mathematical prose, we would call it 'the series of natural numbers generated by the immediate successor operation'. The generality expressed by the variable 'x' in the first two formulations and by the signs '. . .' and 'etc.' in the last two formulations is *the generality of the form of a series generated by an operation*. It does not express the general applicability of a function or a law to some independently given objects, because it is precisely how the natural numbers *are conceived as being given* in arithmetic which is expressed.[15]

The *same form* (of the sequence of natural numbers) is expressed in any one of these ways, so it should be clear that this form is no *physical* form of expression. But neither is it literally a 'form of an infinite sequence of individual, abstract objects', because this is only a metaphor. We may want to speak about the form as a form of numbers (rather than expressions) in a context where the particular notation chosen to express it is irrelevant (which is perhaps the normal situation in ordinary mathematics). But the form exists only as the essential features of the use of expressions. It is no 'abstract entity' in the sense of the ontological jargon. *The form of the sequence of natural numbers consists in the essential features of the use of the symbols for the numbers in the language of modern pure arithmetic.*

To possess or to master the concept of a natural number (or to know what it is to use 'x' as a variable for natural numbers) is not to be able to *state* what is essential, or to *refer to* rule (4) (or some of its other formulations). This is neither a necessary nor a sufficient condition. On the contrary, it is to master the practices of arithmetical calculation, to be able to operate with the signs and symbols in the way which is made explicit, for instance, in rule (4) (or any of its alternative formulations).

But more important, to master the concept of a natural number in this sense is a necessary prerequisite for understanding and following rule (4) (or any of its alternative formulations). These rules (as well as other rules expressed in formalizations of arithmetic) are all expressed *within* the language of arithmetic. They express essential features of a form of use of symbols by actually employing them in that use. So, as definitions or (theoretical) explanations of the concept of a natural number, they are circular – which is to say that the words 'definition' and 'explanation' are misplaced. They *describe* conceptually essential features of a form of use of expressions, *within* that form of use, and this is what must be done, because this form of use as a practice of calculation *is* the 'logical foundation'.

Compare this with what Russell called 'the vicious-circle principle': 'No totality can contain members definable only in terms of this totality.'[16] The comparison gives a clue, it seems to me, to the resolution of conceptual problems connected with impredicative definitions. The problems arise through the misunderstanding of a form as a function (or a set), which makes it seem legitimate to ask for the definition of a form in about the same sense as it is legitimate to ask for the definition of a function. But the (*logical*) *forms are what cannot be defined*. On the contrary, it is against the background of an existing form of use of mathematical expressions that there is such a thing as defining in mathematics at all.[17]

The so-called semantic paradoxes (such as Richard's paradox) arise on the syntactic view of language, where the forms of expression are treated as propositional functions defined for syntactic configurations of signs as arguments. Form is conceived of as an external property of a notation. A sentence, for instance, is conceived as a finite sequence of words satisfying certain external criteria of composition. This is obviously the notion of a sentence employed when one is talking about 'the set of all sentences that can be formed with a finite number of words from a certain lexicon and that define a real number' in formulations of the Richard paradox. There is nothing wrong with the argument of this paradox within the formal, syntactic framework within which it is stated. But to experience the 'paradox' as paradoxical, one must be captured by the picture of the language of mathematics as a system of notation.

One must believe that the content of a mathematical sentence is determined by the sentence as a mere expression, and not by a form of its use.[18]

The general concepts 'natural number', 'ordinal number', 'set', 'function', etc. are not concepts in the sense of being functions (or predicates in the sense of the predicate calculus). They are different *forms* of mathematical constructions, or different forms of use of mathematical symbols. The 'logical paradoxes' actually arose through the confusion of forms and functions. Forms like these were treated as though they were functions. The generality of the expression for a form of mathematical construction was misunderstood to be the general applicability of a function, which is the kind of generality expressed by the universal quantifier of the predicate calculus.

If the expression 'f is a function' is considered as a function $F(f)$ of f, then it may seem as though the function F could be applied to itself to yield the meaningful and true proposition '$F(F)$'. If this makes sense, then why should it not also make sense to form the propositional function 'not $f(f)$', which gives Russell's paradox.

A sentence of the form 'f is a function' does not express a 'proposition about a mathematical object' in the sense in which we may say that e.g. a sentence of the form 'x is a prime number' does so. It is a grammatical proposition which asserts the position of f within the mathematical symbolism. It asserts that the position of 'f' is in expressions of the form

$$y = f(x),$$

where y is the value obtained by evaluating the function f according to some rule or law (in the functional notation developed within the calculus). The symbol '$f(x)$' also expresses a *form*, namely the form of the result of applying a function to an argument. It signifies an *operation*, not a function of the two variables 'f' and 'x'.

In what is termed the second-order predicate calculus, where one not only has formulas such as '$(\forall x)f(x)$', but also formulas like '$(\forall X)X(x)$', where X is a 'one-place predicate variable', there is a confusion of application as an operation and a function. In the latter formula, '$f(x)$' is treated as though it were a function of 'f'.

Whether a symbol signifies an operation or a function depends on how it is used, on its position in calculating.[19] In the *Tractatus* notation for the form of the sequence of natural numbers, '$x + 1$' signifies the successor operation. As such it is conceptually different from and prior to the *function* 'x + 1', which we may *define* on the natural numbers. Suppose that the series of natural numbers are given in the form

(5) 0, S0, SS0, . . .

where Sx is the successor operation. Then we may define a function s(x) by the rule that for each natural number x,

$$s(x) = Sx.$$

Like all definitions of functions on the natural numbers, this definition 'presupposes' the form of the values of the variable x, i.e. the form of the series of natural numbers. In particular it presupposes the successor operation, which must not be confused with the function s(x). The latter is a conceptually secondary construction.

From the extensional point of view, the logical difference between the operation Sx and the function s(x) vanishes, and for many practical, mathematical purposes, the difference may not be important (i.e. a failure to observe and to be explicit about this difference need not result in incorrect calculations). But for the original problems in the discussion about the foundations of mathematics, this difference is of fundamental importance. For instance, the misunderstanding of the successor operation as a function, was obviously the source of the mistaken idea that the infinity of the series of natural numbers can be stated as a mathematical *proposition*, as an 'axiom of infinity', as though it were a kind of fact about the 'abstract or immanent reality' that mathematical propositions 'are about'.

The infinity of the series of natural numbers is *part of its logical form*. Being infinite is not one of its external properties, it is *given* as infinite. It is part of what is expressed (not stated!) in rule (5). Understanding the expression 'Sx' as signifying the successor operation, which can be iterated without limit as indicated by the sign '. . .', is to understand what we might also express in prose as follows: 'Every natural number has a successor.'

When this prose sentence is paraphrased in the reading of the predicate calculus:

For each natural number x, there is another natural number y such that y is the successor of x,

it may appear as though we have a mathematical proposition which states that the series of natural numbers is infinite. As though it could be a problem whether the natural number sequence is *in fact* infinite! The *concept* natural number is here misconceived as though it were a propositional function of which we do not know the number of the arguments to which it truly applies.

This is a misconception since the proposition has the intended meaning only if the series of natural numbers is already given as infinite. It is expressed within a *representation* of arithmetic, where the internal relation between a number and its successor has been represented as a (propositional) function which is defined for natural numbers, and which presupposes the form of the series of natural numbers and thus that it is infinite.

This is another example which shows that the techniques of paraphrase of the predicate calculus and set theory are conceptually inadequate. More generally: modern formal logic was based upon the idea of representing logical form as functions. Here one could speak about 'the conception of logic as a calculus of functions' as the result of the confusion of the tasks of mathematical theory construction and conceptual (logical) clarification.

The misconception about infinity discussed here led Russell to make the metaphysical and nonsensical statement: 'It cannot be said to be *certain* that there are in fact any infinite collections in the world. The assumption that there are is what we call "the axiom of infinity".'[20] Russell also expressed the 'axiom of infinity' as follows: 'If n be any inductive cardinal number, there is at least one class of individuals having n terms.'[21] If 'class of individuals' means class of actual things, this is false, or rather nonsense.[22] If 'class of individuals' means 'set of objects or elements' as this expression is used in the pure mathematical theory of finite sets, then the statement is true. It expresses a feature of the way in which we introduce and operate with the mathematical constructions we call finite sets, and there is no further justification for the statement than the fact that this mathematical practice exists and is considered important and interesting, that it has many useful applications, and so on.

If we must call it a 'fact' that 'there are infinitely many natural numbers', then it is a fact about the established practices of doing arithmetic. But it is not the fact that people have *adopted* it as a convention or *stated* it as an axiom or introduced it as a hypothesis about some 'reality'. It is rather a (normative) fact about the way arithmetical symbols are used. It is a fact on the basis of which there is such a thing as the rule or the concept expressed in (5) at all. To inform someone about facts such as these would not be to define or explain something, but *to show him how certain things are done*. It would be to teach him how certain practices of doing arithmetic are performed, by means of *examples* of various forms of use of expressions. In such a lesson the examples would be used to express rules, *ways* of doing things. The examples would be used to express the *generality of the forms* of use of arithmetical symbols.

It is part of the logical grammar of the symbolism of functions that a function presupposes its arguments. This is, it seems to me, what was correct about Russell's doctrine of logical types. A function is determined only when the logical form of its arguments is determined. A function is a function of some previously *given* kind (or type) of objects. In this sense it might be said that the arguments of a function are conceptually prior to the function. It is different as regards the logical forms of objects (constructions or expressions). Objects are not conceptually prior to their form; they appear as, or are given as, objects of that form. And it is only as the form *of the objects* that the form exists.

We might have used the prose expression 'logical type' instead of 'logical form'. But we would not thereby have avoided the problems discussed in this section, because, in the same way as the term 'logical form' has a technical use in modern mathematical logic for *representations* of logical forms as functions, so the term 'logical type' is used in *theories of types* (such as Russell's) for mathematical representations of logical types. The confusion of these technical/mathematical senses of the expressions 'logical form' and 'logical type' with what they are intended to represent is again a manifestation of the mistaken idea of the logical foundation of mathematics as something to be (mathematically) constructed. In this case the confusion is particularly serious because, as already pointed out, logical form (or logical type) is what cannot be defined or represented. Logical forms cannot be considered as being determined ultimately within a theory or by a system of formal rules. Such a representation is always something conceptually secondary. It does not belong to the 'logical foundations'.

We may say that a certain natural number is the form of use of the expressions for that natural number, but a certain logical type is not a form of use of expressions *for* that type, but for the expressions *of* that type. There is no such thing as the formal property 'X is a logical type' as there are formal properties such as 'f is a function' or 'n is a natural number'. It is *in* the mathematical theories of types that expressions *for* types and rules for calculating with these expressions are introduced. In such a calculus it may make sense to talk about the logical type of types (i.e. the logical forms of the use of type-expressions in the calculus), and if the difference between the logical and the technical/mathematical employments of the word 'type' is not observed, 'paradoxes' may result.[23]

7 MATHEMATICAL INDUCTION

Hilbert sometimes expresses himself as though we have to 'assume that there are infinite totalities' in order to prove an arithmetical proposition like the following:

(6) $\forall x(1 + 2 + 3 + \ldots + x = \frac{1}{2}x(x + 1))$

The idea arises from a misleading picture of how this proposition has meaning: 'This formula contains infinitely many propositions,' (as Hilbert puts it in a similar case).[24]

Regarding the proposition

(7) $(\forall x < 5)(1 + 2 + 3 + \ldots + x = \frac{1}{2}x(x + 1))$

it might be said that it 'contains a finite number of propositions', namely the four equations

$$1 = \frac{1}{2}*1*(1 + 1)$$
$$1 + 2 = \frac{1}{2}*2*(2 + 1)$$
$$1 + 2 + 3 = \frac{1}{2}*3*(3 + 1)$$
$$1 + 2 + 3 + 4 = \frac{1}{2}*4*(4 + 1)$$

But the general proposition (6) is not 'an extension of (7) into the infinite'. To think that it is, is to conceive of an infinite sequence as a very large finite sequence. In proposition (6) we have to do with a categorially *different sense* of the expression 'for all x, . . . x . . .', which is determined within a different form of use of this prose expression, namely within the context of *proofs by induction*, which is connected to the concept of the totality of numbers as generated by the iteration of an operation and not as an extension of individual objects.

Hilbert relies on the extensional view of the infinite. His way of posing the problem presupposes that proposition (6) about all numbers has a precise, mathematical meaning which is based on the analogy with the finite case. He is misled by the idea that the prose expression 'for all x, . . . x . . .' has a constant meaning (being the reading of a 'logical constant') in these different forms of use, in the context of finite, actual extensions as well as in the context of the infinite. He is led to think that, since we cannot actually 'run through' and 'overview' infinite totalities and verify that 'they exist' by direct observation, we seem to be forced to adopt their existence as a *hypothesis*, as a kind of mythology on which the sense of 'ideal' mathematical propositions is based.

To give an epistemological justification of this mythology on the basis of the finite case was the aim of Hilbert's meta-mathematical programme. So it is clear that Hilbert's programme was based on a fundamental misconception of the infinite from the start. More generally, Hilbert's dichotomy beween 'real' and 'ideal' propositions was built upon the mistaken views about 'idealization' in mathematics which I have discussed several times: misled by mere linguistic analogies, the 'ideal notions' of higher mathematics are seen as extending the 'real' notions from which they are obtained by 'abstraction', or they are seen as capturing the essential properties of the notions from which they are 'idealized'. As I have shown in several examples, the truth is rather that essential properties of the original notions are being disregarded in these idealizations, and the idealizations are therefore *wholly new concepts* which do not require support from any mythology of ideal objects or methods.

According to Hilbert's interpretation of the generality of proposition (6), it expresses a kind of 'accidental generality', i.e. a generality of the same kind as in an empirical generalization about some phenomena in nature. But if the precise sense of the concept of natural number in arithmetic is that of a series generated by the iteration of an operation, then this accidental generality, which is derived from finite extensions, cannot be the precise sense of generality about numbers. This is not to say that the extensional picture is wholly irrelevant to the sense of the proposition as a mathematical *problem*, e.g. in arriving at the formulation of the problem and in the search for a proof of the proposition. But since the extensional picture is not literally applicable, the general proposition must be given a precise arithmetical sense, and that is what is done in its being proved by mathematical induction.

Crucial in this proof is the inductive step: We assume that the equation holds for an arbitrary number n and then, for $n + 1$, we calculate as follows:

$$1 + 2 + \ldots + n + (n + 1)$$
$$= \tfrac{1}{2}n(n + 1) + (n + 1)$$
$$= (n + 1)\tfrac{1}{2}n + (n + 1)$$
$$= (n + 1)(\tfrac{1}{2}n + 1)$$
$$= \tfrac{1}{2}(n + 1)((n + 1) + 1)$$

Someone may say that there is an assumption of the existence of an infinite totality in this proof, namely in the conclusion that the step from n to n + 1 holds *for all* numbers n. This 'ontological' interpretation is again made with reference to the view of the generality of the inductive step as 'containing an infinite number of individual calculations' (as though we have managed to 'run through' all of them in a few lines). The generality of the inductive step is misunderstood to be the general applicability of a law or procedure to the numbers as individual things, when in actuality *it is the generality of the form* of an arithmetical calculation.

If we examine what is going on in the proof, we see that the inductive step is a calculation or *transformation* of the mathematical expression

$$1 + 2 + \ldots + n + (n + 1)$$

to the mathematical expression

$$\tfrac{1}{2}(n + 1)((n + 1) + 1),$$

and in this transformation, apart from ordinary rules for calculation and substitution, the equation

$$1 + 2 + \ldots + n = \tfrac{1}{2}n(n + 1)$$

has been used. The generality of the inductive step is expressed in the use of the letter 'n' as a variable, as signifying (as we say) an arbitrary number.

The misleading idea is to think that the variable somehow *represented* ('stood for' or 'ranged over') 'all individual numbers', and that the inductive step therefore represents an infinite number of numerical calculations with individual numbers, calculations which have the common form expressed in the step. But the idea of an infinite number of numerical calculations does not make sense, even though the calculations are uniform. There is literally no such thing (as everyone knows). The inductive step and the rules used in it cannot, in general, be reduced to or justified in terms of numerical calculations on individual numbers. The opposite idea is part of the misconception of the generality expressed by the variable as the general applicability of a law to a totality of individual objects. The function of the variable is not to represent, but to be substituted for and calculated with according to the rules and practices for calculating with numerical expressions (including ones containing variables). These rules and practices are the ultimate basis for the sense and the correctness of the inductive step.

We must not think as though the arithmetical calculus which uses variables is merely a kind of convenient abbreviation for an arithmetical calculus without variables but with 'infinitely long lists of numerical calculations'.

I am not saying that the variable 'n' is just a letter or typographical configuration. It is a mathematical *symbol*; an expression in a certain use. It would be possible (but perhaps inconvenient) to use the numeral '2', say, as a variable or as an arbitrary number in a calculation, namely if no other property of the number 2 was being used in the calculation than the ones which 2 shares with all other numbers. This shows that it is the particular use of the letter 'n' in the calculus which constitutes its being a variable.

Someone might want to say that 'the variable n ranges over a domain of objects, namely over the totality of all natural numbers'. This expression need not be understood with reference to the extensional picture, but as it is used in mathematical logic (in model theory in particular) it is definitely understood in that way. The expression may be harmless and even useful in ordinary mathematical communication, but when it is given a conceptual or philosophical significance, it misleads.

The variable 'n' and the expressions in the proof do of course have a physical or typographical form, but this form is what is inessential and accidental about the expressions in the sense that they could be replaced by other expressions of other typographical shapes. We could have used another letter as a variable, we could have written the transformation in other ways, but in such a way that we would still say that it is *the same* proof, the same calculation. So the essential thing about this transformation is not its physical form, but its logical form as a mathematical use of expressions. This 'logical form' is no 'abstract structure'; it consists of the features which are essential to the transformation when it is placed in its proper context, i.e. within the practice of proving arithmetical propositions by induction. We do not have to introduce a mythology of numbers as 'abstract objects' and their logical form as an 'abstract structure' in order to account for the fact that the *same* proof could be expressed in another notation.

The transformation, as a mathematical operation, as a calculation, also involves a physical transformation of typographical expressions. We can of course 'step outside' the mathematical calculation and pay attention to this aspect of it. In formalizations of arithmetic this aspect is even developed systematically. But *this* is an (imposed) interpretation of the mathematical transformation.

The logical form is determined only in relation to rules and practices of calculation and of operating with the expressions in the language of arithmetic. In the current concept of 'syntactical form' with roots in the meta-mathematical tradition, the idea is the opposite: the syntactical form is the external form, determined prior to the rules and the practices of employing the expressions. When the word 'form' in 'transformation' is conceived as a syntactical form and the calculation as a 'mechanical manipulation of syntactical expressions', it appears as though the proof does not prove what it is meant to prove unless the syntactical transformation is supplied with a 'semantic interpretation', which will 'assign an infinite domain of objects as values of the variable'. So here we see how the formalist conception of the language of mathematics as a system of notation, detached from the forms of the normal use of the notation in mathematics, is connected with the platonist conception of the realm of abstract objects which mathematics is supposed to 'be about'.

With the interpretation of the proposition

$$\forall x(1 + 2 + \ldots + x = \tfrac{1}{2}x(x + 1))$$

according to which it appears as though the proposition and its proof require the 'assumption of an infinite totality', it also appears as though the inductive proof involves a third part (besides the basis of the induction and the inductive step) which might be expressed as follows: 'We have verified the equation for $x = 1$. By the inductive step, if the equation is true for $x = 1$, then it is true for $x = 2$, so by *modus ponens* we conclude that it true for $x = 2$. By applying the induction step and *modus ponens* once more to this result, we conclude that the equation is true for $x = 3$, etc., *ad infinitum*. Hence, the equation is true for all natural numbers x and the proposition is proved.'

This 'Hence, the equation is true for all natural numbers' is, however, not a conclusion. It appears so when the proposition is

171

considered to have a precise mathematical sense by itself outside of the context of its proof, a sense in which the generality of the proposition would be accidental generality, as though the proposition stated something about each one of a totality of individual objects. But that is not the precise conception of the totality of all natural numbers in pure arithmetic. The extensional picture is not literally applicable. The generality of this proposition is not mathematically 'well-defined' on the basis of this picture, but by the sense given to it in the inductive proof. The word 'hence' is therefore misleading.

This 'third part' of the proof is just a way of summarizing in prose what is expressed in the basis and the inductive step. But what it means mathematically is determined by the details of the proof, not the other way round. Instead of saying: 'Hence, the equation is true for all natural numbers', we should say: 'This is what it means that the equation is true *for all natural numbers.*' The inductive proof displays the criterion of general validity of the equation and shows at the same time that it is satisfied. The generality of the proposition is the generality of an induction (recursion or iteration), and not of an immensely long list of valid numerical equations.

It might perhaps be said that there is 'something more' in this 'hence', namely a reference to an established *linguistic* practice of using mathematical prose. On the basis of these linguistic conventions, it appears 'intuitively correct' and very natural to employ the expression 'the equation is true for all numbers'. But the reason for the 'naturalness' of this expression is not that we have a precise and general notion of generality which is immediately applicable to infinite as well as finite domains. It is based rather on formal analogies with other situations where we employ the expression ' . . . is true of all . . .'. The word 'hence' signifies no conclusion, but an agreement with linguistic conventions for using this prose expression. But the mere reading of this expression may be a natural reading of logically *different* senses of generality.

The misunderstanding of this 'hence' as a conclusion, is also connected with the idea of 'justifying mathematical induction' (Hilbert, Heyting, Kleene, Dummett, and others). By rewriting a proof by induction

$$\cdot$$

$$\frac{A(0) \qquad \forall x(A(x) \to A(x + 1))}{\forall x A(x)}$$

(where we assume that induction is not used in the proofs of the premisses) as a series of proofs,

$$\frac{A(0) \qquad A(0) \to A(1)}{A(1)} \quad , \qquad \frac{\dfrac{A(0) \qquad A(0) \to A(1)}{A(1)} \qquad A(1) \to A(2)}{A(2)} \quad , \ldots$$

it appears as though a proof by induction condenses an infinite number of proofs into one. Since the proofs in this infinite sequence do not contain induction and since the sequence can be continued indefinitely, it appears as though we have justified the inductive proof in a non-circular way, i.e. without using induction. We already have a proof of $A(0)$ and since the infinite sequence contains a proof of $A(x)$ for any $x > 0$, we seem to be justified in concluding: 'Hence, $A(x)$ is true for all natural numbers x.'

The non-circularity of this 'argument' is, however, illusory. It is a 'justification' of mathematical induction by means of mathematical induction, so the word 'justification' is misplaced. To see this, let $I(0)$ be the proof

$$A(0)$$

and let

$$I(n + 1) = \frac{I(n) \qquad A(n) \to A(n + 1)}{A(n + 1)}$$

then this formula is a 'recursion formula' for the sequence of proofs. The 'justification' could then be written

I(0) is a correct proof of A(0), and if I(n) is a correct proof of A(n), then I(n + 1) is a correct proof of A(n + 1). Hence: For all n, I(n) is a correct proof of A(n).

So the argument *uses* induction. A 'justification' which is circular in this way is no justification at all (even though the argument may have an illustrative function). To rewrite the inductive proof as an unending series of proofs is just another, 'more intuitive', way of expressing *the same proof*. But this intuitiveness is conceptually misleading when the argument is conceived as a justification, because this idea is based on the misconception of the infinite sequence of proofs as an actual list of individual proofs in which there is no induction (except perhaps in the proofs of the premises).

The important thing here is the following: *the mere conception of this infinite sequence of proofs involves an induction* (or recursion). In order to understand this expression as an expression for an infinite sequence of proofs, you must understand the induction or recursion in it. The logical form of this expression is not that of an actual list of individual things, but of a series generated by the unlimited iteration of an operation. With reference to the examples discussed in section 5, we may say that the employment of the notation ', , , . . .' in the expression for this sequence of proofs is logically of the same kind as in the sequence 2, 4, 6, . . . , but *not* of the same kind as in the sequence a, b, c, ...

If we assume that there is no induction in the proofs of the premises, we may say: 'There is no induction in proof I(0), there is no induction in proof I(1), there is no induction in proof I(2), etc.' So it may appear as though this sequence of proofs involves no induction at all. But this is wrong because *in this 'etc.' there is an induction*!

We may also say: 'For an arbitrary number n, there is no induction in the proof I(n) of A(n).' But the generality expressed by the variable n is the generality of an induction! Without this induction, the precise mathematical *meaning* of this general statement is lost.

This kind of criticism of the attempts to 'justify' mathematical induction is not new. The circularity in Hilbert's attempts to justify mathematical induction by giving a 'finitary' consistency proof was pointed out by Brouwer and Poincaré.[25] About Hilbert's way of working in his meta-mathematics, Brouwer correctly points out:[26]

in the reasonings . . . on the consistency of axioms, he applies again and again intuitive terms such as *one, two, three, some* (by which he means *a certain finite number*), and further he intuitively applies all the laws of logic and even complete induction.

The fundamental mistake among the proof theorists in the Hilbert tradition was to think that the generality expressed by 'schematic variables' within meta-mathematical reasonings can be interpreted according to the extensional picture on the grounds that meta-mathematical inductions always 'stop in the finite' (as Herbrand[27] expresses it).[28] The extensional picture would be literally applicable since meta-mathematics was said to be confined to the concretely given and finite. Like Brouwer, Poincaré realized that it is not true that meta-mathematics is confined to the concretely given and finite. It involves the concept of an infinite series; and the generality expressed by variables in the meta-mathematical reasonings is the generality of 'complete' mathematical induction. Poincaré saw that even if Hilbert were to have succeeded in justifying the induction axiom expressed within the formal systems, he would not have justified the induction used in the meta-mathematical reasoning.

In an attempt to meet Poincaré's objection, Hilbert accused Poincaré of having missed the distinction between these two senses of induction:[29] on the one hand, what Hilbert called 'contentual induction', and which was said to be the only sense of induction employed in 'finitary reasoning about concrete objects' (e.g. about the construction and decomposition of numerals). But there is also, according to Hilbert, 'formal induction', which was said to be 'induction proper', and which is stated as an explicit axiom in the formal systems. Obviously Hilbert held the (mistaken) view that 'contentual induction' is not really mathematical induction, since it 'stops in the finite'. He was thinking as though the concept of the 'for all' of a meta-mathematical induction coincides with the concept of 'for all' of a finite extension of concrete things, as long as we confine ourselves to finite segments of an infinite sequence. But this is to think about the infinite as an extension of, or a continuation of, the finite, and of the generality of an induction as determined by the extensional picture.

It is clear that Poincaré, already in his criticism of Hilbert's programme in 1905, recognized this difference between the induction that is applied in meta-mathematical arguments about 'concrete objects' and the induction that is stated explicitly as an axiom in the formal system. He also recognized that the generality of an infinite sequence is involved in Hilbert's meta-mathematical reasoning, and therefore that 'contentual induction' is mathematical induction 'proper'. This was emphasized by Hermann Weyl in a defence of Poincaré's criticism, where Weyl says:

> When Poincaré claimed that *mathematical induction* is for mathematical thought an ultimate basis that cannot be reduced to anything more primal, he had in mind precisely the process, of composition and decomposition of numerals, that Hilbert himself employs in his contentual considerations and that are completely transparent to our perceptual intuition. For after all Hilbert, too, is not merely concerned with, say, $0'$ or $0'''$, but with any $0''\cdots'$, with an *arbitrary concretely given* numeral. One may here stress the 'concretely given'; it is just as essential that the contentual arguments in proof theory be carried out *in hypothetical generality*, on *any* proof, on *any* numeral.[30]

It is essential that the arguments in meta-mathematics be carried out on any proof, on any numeral *of a series of proofs (or numerals) generated by iterating operations an arbitrary number of times*. So this 'arbitrariness' is the generality of an induction (or recursion). Furthermore, inspection of the arguments of proof theory (for instance, in the arithmetization of meta-mathematics) shows that the concept of the 'finite' in meta-mathematics is *not* that of the finite that can be 'concretely given', i.e. is not what can be realized as a list of concrete things. It is rather the notion of the finite in the sense of the finite sequences of the pure mathematical theory. But 'most' sequences of this kind cannot be 'concretely given' – even 'in principle'. So we can sharpen Weyl's statement and say that it is *not* essential that the constructions dealt with in meta-mathematics can be concretely given, any more than it is essential in ordinary number theory that all the natural numbers can be 'concretely given' as actual numerals in some canonical notation.

In a defence of Hilbert's view that meta-mathematical induction is not 'mathematical induction proper', Herbrand explains:

> We never consider the totality of all the objects x of an infinite collection; and when we say that an argument or a theorem is true for all these x, we mean that, for each x taken by itself, it is possible to repeat the general argument in question, which

should be considered to be merely the prototype of these particular arguments.[31]

The generality expressed in a prototype (or a paradigm case) is the basic sense of generality in ordinary arithmetic as well, and the 'for all' of an induction in ordinary arithmetic *is* a generality of this kind. The step 'from n to n + 1' in a proof by induction expresses the generality of a paradigm case – before it is reinterpreted as the general applicability of a propositional function by being paraphrased into the notation of the predicate calculus.

Herbrand suggests that the extensional view is essential to the sense of general statements proved by mathematical induction in ordinary arithmetic. It is clear that Herbrand, like Hilbert and other proof theorists, conceives ordinary mathematics through the formalizations and the techniques of paraphrase of formal logic, where the mathematical sense of a proposition is meant to be determined by its mere formalization, regardless of the ways of proving it. But many conceptual differences, which depend on methods of proof and calculation, are lost in these formalizations. Herbrand speaks from the point of view that the fundamental sense of generality in mathematics is the generality of the universal quantifier of the predicate calculus with the usual interpretation according to the extensional picture. But with that notion of generality, which is based on similarities in mathematical prose, we cannot differentiate between the conceptually different senses of generality in the finite and the infinite. And this is unfortunate, since confusions about the dividing-line between the finite and the infinite were largely responsible for the original problems concerning the foundations of mathematics.

8 NUMBERS AND NUMERALS

One might say that Hilbert, in the 'finitary viewpoint', is trying to reduce the internal or logical properties of the series of natural numbers to external properties of the expressions for the numbers. He does not seem to realize that in this reduction he is presupposing and using the logical principles of the series of numbers. He is standing within the conceptual system of arithmetic when he is describing the process of iteration (*Fortschreitungsprozess*) through which each numeral has a unique composition (*Aufbau*), to which there is also a corresponding unique step-wise decomposition (*schrittweisen Abbau*).[32] The logical grammar of Hilbert's use of these words, to judge from his meta-mathematical arguments, is the logical grammar of the arithmetic of natural numbers. Already at this stage, the notion of the generality of mathematical recursion is involved.

Hilbert seems to think that the 'full' generality of an infinite sequence is only partially involved, since on the finitary point of view the meta-mathematical methods and results are applied to concretely given sequences of signs. But as is made clear in the statement by Hermann Weyl quoted above, this is a mistaken idea. The arithmetical *notion* of generality involved in the methods and results of meta-mathematics (in the *sense* of these methods and results) is not used only partially in these applications. There is no such 'partial use'. (Compare: when geometrical concepts are being applied to visual space, which is limited by our visual capacities, this does not mean that only parts or 'segments' of the geometrical *concepts* are being used.) Hilbert is misled by the idea of the finite as being part of the infinite, or the infinite as being an extension of the finite.[33] His distinction between 'the real' and 'the ideal' is built upon this idea.

In finitary meta-mathematics it is said that the numerals

$$1, 11, 111, \ldots$$

are being treated as concrete, physical objects. And then one may ask: 'Why should the numerals look just like this? Why not like this

$$-, =, \equiv, \ldots,$$

or like this

$$*, **, ***, \ldots?'$$

And the answer would be that we could very well write the numerals in one of these ways. 'How do you know that?' The answer to this question would presumably take the form of a description of what is *essential* to the different notations; the answer would describe the structure that is *common* to the different notations. But this structure is not a visual or physical structure that someone ignorant of arithmetic could discern immediately. The description of this structure, of what is essential about these notations as numerals, is a description of what is essential about *their use as numerals* in meta-mathematics. The description must be based on the logical form of the series of natural numbers.[34]

This is almost explicit in S.C. Kleene's explanation of the numerals:

178

'The terms 0, 0', 0", . . ., which represent the particular natural numbers under the interpretation of the system, we call *numerals*, and we abbreviate them by the same symbols "0", "1", "2", . . ., respectively, as we use for the natural numbers intuitively.'[35] Whether or not the numerals are conceived as 'formal objects' (i.e. their 'intended interpretation' being disregarded or not), the generality expressed by the sign '. . .' in '0, 0', 0", . . .', is the generality of a recursion.

Hilbert explains: 'In number theory we have the numerals

$$1, 11, 111, \ldots$$

each numeral being perceptually recognizable by the fact that in it 1 is always again followed by 1 (if it is followed by anything).'[36] What he overlooks is that these signs *as numerals* belong to the arithmetical symbolism and not just to visual or physical space. The signs are perceptually recognizable objects, but if we want to make explicit which of the features of these 'objects' are essential to them as the *signs* they are meant to be, we cannot place ourselves outside of the language of mathematics.

The concrete and finitary employment of the expression 'always again followed by', which Hilbert suggests, is of course one possible way of understanding this expression, and it makes sense when applied to written configurations on paper. But this is not the sense it has in proof theory. The concrete sense of the expression 'followed by' is a notion *different* from the arithmetical notion of 'followed by', which refers to the arithmetical successor operation or to the mathematical notion of a finite sequence. The latter notions are not conceptually limited by physical circumstances and by facts about our visual capacities in the way that the concrete, spatial notion 'followed by' is so. And this is a *categorial* difference: the concrete sense of 'followed by' is not a part of the mathematical sense (whatever that would mean). If we call the mathematical notion an 'idealization' of the physical one, we are not referring to a logical relationship between the two notions (but perhaps to a fact in the history of the invention of the mathematical concept, or to one of its possible applications). So contrary to what Hilbert suggests, it is the mathematical and not the concrete sense of 'followed by' that is essential in the methods and results of meta-mathematics. And when these methods and results are being applied to concretely represented sequences of signs, the 'whole mathematical sense' of these methods and results is involved in the applications. This is clear, for instance, by the way in which the following abbreviations are introduced and employed:

> 2 for 11
> 3 for 111
> etc.

From the way these 'abbreviations' are used in the meta-mathematical arguments, it is evident that the generality of this 'etc.' is not some kind of empirical generality of visual or physical shape, but the generality of a mathematical induction or recursion. This means that the sequence 1, 11, 111, . . . is supposed to have the form of the series of natural numbers and not of a list of concretely realizable things. It is part of the conception of the series 1, 11, 111, . . . as the series of numerals that the expressions have a certain structure; they are conceived as being 'built up' by iteration of an operation in the arithmetical sense. But no such structure is involved when they are regarded as mere physical or visual configurations, unless of course a mathematical structure is *applied* in the description of the expressions (as e.g. in the construction of their syntactical representations).

A description of the logical form of the constructions called numerals in modern meta-mathematical treatments (for instance, in the proofs of the 'numeralwise representability' of recursive functions), would take the form of an inductive or a recursive definition:

> (i) 1 is a numeral,
> (ii) If x is a numeral, then x1 is a numeral.

The structure of the series 1, 11, 111, . . . – as a series generated by the unlimited iteration of a successor operation – is not *created* or brought about by such a definition. In giving the inductive definition, the 'inductive structure' is being *used* and at the same time being made explicit. The definition only exists *within* the conceptual system of arithmetic. There is no such thing as an inductive definition of objects in visual or physical space.[37] That the word 'numeral' is used, rather than the word 'number', is based on the mistaken idea that it is something essential for meta-mathematics that numerals be treated as concrete, physical things. But the truth is, on the contrary, that the numerals are treated as *mathematical* 'objects': numerals, conceived according to this inductive definition, *are numbers.*

Someone might perhaps object to this that it was indeed essential to Hilbert's finitary point of view that the numerals are concrete things, and more generally, that the 'real propositions' admissible in the finitary point of view are about concrete things. But then we must say that the finitary point of view cannot be essential in meta-mathematics; it is in fact incompatible with the ways in which one actually works in meta-mathematics. The notions, methods, and techniques actually used are not extensions or idealizations of the strict finitary methods that Hilbert suggests, but categorially differ-ent forms of use of expressions which belong to mathematics.

S.C. Kleene seems to feel this incompatibility when he says (after having emphasized that the objects studied in meta-mathematics are concrete objects):[38] 'Proof theory must be to some extent abstract, since it supposes arbitrarily long sequences of symbols to be constructible, although the quantity of paper and ink in the world is finite.' To some extent! Here one would like to ask: 'Are the objects of meta-mathematics concrete things or are they not?' It is essential that there is no limit to the length of terms and formulas at all, and thus no limit to the amount of terms and formulas that are not realizable as concrete lists of signs. The notion of generality used in the formation rules is a *mathematical* notion.

The mathematician engaged in proving theorems in meta-math-ematics is not worried by the suspicion that the expressions and formulas he deals with may be too long to be realizable as actual lists of concrete signs, because he is not concerned with expressions as lists of concrete signs at all, but with expressions as mathematical constructions (like the natural numbers). He is standing within a mathematical conceptual system.

The important thing about the various notations for numbers

$$1, 11, 111, \ldots$$
$$0, 0', 0'', \ldots$$
$$0, S0, SS0, \ldots$$

which have been used in mathematical logic is not that they are concrete objects (that is not more important about these signs than it is about other signs). What is important about these notations is that they give a more distinct articulation of a conception of the series of natural numbers within pure mathematics, namely of this series as generated by the unlimited iteration of a successor oper-ation, and also that they give a way of representing each numeral as a 'formal object', as a finite sequence (or list or 'string'). The former, recursive structure is used, for instance, in the proofs of the 'numeralwise representability' of the recursive functions in formal systems, and the latter, formal structure is used in the arithmetization of meta-mathematics.

We do of course have a general concept of a list of concrete signs, which is literally a list or a row. And this concept is limited by the physical possibility of constructing, surveying, and 'running through' such lists. How would it otherwise be a concept of a list of *concrete* things? The upper limit to the length of such a list is determined within the human practices in which it occurs, by the methods for constructing it, by the way it is perceived and described as a concrete object. So it is clear that the notion of 'a list of arbitrary length' in this concrete sense involves a sense of generality which is conceptually different from the one occurring in the notion of 'an arbitrary long expression' that can be constructed by the inductive definitions in meta-mathematics. And the fact that the meta-mathematical methods and results *can be applied* to concrete expressions does not change this fact.

The operation 'followed by 1' in the inductive definition of the numerals is meant to be applicable without limit (independently of what mathematicians and philosophers might *say* about this; it is what they *do* with the definition that counts). But the physical possibility of realizing the numerals as concrete lists of signs is of course limited. The confusion of the physical and the mathematical perspectives in the idea of a finitary proof theory sometimes comes out in reactions like this: 'But are there numerals that cannot be physically realized? Are not numerals, as distinguished from numbers, concrete, physical things?', which invites the misleading picture of the numerals and the numbers as forming two parallel sequences of things, of which the former is concrete and (perhaps) finite, while the latter is 'abstract' and endless, and between the two sequences there are external relationships of denotation or reference.

This picture and its generalizations – let us call it *the referential picture*[39] – is the source and the basis for several questionable technical concepts in current philosophy of language and linguistic theory, such as the distinctions 'use/mention', 'name/thing named', 'syntax/semantics', 'object-language/meta-language'.[40] It is clear that Hilbert's idea of finitary reasoning was the main source of inspiration for the invention of the notion of 'syntactical form', i.e. the notion of the form of a linguistic expression as a concrete, physical structure, which is being 'connected to' the content (or objects referred to) through semantic rules. (We do not find this technical notion of 'form' in Frege's and the early Russell's writings.) This notion of the form of expressions created the need for a new science, 'semantics', whose task was to explain the 'mechanism' whereby the 'uninterpreted, concrete expressions' are connected to their meanings or references.

Current views in the philosophy of mathematics, such as realism and platonism, as well as their counterparts, anti-realism and formalism, are to a great extent conceptions *within* this way of thinking about the form and content of mathematical expressions. Hilbert's conception of expressions and their form, of calculation as mechanical manipulation, was not questioned when it was realized that the formalistic view of mathematics as a game with expressions *qua* concrete, physical things, is untenable. Instead, many mathematicians and philosophers were misled by Hilbert's epistemological programme into thinking that there must be some *other* kind of things which mathematics 'is about', other things which are not just 'our idealizations' but real things. One was led to think that, besides the realm of concrete things to which the expressions belong, there must be 'abstract objects' to which the expressions of mathematics 'refer'. One might say that Hilbert's 'ideal objects' were appointed 'real objects' in this realism, but within a conception of the language of mathematics which is essentially the same as Hilbert's, namely, as a system of notation (or physical forms of notation) separated from the forms of their use.

9 LANGUAGES AND FORMAL SYSTEMS

Hilbert's proof-theoretical programme was partly a mathematical research project and partly an epistemological programme framed within a naturalistic perspective. The two programmes were not, and still are not, kept separate. The epistemological ideas and claims penetrate the technical notions and methods of the mathematical project via the prose used to express the significance of technical notions and results (e.g. when the word 'formal' is used to signify a concrete, physical structure). Thus, proof theorists sometimes claim to be concerned with 'the concrete signs and their syntactical relationships', as though 'the syntactical relationships' were something extra- or pre-mathematical which would not involve mathematical concepts.

In the advanced textbook on mathematical logic by J.R. Shoen-field,[41] it is said:

> In our study of formal systems, we shall be studying expressions, just as an analyst studies real numbers. . . . an analysis text uses names for certain real numbers. . . . Similarly, we shall need names for expressions. We are in the fortunate position of being able to provide a name for each expression with one convention: each expression shall be used as a name for itself. This convention is not available to writers of analysis texts; for a name must be an expression, and a real number is not an expression.

This statement indicates the pattern according to which the syntax and the semantics of a 'language' in the sense of Tarski and Carnap is being built up according to the referential picture: the expressions belong to the realm of concrete objects, while the real numbers are 'abstract objects' and the two kinds of things are connected through external relations of denotation or reference. Once such a connection is brought about through a stipulation or 'convention' in the 'meta-language' such as ' "N" is the name of . . .' or 'Let "N" denote . . .', we may use 'N' as a name of the object which has been made the 'bearer' of this name through the stipulation. In this way the mistaken idea arises that naming or referring, as functions of expressions in language, are ultimately brought about or created through a stipulation of this kind; as though naming or referring were conceptually determined as being the application of stipulations such as the foregoing. That 'N' be a name of an object is conceived as consisting in *the fact* that an external binary relation of reference holds between the name *qua* physical object and the thing named, regardless of whether 'N' is ever *used* as a name. If one were to ask what such a 'semantic fact' consists in, one would presumably receive the answer that naming and reference are 'primitive concepts'.

In this semantic jargon, naming and referring are forgotten as functions of expressions in language, which are ultimately determined as practices, as forms of use of expressions. Only against the background of these practices is there such a thing as giving, applying, or using the stipulations at all.

The meta-mathematical conception of the name-relation under-lies the distinction between use and mention as expounded, for instance, by Quine.[42] What Quine does not mention in his explanation of 'Boston' as a name for the name of the city of Boston, is that it presupposes that the expression within the quotes has the linguistic function of *being a name*, and not just that it is a 'physical object' or a spatial or visual configuration. One might say, with Quine, that 'the discrimination between one name and another is a visual operation of an elementary kind',[43] but only if it is understood that this capacity to discriminate is part of the linguistic practice of using expressions as names.[44]

If something is given a name, it must be determined in some way; the thing to be named must be *given* in some way. It may be described, it may be shown concretely, it may be pointed to, etc. How are the expressions in mathematical logic given which are assigned names in the 'meta-language'? Well, certainly not as concretely displayed, physical objects. Only 'a few' of them can be realized as concrete expressions even 'in principle'. No, they are given as constructions generated by the unlimited iteration of certain operations. The generality expressed by the 'syntactical variables' for 'expressions', terms and formulas is the generality of generalized *mathematical* inductions. Since it is not essential that these constructions at all be realized as actual expressions of some language, we may even say that it is this structure that is the essential thing; it is the actual object of study. But this means that the 'expressions', the numerals and the formulas in metamathematics, are as much mathematical constructions or mathematical 'objects' as are numbers.

In stating the formation rules, certain signs, and notations are being *used*. For instance, in the rule for the construction of the numerals, certain signs are being used to express zero and the successor operation. *These* signs are expressions in the language of mathematics in the ordinary sense. It is essential that they be perceptually realizable, surveyable, and so on. But the 'expressions' in the sense of the 'objects' obtained by applying the formation rules – as something other than the expressions *used* to express the rules – *are not linguistic expressions* in the ordinary sense, but mathematical constructions.

When (in mathematical logic) we talk about the results obtained by applying the formation rules, regardless of the notation used to express these results, we are talking about the *logical form* of the constructions obtained (or about the constructions as expressions for that logical form). In that sense mathematicians speak about this term or that formula as being *the same* term or formula as may be written somewhere else, possibly in some other notation. They speak about 'the Gödel formula' as a mathematical construction and not as a certain expression in the particular notation used by Gödel. They speak about terms or formulas as *forms* (of expressions or constructions), with the understanding that the particular notation used is unimportant as long as it is capable of expressing the structure that is essential in the meta-mathematical proofs and results. This is the logical (not spatial or typographical) form of the expressions.[45]

The idea of the 'expressions' in the 'object-language', which are said to be obtained by the formation rules, is the idea of a concrete *representation* of these logical forms as physical forms. It is the idea of a mechanization of the logical forms in the spirit of Hilbert's finitism. Now, provided that we do not mean reduction by 'representation', such concrete mechanical representations can in a certain sense be given,[46] but this fact is not something essential to mathematical logic and proof theory. The proofs and the results about, for instance, the incompleteness and the undecidability of first-order arithmetic do not depend on the existence of such a concrete 'object-language'. It is not important that the constructions are physically represented in these proofs, because they are treated as mathematical constructions (like numbers or well-founded trees).[47]

The so-called syntactical variables in mathematical logic do not 'vary through the expressions of the language being discussed',[48] considered as written configurations on paper. They are used to express the *form* of the mathematical constructions with which meta-mathematics is concerned.

Shoenfield introduces the syntactical variables 's', 'u', and 'v' for 'expressions of an object-language' and explains: 'we shall use uv to stand for the expression obtained by juxtaposing u and v, that is, by writing down u and then writing down v immediately after it.' So this must mean that in an expression of the form uv there is an order between u and v which is an essential feature of this expression. But is it an order that u and v have as physical or visual objects, as actual written signs on a paper? Is it a spatio-temporal order? No, the truth is rather that certain physical properties of and relationships between the written signs 'u' and 'v' have been used to express a certain *mathematical* structure.

By ignoring the prose explanations and looking instead at the way this 'juxtaposition system' is being *used* in mathematical work, we find for instance the following: the fact that 'u' and 'v' are two

different letters written close to one another from left to right signifies a binary (algebraic) operation. That *these* letters have been
used is inessential and arbitrary, but that they are *different* letters
is essential (it is a feature that belongs to the logical form of the
expression uv). That 'u' and 'v' have a definite spatial relation as
regards left–right is also something essential: it expresses that uv is
not in general the same construction as vu. But the 'grouping' in
an expression like suv is not essential: The operation 'juxtaposition'
is obviously meant to be associative; s(uv) is meant to be the same
construction as (su)v.

All this could be expressed by means of other signs and other
physical relations between them. The interpretation of uv as the
juxtaposition of actual, written signs is not essential, even if it is
one possible application of the algebraic system. But this application
is never used in an essential way in the theorems and proofs in
mathematical logic. So what we have is an algebraic system with
a binary operation *called* 'juxtaposition' which can be iterated (without limit) to form mathematical constructions called expressions
(let us call them *formal expressions* to indicate that we have to do
with a technical/mathematical sense of the word 'expression'). And
there are statements of the form 'u is the same expression as v' for
which the following rules are taken for granted:

(su)v is the same expression as s(uv).

If s is the same expression as u, then sv is the same expression
as uv and vs is the same expression as vu.

What 'u is the same expression as v' means for 'atomic expressions'
is something that does not need to be specified in physical or
typographical terms, because one is not concerned with that application of this algebraic structure in mathematical logic.

Using this algebraic structure, Shoenfield proves a 'Formation
Theorem' which states that every term and formula of the formal
systems can be written in the form $uv_1 \ldots v_n$ in a unique way,
where u is a symbol with 'arity' n and $v_1, \ldots, v_n$ are terms or
formulas. This theorem will guarantee that commas, parentheses,
etc. are not necessary to determine 'groupings'. However, the
expressions 'unique way', 'grouping', etc. do not signify – as Shoenfield wants us to believe – a physical or typographical notion of
form, but the form of the meta-mathematical 'expressions' as mathematical objects (or constructions). This is obvious from the fact

that the theorem is being *proved* by mathematical induction. The essential thing about these 'expressions' in the proof is that they are finite sequences in the mathematical sense and that terms and formulas are conceived as being constructed by generalized inductions.

Shoenfield introduces this juxtaposition system as a mathematical system for the 'syntactical' representation of terms and formulas as finite sequences ('lists' or 'strings'), presumably because it simplifies the 'arithmetization of meta-mathematics'. His concern is to prove that terms and formulas (as generated by generalized inductions) can be represented in a unique way within it. It is clear that it is only the *mathematical* structure of this juxtaposition system which is being used. The concrete interpretation of juxtaposition as concatenated written expressions is not involved at all; nor is the syntax of an actual language involved. These ideas are only parts of an inessential and misleading picture which accompanies the mathematical treatment (and which is first sketched in Hilbert's epistemological programme).

What the proofs are concerned with are the properties of and relations between two mathematical systems. A formula belongs to the one system by being generated by iterating the logical operations, and to the other through being constructed by juxtapositions of formal expressions. In either case, it is the formula as the mathematically determined *form* of such a construction which is the object of study in mathematical logic, not some physical representation of it.

The real content of the 'name-relation' or the distinction between use and mention in mathematical logic has to do with this double meaning of 'term' and 'formula': On the one hand, a formula is a construction obtained by iterating logical operations. On the other hand, as a 'formal object',[49] a formula is a finite sequence or a formal expression ('string') in the juxtaposition system. These are *different* mathematical constructions (or 'objects') and the 'name-relation' is an external relation between them. The quotation convention used to distinguish between use and mention is based on a systematic method for associating a formal expression in the juxtaposition structure with each term and formula in the former sense. And for the expressions which already are formal expressions within the juxtaposition system, the quotation notation is not needed; they are 'used as names of themselves'.

'But is it not essential in the definition of formal systems such as

the first-order languages that the languages be carefully specified?'
What is important is that the *notation* to be used is specified; there
must be a fixed list of symbols to be *used* in the mathematical
symbol-roles of constants, variables, and auxiliary symbols. And
there must be a (mathematical) system like Shoenfield's juxtapo-
sition-system for formal representation of terms, formulas, and
proofs as formal objects. That the formal system is *formal* means in
meta-mathematics that the rules can be stated with reference to the
terms and formulas as formal objects only, i.e. as rules for replacing
certain finite sequences (or strings) by others. The formal rules are
rules for calculating within the system for formal representation.[50]

What is important to realize about this is that calculating in this
sense within the formal representations is as much mathematical
calculation as calculating in ordinary arithmetic. It is not a more
'mechanical' sense of calculation, if this is supposed to mean that
it is a kind of physical, pre-mathematical manipulation of concrete
symbols. It is calculating within mathematical systems *different* from
ordinary arithmetic, which we may agree to *call* 'mechanical' with
a view to applications in computer science; but no result in mathematical logic or proof theory depends on the possibility of these
applications.

The forms of use of the expressions in these 'mechanical calculi'
are mathematical, and so is the notion of generality in the rules of
calculation. The concepts 'expression', 'string', 'finite sequence',
'length', 'juxtaposition', 'occurrence', 'grouping', etc., as used in
the system for formal representation, are technical mathematical
concepts. Consider for instance the notion of occurrence. When we
talk about 'the second occurrence of the variable x in the formula

$$x + y = y + x'$$

we are not referring to an event or an object or a position in physical
space, but to a feature of the form of a mathematical construction.
It is not the same notion of occurrence as when we say 'there are
several occurrences of the letter a on this page', which refers to
written signs on a piece of paper. Instead, we could say that a
certain occurrence of the letter x on this page marks the second
occurrence of the variable x in the formula. If I were to write the
same formula in the same notation on the next page, it would be
correct to say 'an occurrence of the letter x on the next page
indicates the same occurrence of the variable x in the formula'.

It is a mistake to think that the words 'occurrence', 'place' (in 'argument place'), etc., as used in mathematical logic, refer to positions, events, or things in physical space, in the same way that it is a mistake to think that a theorem about triangles in a book on geometry is about the physical triangles that are printed in the book; this, however, is not to suggest that the theorem is about some 'abstract triangles', but that we have a confusion of conceptual systems.

The technical mathematical employments of the words 'use', 'mention', 'syntax', 'name', 'reference' in mathematical logic have little to do with the ordinary employments of these words in connection with actual linguistic functions. The point of the idea of the 'object-language' is to make us believe the opposite, and unfortunately this belief is the foundation for dominating trends in current philosophy of language and linguistic theory. When the technical notions of use versus mention and of syntax versus semantics are transferred to the study of actual languages, one is led to assume that there is a general technique for representing linguistic expressions as formal or syntactical objects, because that is what this meta-mathematical notion of syntax requires. Since 'natural languages' are not artificial constructions, it is even supposed that there is such a formal syntactical structure in a language as it is given, and that it is the task of linguistic theory to make it explicit. The idea of the 'object-language' is introduced to make it look as though the syntactical representation were not just a construction, but a description of a basic structure which exists in the language as it is given. A language as an 'object-language' is a projection of the methods of a syntactical representation. As though actual languages were, after all, 'built up' according to the methods for constructing syntax and semantics for formal systems. The real purpose of the idea of an 'object-language' was to cover up the conceptual difference between languages and formal systems in order to 'justify' the use of the methods of formal logic and meta-mathematics in the study of actual languages.[51] This has resulted in a widespread inability to see the difference between a linguistic expression in the ordinary, non-technical sense, and an expression as an object in some system for syntactical representation. It is common among theorists of language to think that people are actually using a system for syntactical representation in the ordinary employment of language. This way of thinking was, it seems to me, and still is an idea fundamental for the Chomsky tradition. It is also a presupposition in current attempts to produce theories of meaning (as shown in part 2 of this book). And it is this false perspective on actual language that creates several problems discussed in current philosophy of language (e.g. the problem of the 'productivity of language' or such problems as 'how can sequences of physical sounds have meaning and express thoughts?', etc.).

The confusion of 'sentence' or 'expression' in the ordinary sense and in the sense of formal or syntactical representations of linguistic expressions, is a parallel to (and perhaps a consequence of) the confusion of the different concepts of a term and a formula mentioned above. As already explained, in the proof theory of first-order arithmetic, as presented by Shoenfield, there are (at least) three conceptually different kinds of mathematical constructions: formal expressions generated by the juxtaposition operation, numerical terms which express the result of applying operations on numbers, and formulas generated by iteration of the logical operations. This is the way terms and formulas are conceived in 'proofs and definitions by induction on the construction of terms and formulas', and this is the way they are given when they are assigned syntactical representations in the formation rules. However, in this sense the class of terms and formulas is not a subclass of the class of formal expressions generated by juxtaposition. It is the syntactical representations of the terms and formulas as 'formal objects' which is such a subclass.

We may also express this as follows: terms or formulas are not given as finite lists or strings with the external property of being terms or formulas. For instance, the numerical term SS0 is not given as the result of the juxtaposition of symbols. That is true rather of its representation as a formal object. As a numerical term it is given as the expression (in the ordinary sense) for the result of applying the successor operation to zero and its successor.

This means that the notation 'uv' has two different senses in Shoenfield's exposition. In the *numeral* S0 it does not signify the result of applying the juxtaposition operation but the result of applying the successor operation to zero. But in the formal expression S0, it signifies the result of applying the binary operation of juxtaposition to the formal expressions S and 0. When Shoenfield says: 'The terms 0, S0, SS0, . . . are called *numerals*,'[52] he is *using* the expression 'S0' in the former sense. Similarly, in the formation rules for formulas the logical constants are given as operations generating formulas, and the rules describe a method for associating with each formula a formal expression in the juxtaposition system. The

191

formation rules define the predicate 'u is a formula' as an external property of formal expressions.

The fact that Shoenfield sometimes uses the symbols in their intended mathematical sense is concealed by his notation, which does not distinguish between a formula (a term) and its representation as a formal expression. It looks as though everything were being done within the system for syntactical representation. It seems to me that a conceptually more correct way of presenting the proof theory of first-order arithmetic would be to start by formulating the rules and axioms using the symbols in their intended mathematical sense, and then to introduce the system for syntactical representation and to give a method for associating with each term, formula, etc., a formal expression. For instance, if '∼' and 'A' are the formal objects associated with the negation operation ∼ and with the formula A respectively, then '∼A', the formal object associated with the formula ∼A, is the result of applying the operation of juxtaposition to the formal objects '∼' and 'A'. The rules are then transformed into rules for operating with formal expressions within the juxtaposition system (or within a calculus of finite sequences).

Note, however, that by 'the intended mathematical sense' I do not mean what logicians call 'the intended interpretation', where numerals are assigned 'denotations' in the 'standard model' and formulas are interpreted as propositions. This is another interpretation or translation which is based on the familiar techniques for paraphrasing terms and formulas into mathematical prose (e.g. '∼A' has the reading 'it is not the case that A' and '∃xA' has the reading 'there exists an x such that A', etc.).

There is a parallel to what I have been trying to say here for actual languages: a meaningful sentence of a language is not a sequence of words (or marks on paper or sounds) with the external property of being meaningful. Using Tarski's jargon one would say: 'the class of meaningful expressions is not a subclass of the class of all expressions.' This is rather the way one wants to have it within a syntactical representation of a 'language with a specifiable structure', when one pretends that the syntactical representation were the conceptual basis of actual languages, as though a sentence were basically a finite sequence of marks on a piece of paper which is being interpreted or endowed with sense later on. But as I have tried to show, the formal or syntactical representations are conceptually secondary constructions, which are not involved at all in our normal use of language.

The myth of the 'object-language' is also the basis for the interpretation of the significance of many results in mathematical logic and proof theory. By generalized inductive definitions, syntactical predicates and relations like 'a is a numerical term', 'u is a formula', 'A is an axiom', 'A is an immediate consequence of B', 'Y is a proof' are defined in meta-mathematics as external properties (i.e. as functions) of formal objects (which, we remember, are really finite sequences or lists in the mathematical sense of these terms). It is clear that the readings of these syntactical predicates in mathematical prose is the basis for the statement of many results in meta-mathematics and for the interpretation of their significance, as for instance in the statement that 'Gödel constructed a sentence expressing its own unprovability'. What notion of 'expressing' is this, and what is meant by a 'sentence' here? It is not the more common senses of these words. They do not mean what they usually mean when we say that 'a sentence expresses so and so'.[53] One has to inspect the mathematical construction in Gödel's proof to see what it means.

The syntactical predicates are defined as external properties (functions) on certain mathematical objects, namely formal expressions in the juxtaposition system. To call such mathematical constructions 'formulas', 'numerals', 'axioms', 'proofs', etc., is of course not in agreement with the ordinary ways of employing these words in mathematics. The readings are based on the 'identification' (or the failure to distinguish) between the syntactical representations and what they represent. This means of course that the prose used in the readings of the syntactical predicates, as well as in the statements of many results in meta-mathematics, is highly figurative.

The confusion of syntactical constructions with what they represent is connected with the mistaken idea that we are somehow applying or using (perhaps tacitly) a system for syntactical or formal representation when we use a language in mathematics and elsewhere. (Some people seem even to think that there exists such a system for 'sentence parsing' in the human brain comparable to the programs of computers.) As already suggested in part 1 of this book, it seems to me that one important origin of this idea is to be found in Hilbert's naturalistic conception of formalization. Let us take a look at this again in the light of what has been said here.

Hilbert refers to algebra when he explains his conception of formalization. In algebra, says Hilbert, we regard 'the expressions formed with letters to be independent objects in themselves'.[54] And if we regard the expressions of ordinary arithmetic in that way, they will be 'concrete objects that . . . are considered by our perceptual intuition, and the derivation of one formula from another in accordance with certain rules takes the place of the number-theoretic proof based on content.' What is wrong here is the idea that calculation in algebra is something essentially different from calculation in ordinary arithmetic. Algebraic calculation is not more mechanical or more concerned with the manipulation of concrete objects than is ordinary calculation in arithmetic. Hilbert is thinking in terms of a formal representation or mechanization of ordinary algebraic calculation. He speaks as though the ordinary human practice of calculation in algebra (e.g. in Boolean algebra) were the application of such a formal representation. But in the ordinary practice of calculation in algebra the expressions are *not* considered as concrete and 'independent objects in themselves' any more than in ordinary arithmetic. The features of the expressions in algebra (as in arithmetic) which are essential are determined by the mathematical rules for operating with them. The difference is that the rules are different.

It seems to be this confusion of a formal representation of calculation (e.g. as a Turing machine) with the ordinary mathematical practice of calculation which leads some people to forget that we have to do with a metaphorical or technical employment of the word 'calculation' when we say that computers calculate. When this is forgotten it may seem as though the ordinary human practice of calculation were the application of a formal representation. The human activity of calculating is misconceived as consisting of two parts, a physical (mechanical, formal, syntactical) part (mechanical symbol-manipulation), and on top of that another mental (intentional, intuitive, semantical) part (interpretation, understanding); and the latter, according to some advocates of mechanism in the philosophy of mind,[55] is ultimately to be reducible to the former. The idea of the physical (or behavioural) part of a human action is a direct counterpart to the idea of a language as an 'object language'; both ideas are projections of certain methods for constructing formal representations.

10 COMPUTABILITY AND DECIDABILITY

Most problems in the philosophy of mathematics discussed in the foregoing sections have been concerned with conceptually misleading ideas rooted in the view of ordinary mathematics as a science about some sort of 'ideal objects' and as employing such notions as 'iteration', 'list', 'run through', etc., in an 'idealized sense'. Other examples are the notions of computability and decidability used in connection with Church's thesis, Turing machines and in statements of the significance of results in recursion theory. These notions are sometimes claimed to have senses which are 'idealizations' of the ordinary senses of computability and decidability that refer to actual practices of calculation. It is sometimes said that a 'mechanical procedure', in the idealized sense, is a procedure 'which could be carried out by a suitably designed machine'. But then it must be added that 'we have in mind an ideal machine, not limited, as real machines are, by problems of size, mechanical breakdown, etc.'[56]

It is of course true that features of algorithms and actual numerical calculation, performed by human beings with or without the help of some mechanical means, influenced the development of the notions and techniques of the theory of computability in mathematical logic, but it seems to me that mistaken conceptual conclusions concerning what is essential about these notions are often drawn from such facts about their origin.

Hilary Putnam comes in contact with one conceptual issue involved here when he raises the problem:

> If the physical universe is thoroughly finite, both in the large and in the small, then the statement '$10^{100} + 1$ is a prime number' may be one whose truth value we can never know. For, if the statement is true . . ., then to verify that it is true by using any sieve method might well be physically impossible. . . .
>
> Now, although many people doubt that the continuum hypothesis has a truth value, everyone believes that the statement '$10^{100} + 1$ is a prime number' has a truth value. Why? 'Because the statement is decidable.' But what does that mean, 'the statement is decidable'?[57]

Putnam's answer is that it means that 'it is *possible* to decide the statement'. The statement is 'an assertion of mathematical possibility'. But what notion of possibility is this? Obviously it is not the possibility of practical calculation; it does not refer to what may come out as an actual result of applying a technique of calculating products of possible factors of $10^{100} + 1$.

Putnam tries to clarify this point by saying that someone who makes this assertion believes that just one of two statements is a 'necessary truth'. One of these statements is the following: 'If all pairs n, m (n, $m < 10^{100} + 1$) were "tried" by actually computing the product nm, then in some case the product would be found equal to $10^{100} + 1$.' The other statement is that in no case would the product be equal to $10^{100} + 1$.

Now, what is really 'believed' here? That under certain conditions an actual process of numerical calculation will produce one of these two results? No, because the example was chosen in such a way that these conditions will never obtain![58] To this it would perhaps be answered that the conditions will never be *physically* realized, but that they have a mathematically well-defined sense. That is true, in a certain sense, but this mathematically well-defined sense of decidability is a concept *different* from the notion of decidability which refers to the practice of the numerical calculation of products. For this technical notion of decidability (or computability) the existence of a real process of numerical computation that ends up in an actual result is something inessential, and something that we will not have in our example (as it was chosen). About this technical notion of computability it is simply agreed that 'any finite number of steps can be run through' (with the purely mathematical sense of 'finite' discussed in section 5) as a convention for a new technical employment of the word 'computability' (or 'decidability').

There is no justification for this convention in the ordinary, literal sense of decidability or solvability which refers to what can be done by humans (perhaps with the help of 'real machines') in practice. And this is a fundamental sense of computability and decidability, because mathematics, as well as its applications, is after all a family of human activities, practices, techniques. The convention mentioned above is not an 'idealization' in the sense that an essential feature of the literal notion of 'can be decided (solved)' is being isolated; on the contrary, it is an institution of a completely different notion - different, because the existence of a 'physically realizable' and an actually ending process of computation is an essential feature of the concept of 'reaching a decision or result by means of a technique of computation', which we apply to humans (or computers).

When Putnam expresses himself as though the assertion of the decidability of the statement '$10^{100} + 1$ is a prime number' would involve the belief in the truth of one of two statements which refer to processes of 'actually computing products', which cannot all of them be physically realized, he is confusing the different concepts of decidability. He is led to express himself as though there were 'idealized processes of numerical computation' with which pure mathematics is concerned, and which we can (or rather, 'ideal machines' can), as it were, perform without running through the individual steps of the computation in time and space.

Since the expression 'actually computing the products . . .' occurs in the statements beginning with 'If all pairs m, n (m, $n < 10^{100} + 1$) were "tried" by actually computing the products . . .', it is clear that the statements should be understood as statements about deciding by actual computation in the literal sense. So, if the assertion of decidability is an assertion of 'mathematical possibility', then this possibility must be conceptually determined through some practice or technique of numerical computation, otherwise it is *not* a well-defined *mathematical* possibility. But techniques for numerical calculation – the existing ones as well as those which will be invented in the future – do of course have their physical and technical limitations. The activity of deciding numerical problems on the basis of an 'actual process of numerical computation' *is bound to have physical limitations*, as do other human activities. 'Actual processes of numerical calculation' where any physical and technical limitations 'are abstracted away from' is a chimera, a false picture. Now, Putnam's example was chosen in such a way that the physical limitations are transgressed. This means that the statements, one of which is believed to express a 'necessary truth', do not make sense, they do not express a well-defined mathematical possibility.

In what sense then is it correct to say that the statement '$10^{100} + 1$ is a prime number' is decidable? It is correct in the sense in which we say that the *predicate* 'n is a prime number' is 'decidable' or that a *statement of the form* 'n is a prime number' is a 'computational statement'. But these are technical employments of the words 'decidable' and 'computable' which refer, not to numerical calculation, but to calculation procedures with expressions for functions within certain calculi of functions. The problem of defining the 'computable functions' became particularly important in connection with the new, general concept of a *function* in mathematical logic, which included *predicates* as 'propositional functions'.[59] Many conceptual confusions and much philosophical nonsense have resulted from the assimilation of this notion of decidability with the ordinary literal sense of solvability of certain kinds of problems by means of a technique for numerical calculation.

In the ordinary or literal sense of 'decidable', the statement '10^{100} + 1 is a prime number' is not decidable. It is not decidable in the sense in which the statement '13 is a prime number' or '233 is a prime number' are. The techniques which work for deciding the latter statements do not work for the first statement. So, in this literal sense of 'decidable' or 'computable', there is no explanation, uniform in 'n', of the statements of the form 'n is a prime number' as computational statements. However, there is such an explanation or definition of 'n is a prime number' as a *recursive predicate* (even a primitive recursive predicate), and of the 'characteristic function' $p(n)$ of this predicate as a primitive recursive function, with which we operate according to the rule that, for any number n, $p(n)$ has a value which is 0 or 1 (and not both), regardless of whether there exists, for a certain number n, a technique for actually working out a numerical value of $p(n)$. We operate with $p(n)$ according to this rule in the calculus of recursive functions, but *not* because we can give a (non-circular) verification or justification of the rule by means of a technique for actually working out the value of $p(n)$ for an arbitrary n (in general we cannot), but because this is the way we operate with functional expressions in the calculus of recursive functions.

When this rule is applied to the function $p(n)$, and the result is translated into mathematical prose, it can be read: 'The statement "10^{100} + 1 is a prime number" has a truth-value, it is either true or false, and not both.' That the predicate 'n is a prime number' can be represented as such a primitive recursive predicate (or function) is the essential mathematical content of the statement that the predicate 'n is a prime number' is decidable; and, as a special case, this is the sense in which it is correct to say that the statement '10^{100} + 1 is a prime number' is decidable. It all falls back upon the calculus of recursive functions. What someone who makes this assertion expresses besides this is only adherence to the linguistic convention in mathematical logic of calling recursive functions (predicates) 'computable' ('decidable').

There may be some good reasons for this linguistic convention,

198

but it is also a source of confusion. It is often claimed that it is something more than a linguistic convention. It is maintained that the statement 'every recursive function is computable' can be given, if not a strict mathematical proof, at least a convincing argument, which is not just an argument for the suitability of a terminological convention but is meant to make the statement 'epistemologically evident'. This would mean that mathematicians were in possession of an 'intuitive concept' of the computability of functions, independently of the concept of a recursive function. This is, it seems to me, a mistaken idea. (The issue is similar to the situation in set theory discussed in section 2, where one claims to have an intuitive concept of a set on the basis of which the axioms of set theory are 'justified'.)

Let us take a look at the alleged argument for the computability of the primitive recursive functions. Suppose that the function $f(x)$ is defined by a rule of the form

$$f(0) = k$$
$$f(n+1) = g(n,f(n)),$$

where we know the number k and where we know that the function $g(x,y)$ is 'computable'. Then the 'argument' for the 'computability' of f may run like this: 'For an arbitrary number n we calculate the value of $f(n)$ by first noting that $f(0) = k$. If $n = 0$, we are finished. Otherwise we calculate $f(1) = g(0, k)$. Since $g(x,y)$ is computable we can find the value k', say, of $f(1)$. Then, in the same way we calculate $f(2) = g(1, k')$, etc., and *after a finite number of steps* which are fixed in advance by the rule, we will arrive at the value of $f(n)$.' However, these 'finite number of steps' may be so large and the function $g(x,y)$ may be so complicated that it is actually impossible for people as well as machines to run through these steps. It may not be possible to realize this 'computation' as an actual process of numerical calculation. Now, this is precisely what one is supposed to disregard about this notion of computability, which of course means that *the argument does not refer to actual processes of numerical calculation* (which were, somehow, only summarized in the argument). The prose expressions 'we calculate . . .', 'we can find the value . . .' occurring in the argument do not mean what they normally mean when we are talking about actual numerical calculation. We may *not*, in general, be able to 'find the numerical value of expressions of the form $f(n)$'.

What this means is not that the argument refers to some 'abstract processes of numerical calculation which cannot be physically re-alized', but that we have to do with a new use of words and expressions like 'computable', 'we can calculate . . .', 'we can find the value . . .', etc. In this new use the expressions have their precise meaning *on the basis of rules and techniques for operating with expressions for functions and finite sequences* (sequences, which may not be physically representable as actual lists) in some calculus of functions. But the computations according to these rules are of course as much 'physically realizable' as ordinary numerical calculations.

If we accept this new use of the word 'computable', then the real reason for saying that f(n) is computable is the *form* of the sequence of 'computations'

$$f(0) = k,$$
$$f(1) = g(0, f(0)) = g(0, k),$$
$$. . .$$
$$f(n) = g(n-1, f(n-1)) = g(n-1, g(n-2, . . . g(0, k) . . .)),$$

i.e. the uniform relationship between one value and the next, as expressed by the equation $f(x+1) = g(x,f(x))$, and the finiteness of the sequence of computations. It is not that this algebraic calcu-lation summarizes an immensely long list of numerical calculations (which may not be 'physically realizable').[60]

So the 'argument' for the computability of the primitive recursive function f is no argument. It is a way of introducing the new technical employments of the words 'computability', 'computation', etc., by means of an example of their use. It is more of a paradigm for a way of speaking than an argument. But these terminological conventions are misleading since they suggest conceptual connec-tions with actual numerical calculation which do not exist.

That these terminological conventions are misleading is even more obvious in connection with the converse statement 'Every computable function is recursive', known as Church's thesis. It is generally admitted that this is a statement we cannot hope to prove, but (as Shoenfield[61] puts it) 'lacking such a proof, we can still hope to find evidence that Church's thesis is true.' But how could there be such a thing as evidence here? It is as though we had to do with a kind of hypothesis about some already existing but partly hidden state of affairs, which, however, is not wholly a mathematical state of affairs, since it cannot be proved.

Behind this idea is the false comparison with the ordinary, literal sense of computability or solvability of certain kinds of problems by means of an actual numerical calculation procedure. Certain procedures for operating with expressions for functions are conceived and judged in terms of procedures for operating on individual numbers, as though the rules for calculating with functions described or summarized such operations. Since these operations cannot literally be carried out as operations on numbers (i.e. they are 'idealized procedures'), it is clear that the intuitive concept of the computability of functions refers to (extensional) *pictures* of procedures for operating with individual numbers.

From where do these pictures arise? Are they recollections of a previous contact with the platonic ideas? They are rooted in the prose readings of expressions for functions and of the rules for operating with functions.

The 'intuitive concept' of the 'effective calculability of functions' developed *together with* and *on the basis of* the technical work on the methods for defining and operating with recursive functions. This is clear, it seems to me, from the work of Hilbert, Skolem, Ackermann, Herbrand, Gödel, Kleene, and Church, despite the fact that they often express themselves in prose – in the manner characteristic of mathematicians – as though the precise sense of the notion were there from the start waiting to be discovered.[62] But the concept was invented and the 'intuitions' of mathematicians about effective computability were shaped by their work with the construction of formal systems and the calculus of recursive functions. So it is hardly surprising that Church's thesis is found to be 'a reliable heuristic principle' for inferring that a function is recursive when it is felt to be 'intuitively calculable'. But it is misleading to describe it as an inference on the basis of a hypothesis which could be supported by evidence.

In what way is the notion of computability that occurs in Church's thesis an important concept for mathematics? Church's thesis, as the kind of semi-mathematical hypothesis it was originally meant to be, is used in mathematical logic and in meta-mathematics where it is said to be the basis for 'many important negative results: there are no effectively computable functions or decision procedures for such and such questions';[63] and according to Shoenfield: 'In order to use recursiveness to discuss decision problems, we must be convinced of the truth of the following statement: every calculable function or predicate is recursive.'[64] But it is easy to see that Church's thesis is never used in the proofs of these negative results. What is, for instance, the mathematical content of Church's theorem (as presented by Kleene)[65] besides the result that the predicates

$$(y)\overline{T}_1(x, x, y) \text{ and } (\exists y)T_1(x, x, y)$$

are non-recursive? Someone would perhaps want to say that it also contains the following conclusion: 'There is no decision procedure for these predicates; they are undecidable.' But this is no mathematical conclusion, it is just another reading of the same mathematical result in the prose of meta-mathematics.

The function of Church's thesis, for these kinds of negative results, is to give them a more suggestive reading as results about undecidability (when they are really technical results about recursive unsolvability). This reading misleads when it is claimed to express the 'epistemological significance' of the results on the basis of the 'truth of Church's thesis'.

'But does the notion of Turing computability not capture the intuitive notion of computability according to an algorithm?' In a certain sense, yes, but not in the sense that the definition of the technical/mathematical concept of Turing computability is somehow justified on the basis of some pre-existing and independent 'intuitive concept' of mechanical computability. The notion of Turing computability was defined on the basis of the meta-mathematical methods and techniques for constructing the systems for syntactical representation discussed in the foregoing section. This mathematical practice is the conceptual foundation for the notion of Turing computability. The 'intuitions' of mathematicians about the mechanical calculability of functions were imprinted on them by the methods and techniques of Hilbert's meta-mathematics. For this reason, the equivalence of Turing computability and recursiveness is a purely mathematical result that does not support any epistemological thesis.

It is important to note that a Turing machine is a *mathematical* system of rules for operating with expressions. The rules are called 'mechanical', but this employment of the word 'mechanical' is not opposed to mathematical; it does not mean physical or pre-mathematical. The forms of use of the expressions are mathematical ones. For instance, it is said that the computations can have 'arbitrary finite length', but this concept of 'length' is not physical length, i.e. length that we could, in general, determine by actual counting and empirical observation. It is the notion of length connected with the purely mathematical concept of a finite sequence.

This, in turn, does not mean that Turing machines are idealizations of actual, physical machines. Turing machines are formal systems. The difficulty here, as elsewere, is to avoid confusion of the logical foundation of the concept and a source of inspiration for its construction. What misleads is the 'intuitive picture' of a Turing machine which comes out in the prose used in connection with Turing machines, i.e. 'machine', 'input', 'output', 'tape', 'internal state', etc. The connection with actual machines suggested by these expressions is not a logical connection. 'A Turing machine which calculates products' refers to a formal representation of an arithmetical operation, a system of rules which human beings can follow in order to calculate products.[66] As already remarked in part 1 of this book, it is a misleading analogy behind the conception of a Turing machine (or a program) as the agent of an activity of calculating. The distinction which is sometimes made between 'human computability' and 'mechanical computability', as two species of computability, is based on this false analogy.

This analogy is even worse when it is used in the opposite direction, i.e. when the human activity of calculating is conceived as the execution of a program implemented in the human mind. This idea is behind the nonsensical question: 'Is Church's thesis true about the human mind?'[67]

It may be tempting to think that the idea of a computation, which cannot be physically realized but which is finite, is epistemologically more acceptable than the idea of a computation involving an infinite number of steps. But it is a mistaken thought, since the two ideas involve the same conceptual mistake when they are compared in this way. The technical notion of computability which applies to functions is conceived, on this way of thinking, as though it were somehow a continuous extension of the ordinary notion of actual computability. But it is a different concept, which, though, has *applications* to actual numerical calculability. The definition of a recursive function may yield a technique which can be used in practice for finding the numerical value of the function for certain arguments. However, what makes *the function* computable is not the existence of such techniques, but the ways it is defined and operated with as a function in the calculus of functions. The reason for 'accepting' processes of computation involving any finite number of steps, no matter how large, is to obtain a notion of computability that applies to functions uniformly in their arguments.

According to Gödel: 'Recursive functions have the important

property that, for each set of values of the arguments, the value of the function can be computed by a finite procedure.'[68] The notion of 'finite' occurring here is of course the pure mathematical notion. So it is clear that the problems with the notion of computability discussed here are closely connected with the confusion of the different senses of 'finite' discussed in section 5. The word 'finite' is used in the technical mathematical sense which we find in the calculus of finite sequences and in the theory of finite cardinal numbers. The 'finite' as what can be actually realized as a totality of individual things is conceived as just a special case of the technical mathematical notion, on the grounds that the latter has *applications* to finite sets and sequences of actual things. But, as explained in section 5, the 'finite', in this sense, is a *different* concept which is in a certain sense prior to the technical/mathematical notion. Actual computations, calculations, lists, proofs, etc., performed and constructed by humans, are finite in this sense, even if they are computations in the calculus of infinite sequences.

Since the pure mathematical notion of 'finite' is taken as the fundamental notion, the rules governing the talk of 'finite processes of computation' in mathematical logic are the rules of the mathematical theory of finite sequences, and not the rules for our notion of computation as it is performed in actual human practices (with or without the help of computers). This talk is felt to make sense against the background of the extensional picture of these 'idealized finite processes of computation' as being a series of individual computational steps. So we may also express the misconception involved here by saying that the extensional view of the mathematical notions of a finite sequence and a finite set is as mistaken as the extensional view of infinite sets and sequences.

The opposite view, the idea that the mathematics of the finite, conceived extensionally, is epistemologically safe ground, was the fundamental idea behind Hilbert's finitism. Hilbert argued[69] for this idea from a naturalistic point of view, where the different senses of 'finite' were assimilated, i.e. from the point of view of applied mathematics, where the mathematical concept of the finite was used as fundamental. It is strange that this idea has been so generally accepted – even among those who are otherwise opposed to Hilbert's views (including the modern intuitionists and proof theorists, who conceive of intuitionistic methods and notions as *extending* those of the finitary point of view).

There is a primitive recursive function $f(x)$ and a number n such that the numerical value of f(n) is not only unknown, but cannot be determined. But there is obviously also a sense in which it is correct to say that 'there is a unique number which is the numerical value of f(n)'. According to the extensional view, this numerical value of f(n) exists as an individual number, an 'abstract object', but one which we cannot actually determine. Now, if we reject the extensional view we seem to be forced to equate the existence of the numerical value of the function with the practical possibility of actually determining it according to some technique for numerical calculation. But then, must we not also reject the statement that there is a unique number which is the numerical value of f(n), or, what amounts to the same thing, that f(x) is a well-defined numerical function?

Suppose that someone said that he had defined a primitive recursive function with the remarkable property that the function has no numerical value for certain arguments. Our reaction to that information would not be 'That's sensational!' but rather, 'You must be mistaken, you cannot get anything like that if you apply the rules for primitive recursive functions correctly.' There is no *mathematical* problem about whether there are primitive recursive functions that have no values for certain arguments. The proposition that a primitive recursive function has a uniquely determined value for each argument does not express a 'mathematical truth' in the same sense as the mathematical statements that can be verified by proof or calculation. It is a proposition of the logical grammar for functional expressions. It expresses an essential feature of the way in which we operate with expressions for functions in recursive arithmetic. For instance, we may introduce a constant k as the numerical value of f(n) (e.g. 'let f(n) = k, then . . .'), we may operate with k as a constant, we may substitute k for number variables, etc.

For the same reason, there is no mathematical problem, to be solved by proof or calculation, as to whether an instance of the schema of primitive recursion really defines a function, i.e. whether 'there exists a unique function satisfying certain recursion equations'. The method for defining functions by primitive recursion was a new form of use of functional expressions, a new concept of numerical functions – new in the sense that it is not reducible to other mathematical notions. There is no further 'justification' of this concept beyond the fact that it exists as a practice of calculating with expressions for numerical functions. Part of 'accepting' this practice of calculation is to 'accept' the statement that there is a unique function satisfying an instance of the schema of primitive recursion – not, however, as a hypothesis about some hidden reality to which the expressions in the schema refer, but as a statement of the logical grammar of the symbolism of primitive recursive functions.

As is well known, the results of straightforward attempts to justify definition by primitive recursion on the basis of a proof by induction are 'circular justifications', which is what generally happens when one tries to justify or define a logical form.

Frege, who conceived a logical form (or a concept) as a function, also made the connected mistake of conceiving the statement about the existence of a function satisfying an instance of the schema of primitive recursion to be a mathematical proposition to be proved. He objected to H. Grassmann's recursive definition of the sum a + b of two numbers on the grounds that the definition was not justified by a proof of the existence and uniqueness of the function defined.[70] Frege's attitude was connected to his demand for a *reduction* of the basic arithmetical operation to something else.[71]

In what sense, then, is the numerical value of f(n) determined by the rule defining the function? For certain values of the number variable x, it may be literally possible to determine the value of f(x) (even if no one has worked it out). When one says, in the general case, that the value of f(x) is determined for each x, with reference to the recursive rule defining the function, one is employing the expression 'is determined' in a figurative sense. One is alluding to formal similarities between conceptually different situations. On the extensional view one takes this latter employment of the expression 'is determined' nevertheless to be the literal one, but with the difference that it is used about another 'ideal or abstract realm of things', where all values of the function are somehow already determined, but beyond our reach. The conceptual difference is transformed into a 'factual' or 'ontological' one.

In the literal sense the numerical value of f(n) is not determined before it is actually calculated, and that the numerical value of f(n) *can* be determined means that there is a technique for actually working it out. But to say in the figurative sense that all numerical values are determined, or can be determined, by the rule defining the function, *is to say nothing more than that the rule defines a function*, the function is a 'well-defined' primitive recursive function. We recognize the rule as an instance of the schema of primitive recursion; we operate with f(x) as we operate with primitive recursive functions, etc. On the extensional view the assimilation of these different senses of 'is determined' makes it look as though the function itself had worked out all its numerical values.

We operate with f(n) *as though* we could literally run through any finite number of computational steps; we substitute f(n) for number variables *as though* the value of f(n) could be literally determined; we talk about the numerical value of f(n) *as though* it actually existed. Here 'as though' means: using rules that we employ in those cases where the value of the function *can* be literally determined, rules which *can* be verified by numerical calculation in some of these cases.

The usual explanations of a function, for instance a function whose arguments and values are numbers, as a mapping of numbers on numbers or as a correlation of numbers, are usually based on the extensional picture.[72] What is conceptually important is that functions (like sets) are a separate form of use of mathematical expressions, a form of use which cannot be reduced to or defined in terms of rules for operating with individual numbers. For instance, the function $y = f(x)$ defined by the equation $y = 2x$ is not explained as a correlation of individual numbers in the infinite list $(1, 2)$, $(2, 4)$, $(3, 6)$, . . ., because this is not literally a list of correlated individual numbers but another expression for the function.

In the literal sense of 'is determined', one would perhaps agree if we say: the fact that the value of a function is determined can be completely expressed as a computation on paper (or on a computer). My point is that a corresponding claim is true about the other sense in which 'f(n) is determined', though it cannot generally be expressed in terms of numerical calculations, but is rather completely manifest in our ways of operating with expressions for functions and finite sequences.

Expressions for 'infinite objects' such as sets and functions do not represent entities in some transcendent realm which are only partially or indirectly accessible to us. There is nothing (by necessity) hidden about the infinite or ideal objects of mathematics. This is just the way it looks before a certain problem has been solved, before certain expressions have been given a precise mathematical sense. It is the way it looks when our understanding of the problem is based on analogies with other situations, which may be of a conceptually different kind despite similarities in linguistic form. In the problem situation we tend to think as though the solution to the problem already exists somewhere, only not here with us, or as though the precise sense of the expressions (e.g. of 'computability') is there to be found before it is created through the invention of a method or a technique which determines the sense. This is to think as though new notions, methods, and practices in mathematics were not really new, but only new to us.

NOTES

1 LANGUAGE, MIND, AND MACHINES

1 This calculus conception of language is a special case of the more general view of language which Roy Harris calls 'the myth of the language machine'. In R. Harris, *The Language Machine*, (Cornell University Press, New York, 1987), the historical origin and evolution of this view is explored.

2 These features of the calculus conception of language are discussed in my paper 'On the concept of language in some recent theories of meaning', Synthese, 79 (1989), 51–98, and in my book *Undersökningar i Matematikens Filosofi* (Bokförlaget Thales, Stockholm, 1988), as well as throughout the present work.

3 For a critical exposition of the conceptual incoherence of pragmatics in this respect, see Pär Segerdahl, E*n kritik av den logiska ordningen i pragmatiken*, Department of Linguistics, Uppsala University, 1988.

4 This is connected with various 'negative results' in modern philosophy of language on 'underdetermination', 'indeterminacy of translation', 'scepticism about rule-following', the impossibility of 'full-blooded theories of meaning', and so on.

5 In Merrill B. Hintikka and Jaakko Hintikka, *Investigating Wittgenstein* (Basil Blackwell, Oxford, 1986), and in Jaakko Hintikka, 'On the development of the model-theoretic viewpoint in logical theory', Synthese 77 1988, 1–36.

6 I do not want to say that this is necessarily to Hilbert's disadvantage. Some of Frege's philosophical ideas were certainly becoming obsolete, especially in his philosophy of mathematics. Frege could not appreciate that *some* of the things in the formalist viewpoint were good. But I doubt that Hilbert's repudiation of some of Frege's views was based on well-thought-out philosophical reasons. It is much more likely that he was guided by his good instinct for what was fruitful for mathematics.

7 In L.E.J. Brouwer, *Collected Works*, vol. 1, ed. A. Heyting (Amsterdam: North-Holland, 1974), pp. 6, 447ff. I do not want to suggest that Brouwer is a major figure in the development of later philosophy of language and philosophy of mind. I am taking Brouwer as an example simply because he is so explicit about certain ways of thinking

concerning the relationship between language and thought, ways of thinking which occur in current philosophy in a more veiled language.

8 Brouwer, *Collected Works*, p. 447.

9 ibid., p. 448.

10 ibid., p. 6.

11 ibid., p. 447.

12 See for instance J.-F. Lyotard, *The Differend, Phrases in Dispute*, G. Van Den Abbeele (trans.) (Manchester University Press, Manchester, 1988).

13 Cf. Jerry A. Fodor, *The Language of Thought* (Thomas Y. Crowell., New York, 1975).

14 This is related to the problem of the conceptual role of the 'mathematical prose' and the 'readings' of mathematical symbolism in mathematics, which will be a main theme in the third part of this book.

15 Brouwer, *Collected Works*, p. 6.

16 Thus, John Searle explains: 'I think of Intentional states, processes, and events as part of our biological life history in the way that digestion, growth, and the secretion of bile are part of our biological life history.' (*Intentionality, An Essay in the Philosophy of Mind*, Cambridge University Press, Cambridge 1983, p. 160).

17 Daniel C. Dennett writes (*Brainstorms*, Harvester Press, Hassocks, 1979, p. xii): 'a philosophical theory of the mind is supposed to be a consistent set of answers to the most general questions one can ask about minds, "are there any?", "are they physical?", "what happens in them?" and "how do we know anything about them?" ', and on p. xiv he continues: 'Philosophy of mind is unavoidable. As soon as one asserts anything substantive about anything mental, one *ipso facto* answers at least by implication one or more of the traditional questions and thus places oneself in the camp of an ism.' Fortunately, this is not true at all.

18 Dennett, *Brainstorms*, p. 82.

19 ibid., p. 83.

20 Kevin T. Kelly, 'Artificial intelligence and effective epistemology', in *Aspects of Artificial Intelligence*. ed. James H. Fetzer (Kluwer Academic Publishers, Dordrecht, 1988), pp. 309–22.

21 Richard Montague, 'Universal grammar', *Theoria* 36, 1970, 373–98.

22 Donald Davidson, 'Semantics for natural languages', In D. Davidson, *Inquiries into Truth and Interpretation* (Clarendon Press, Oxford, 1984), pp. 55–64.

23 This point is discussed by Stuart Shanker in 'The decline and fall of the mechanist metaphor' in Rainer Born (ed.), *Artificial Intelligence, The Case Against* (Croom Helm, London, 1987), pp. 72–131.

24 Dennett, *Brainstorms*, p. 16.

25 Margaret Boden seems to sympathize with this idea in *Artificial Intelligence and Natural Man* (Harvester Press, Hassocks, 1977).

26 John R. Searle, 'Minds, brains, and programs', *The Behavioral and Brain Sciences*, vol. 3, 1980, 417–24, 450–7.

27 James H. Moor, 'The pseudorealization fallacy and the Chinese room argument', in Fetzer (ed.) *Aspects of Artificial Intelligence*, 35–53.

28 ibid., p. 43.

29 D. Hilbert, 'Axiomatisches Denken', *Mathematische Annalen* 78, 1918, 405–15.

30 Hermann Grassmann, *Die Ausdehnungslehre von 1844 oder Die lineale Ausdehnungslehre* (Leipzig, 1878).

31 These ideas in Hilbert's philosophy of mathematics will be discussed in greater detail in the last part of the present work.

32 Jean van Heijenoort (ed.), *From Frege to Gödel: A Source Book in Mathematical Logic, 1879–1931.* (Harvard University Press, Cambridge, Mass., 1977), pp. 379, 381.

33 See Part 3, section 7 below.

34 The most recent trend in AI, so-called 'connectionism', is no exception to this dualism, although one rejects the view of thinking as being symbolic processes, and instead emphasizes physical and causal mechanisms.

35 A.M. Turing, 'Computing machinery and intelligence', *Mind*, vol. 59, no. 236, 1950, 433–60.

36 William J. Rapaport, 'Syntactic semantics: foundations of computational natural-language understanding', in Fetzer (ed.), *Aspects of Artificial Intelligence*, 81–131.

37 Do not think that I am here talking about the ordinary, mathematical sense of calculation as being an 'abstract entity', or about the algebraic rule as an 'abstract object'. This idea results from another misconception of the generality I am referring to.

38 I am not advocating a 'conventionalist view' of mathematics as founded in 'freely chosen conventions'. We are not free to let anything mean anything. When there are alternatives to choose between (different methods of proof, rules of computation, etc.) something is already prepared in the language of mathematics, a logical order is already in existence in the use of the signs and symbols that makes it possible for us to define the alternatives, and *that* order is not freely chosen. For instance, we may choose to reject, like the intuitionists, the law of the excluded middle as a rule of proof, but the fact that there *are* applications of it which we (and the intuitionists) can recognize as such is not dependent on our discretion. The existence of (possible) conventions is founded in the existence of forms of use of symbols in the language of mathematics. These forms of use do not exist as possibilities (of choice) unless they are actualized as practices.

There is no 'ism' in the jargon of the philosophy of mathematics that will do justice to the 'view' I am here taking on mathematics and, in a certain sense, there never can be. Mathematics itself is not an application or realization of some one philosophical ism.

39 Stuart C. Shapiro, 'Representing numbers in semantic networks: Prolegomena', *Proc. 5th Internat. Joint Conference on AI (IJCAI-77; MIT)*, (Morgan Kaufmann, Los Altos), p. 284.

40 Rapaport, 'Syntactic semantics', p. 93.

41 Fred Dretske, 'Machines and the mental', *Proc. and Addresses of the American Philosophical Assoc.* 59, 23–33.

42 John R. Searle, *Minds, Brains and Science* (Harvard University Press, Cambridge, Mass., 1984), p. 31.

43 Bruce G. Buchanan, 'Artificial intelligence as an experimental science', in Fetzer, (ed.), *Aspects of Artificial Intelligence*, pp. 209–50.

44 Thus, Buchanan (ibid., p. 232) explains: 'Even if the *mechanisms* underlying human performance are inexplicable in the vocabulary of computer programs, the *behaviour* of human problem solvers may be adequately reproduced by programs.' The trouble with this statement is not so much what it says about the prospects of computer technology (which may be true in some sense), but the machine conception of human performances which it presupposed in this 'adequately reproduced'.

45 This is related to a common confusion of ideological criticism of the negative and problematic effects of the development of computer technology on the one hand, and the philosophical investigation and exposition of the conceptual confusions of AI on the other. The philosophical investigation is concerned with the boundary between sense and nonsense, with what is logically possible, with what is possible in principle; and not with what is technically or empirically possible or what is desirable and useful. The philosophical investigation is concerned, one might say, with what it makes sense to desire or expect or fear about this technology at all.

The criticism of unsound development and application of computer technology, which confuses these things, is playing into the hands of its opponent, because this confusion is a characteristic feature of some of the most unsound application projects as well as of the pseudo-philosophical claims of AI. People are sometimes persuaded to give up or to reorganize good practices in order to use computers on grounds which are conceptually suspect but which may appear compelling. ('It is only a question of time before computers "*can replace*" this or that human capacity, so let us reorganize . . .'). Conversely, on the basis of confusing ways of describing existing computer projects and experiments it is claimed that empirical evidence and justification are already in existence for some of the boldest pseudo-philosophical claims of AI.

46 Compare this with the situation in the philosophy of language where fragments of ordinary language are explained as species of formal systems.

47 There are problems similar to the problem of 'implementing intuition' in the discussion concerning the possibility of mechanizing so-called 'tacit knowledge'.

48 R.J. Nelson, 'Church's thesis and cognitive science', *Notre Dame Journal of Formal Logic*, vol. 28, no. 4, Oct. 1987, 581–614.

49 Dennett, *Brainstorms* p. 80.

50 This idea rests on the received (but questionable) interpretation of Church's thesis in mathematical logic, which will be discussed in Part 3, section 10.

51 Different manifestations of this 'mythology of rules' are expounded in G.P. Baker and P.M.S. Hacker, *Language, Sense, and Nonsense* (Basil Blackwell, Oxford, 1984).

52 In the *Remarks on the Philosophy of Psychology*, Wittgenstein says about Turing's 'machines' 'These machines are humans who calculate.' This is discussed by Stuart Shanker in 'Wittgenstein versus Turing on the

nature of Church's thesis', *Notre Dame Journal of Formal Logic*, vol. 28, no. 4, Oct. 1987, 615–49.

53 This confusion is behind the following argument by Buchanan ('Artificial Intelligence', p. 232): 'AI programs have obviously been successful at capturing some elements of good problem solving performance – on tasks that require intelligence when people do them.' 'When people do them!' As though it were the identical acts, or acts in the same sense, with the only difference that the agents are humans in one case and computer programs in the other.

54 Saul Kripke, *Wittgenstein on Rules and Private Language*, (Basil Blackwell, Oxford, 1982). Kripke's argument for 'rule-scepticism' will be further discussed in Part 2, section 11.

2 NOTIONS OF LANGUAGE AND THEORIES OF MEANING

1 An exception in the predominance of naturalistic theories of language is the theory of meaning of Per Martin-Löf *Intuitionistic Type Theory* (Napoli: Bibliopolis, 1984), and 'Truth of a proposition, evidence of a judgement, validity of a proof', *Synthese*, vol. 73 1987, 407–20, which is intended as (what I shall here call) an *'a priori* theory of meaning'.

2 W.v.O. Quine, *Word and Object*, (MIT Press, Cambridge, Mass., 1980), pp. 3–4. In this statement of Quine's it is understood that science consists of modern mathematics and natural science, the latter conceived in the perspective of modern empiricism; and with that understanding, Quine's statement constitutes an excellent example of what I mean by 'the naturalistic attitude' in this book.

3 Cf. the criticism of naturalistic philosophy in E. Husserl, 'Philosophie als strenge Wissenschaft', *Logos*, vol. I, 1910–11, 289–341. Translated as 'Philosophy as rigorous science', in Husserl, E., *Phenomenology and the Crisis of Philosophy*, trans. Q. Lauer, (Harper & Row, New York, 1965), pp. 71–147.

4 The affinity of Frege's logical investigations with the Kantian tradition has been elaborated by several authors recently, for instance by Leila Haaparanta, 'Analysis as the method of logical discovery: Some remarks on Frege and Husserl', *Synthese*, vol. 77, 1988, 73–97.

5 Arthur Pap, *An Introduction to the Philosophy of Science* (The Free Press, New York, 1962), p. 5.

6 It could be said that the naturalistic attitude, as a philosophical position, amounts to taking certain current scientific methods – such as the predicate calculus, set theory, game theory, behavioural psychology, classical physics, computer science, neurophysiology – as being the ultimate foundation. This means making this relativism and scepticism into an unavoidable and permanent 'philosophical' position that one just has to live with (postmodernism). What was felt by Frege and Husserl to be the acute problem, the motive for the philosophical investigation, is seen as though it were the philosophical solution.

7 D. Davidson, 'Truth and meaning', in J. Kulas *et al.* (eds), *Philosophy, Language and Artificial Intelligence* (Kluwer Academic Publishers, Dordrecht, 1988), p. 105.

8 This is what linguists call 'giving semantic representations'.

9 Davidson, 'Truth and Meaning', p. 105.

10 This difference between *formalization* in the sense of applying a formal technique for paraphrasing or representing sentences for the purpose of formal theory-construction, or computer implementation, on the one hand, and in the sense of the articulation of logical form as the conceptually essential features on the other, is an often forgotten difference. This is perhaps the most essential point in the difference between *a priori* and naturalistic theories of language.

11 Michael Dummett, 'What is a theory of meaning?', in *Mind and Language*, ed. Samuel Guttenplan, (Clarendon Press, Oxford, 1975), pp. 97–138.

12 The choice of a word such as 'full-blooded' does, however, indicate a spirit of doing philosophy that was foreign to Frege, Husserl, and Wittgenstein.

13 The notion of 'logical syntax' of Wittgenstein's *Tractatus* was therefore an essentially different conception from the (naturalistic) idea of syntax of Carnap and the logical empiricists, which was said to be the science of expressions and their forms 'in abstraction from their content'.

14 For instance in his paper 'On the infinite', in van Heijenoort (ed.), *From Frege to Gödel, A Source Book in Mathematical Logic, 1879–1931* (Harvard University Press, Cambridge, Mass., 1977).

15 In his 'Autobiography' (in *The Philosophy of Rudolf Carnap*, P.A. Schilpp (ed.), 1964.) Carnap explained the purpose of his terms 'object language' and 'metalanguage': 'Whereas Hilbert intended his metamathematics only for the special purpose of proving the consistency of a mathematical system formulated in the object language, I aimed at the construction of a general theory of linguistic forms.'

16 As has been argued by Quine, from a strict naturalistic viewpoint there is no justification for the idea of '*the* linguistic meaning of an expression' in this sense. What remains then for 'meaning-theory' is only the study of 'linguistic behaviour' associated with the expressions of a system of conventional notations by the methods of empirical science. But the results of such a strict causal investigation are bound to be hypothetical and underdetermined by empirical evidence.

17 Husserl relied on traditional grammatical categories in the *a priori* theory of meaning which he presents in his *Logische Untersuchungen* (vol. II, part 1, ch. 4 in the revised version of the second edition of 1913). He uses categories such as 'nominal matter', 'adjectival matter', 'propositional matter'. Bar-Hillel, who has contributed much to the confusion of linguistic and philosophical perspectives, is, however, correct when he remarks: 'we must certainly ask ourselves what Husserl's meaning categories are supposed to be . . . these categories turn out to be nothing else but the objective counterparts of the grammatical categories that were regarded as standard in Husserl's time (at least for Indo-European languages)!' in 'Husserl's conception of a purely logical grammar', in Y. Bar-Hillel, *Aspects of Language, Essays and Lectures on Philosophy of Language, Linguistic Philosophy and Methodology of Linguistics* (North-Holland, Amsterdam 1970).

18 Ludwig Wittgenstein, *Philosophical Investigations* (Basil Blackwell, Oxford 1974), §107.
19. Parts of the rest of this essay have appeared in my paper 'On the concept of language in some recent theories of meaning', *Synthese* 79, 1989, 51–98. Those parts appear here in revised form.
20 G. Evans and J. McDowell (eds), *Truth and Meaning. Essays in Semantics* (Clarendon Press, Oxford, 1976).
21 Dag Prawitz, 'Dummett on a theory of meaning and its impact on logic', in B.M. Taylor, (ed.), *Michael Dummett. Contributions to Philosophy* (Martinus Nijhoff Publishers, Dordrecht 1987), pp. 117–65.
22 Michael Dummett, 'Reply to Dag Prawitz', in Taylor *Michael Dummett*, p. 282.
23 R. Montague, 'Universal grammar', *Theoria* 36, 1970, 373–98.
24 D. Davidson, 'Semantics for natural languages', in D. Davidson, *Inquiries into Truth and Interpretation* (Clarendon Press, Oxford, 1984), p. 59.
25 A. Tarski, 'The semantic conception of truth', *Philosophy and Phenomenological Research*, 4, p. 346.
26 ibid., p. 347.
27 Tarski explained: 'Whoever wishes, in spite of all difficulties, to pursue the semantics of colloquial language with the help of exact methods will be driven first to undertake the thankless task of a reform of this language. He will find it necessary to define its structure, to overcome the ambiguity of the terms which occur in it, and finally to split the language into a series of languages of greater and greater extent, each of which stands in the same relation to the next in which a formalized language stands to its metalanguage. It may, however be doubted whether the language of everyday life, after being 'rationalized' in this way, would still preserve its naturalness and whether it would not rather take on the characteristic features of the formalized languages' (A. Tarski, 'The concept of truth in formalized languages', in *Logic, Semantics, Metamathematics*, Clarendon Press, Oxford, 1956, 152–278).
28 Some people like to call this familiarity 'tacit knowledge' and to speak about it as though we have to do with a new, by science and philosophy hitherto unimagined (or at least neglected) species of knowledge, which is non-theoretical and non-representable, but it is a kind of knowledge which one is nevertheless engaged in defining, explaining, and justifying. The term 'tacit knowledge' is a technical philosophical term which is too coloured by its role in philosophical battles against positivistic and mechanistic views to be useful.
29 The example is due to T. Winograd, 'Is realism for real? – A response to John Perry's seminar', *CSLI Monthly*, vol. 2, no. 5, 1987.
30 Although considerations of application and interpretation may very well have been involved in the process of inventing or constructing the calculus. Cf. the predicate calculus as a purely formal calculus as we have it today, and the considerations in the process of constructing it and formulating it in the past.
31 Prawitz, 'Dummett on a theory of meaning', p. 128.
32 With the exception perhaps of Davidson's theory and certain linguistic

215

semantic theories, such as the one proposed by J.J. Katz and J.A. Fodor in 'The structure of a semantic theory', *Language*, vol. 38, 1962, 170–210.

33 Thus Beardsley explains, 'every declarative sentence has a *primary meaning* by virtue of its grammatical form: it presents a complex of meanings of such a sort that it can be said to be true or false. In short, it is a statement' (M.C. Beardsley, *Aesthetics, Problems in The Philosophy of Criticism*, Hackett, Indianapolis, 1981, p. 122).

34 This is presumably what Wittgenstein was thinking about when he wrote: ' "Mathematical logic" has completely deformed the thinking of mathematicians and of philosophers, by setting up a superficial interpretation of the forms of our everyday language as an analysis of the structures of facts. Of course, in this it has only continued to build on the Aristotelian logic' (*Remarks on the Foundations of Mathematics*, 2nd edn., Basil Blackwell, Oxford, 1989, p. 300).

35 Katz and Fodor explain:'Grammars seek to describe the structure of a sentence IN ISOLATION FROM ITS POSSIBLE SETTINGS IN LINGUISTIC DISCOURSE (WRITTEN OR VERBAL) OR IN NON-LINGUISTIC CONTEXTS (SOCIAL OR PHYSICAL). The justification which permits the grammarian to study sentences in abstraction from settings in which they have occurred or might occur is simply that the fluent speaker is able to construct and recognize syntactically well-formed sentences without recourse to information about settings' (J.J. Katz and J.A. Fodor, 'The structure of a semantic theory', *Language*, vol. 39, 1963, p. 173).

36 In G.P. Baker and P.M.S. Hacker, *Language, Sense, and Nonsense* (Basil Blackwell, Oxford, 1984), there is a detailed account of how the sense/-force distinction and related distinctions are founded in methods for paraphrasing sentences.

37 Pär Segerdahl, in *En Kritik av Den Logiska Ordningen inom Pragmatiken* (Department of Linguistics, Uppsala University, Uppsala, 1988), deals with these problems in detail. I owe much in this section to the work of Segerdahl.

38 Stephen C. Levinson, *Pragmatics*, (Cambridge University Press, Cambridge, 1983, p. 114). An 'implicature' is meant to be a kind of inference which, unlike logical inference, is based not only on 'the semantic content' of sentences, but also on 'some specific assumptions about the cooperative nature of ordinary verbal interaction'.

39 W.v.O. Quine, *Word and Object*, (MIT Press, Cambridge, Mass. 1960).

40 Hilbert, 'On the Infinite', p. 373.

41 ibid., p. 379.

42 This will be discussed in greater detail in Part 3 below.

43 P. Martin-Löf, 'Truth of a proposition, evidence of a judgement, validity of a proof', *Synthese*, vol. 73, 1987, 407–20.

44 Prawitz, 'Dummett on a theory of meaning' p. 129.

45 This will be discussed in Part 3 below.

46 Tarski, 'The concept of truth in Formalized Languages'.

47 D. Davidson (1970, p. 55).

48 M. Dummett, *What do I know when I know a language?*, Lecture held at the Centenary Celebrations of Stockholm University, Stockholm University, 1978, p. 4.

49 S.A. Kripke, *Wittgenstein on Rules and Private Language* (Basil Blackwell, Oxford, 1982).

50 I should perhaps say 'Kripke's interpretation of Wittgenstein's remarks on following a rule'. However, many are those who have shown that Kripke's interpretation is a gross misunderstanding of Wittgenstein, for instance G. P. Baker and P.M.S. Hacker, in *Scepticism, Rules and Language* (Basil Blackwell, Oxford, 1984). I shall not be concerned with this exegetical problem further.

51 Kripke, *Wittgenstein*, p. 28.

52 Thus Chomsky declares: "From now on I will consider a *language* to be a set (finite or infinite) of sentences, each finite in length and constructed out of a finite set of elements. All natural languages in their spoken or written form are languages in this sense, since each natural language has a finite number of phonemes (or letters in its alphabet)'. (*Syntactic Structures*, Mouton, The Hague, 1976, p. 13).

53 A. Heyting, *Intuitionism: An Introduction* (North-Holland, Amsterdam, 1956), p. 8.

54 P. Martin-Löf, 'Truths of a proposition, evidence of a judgement, validity of a proof', *Synthese*, 73, 1987, 407–20.

3 FORM AND CONTENT IN MATHEMATICS

1 See Stuart Shanker, *Wittgenstein and the Turning-Point in the Philosophy of Mathematics* (Croom Helm, London, 1987, chapter 5).

2 This employment of word-language has been very much stimulated by the conspicuous position that popular science has in our times.

3 Some of the ideas presented in this part have appeared in my book '*Undersökningar i matematikens filosofi*' (Investigations in the Philosophy of Mathematics) (Bokförlaget Thales, Stockholm, 1988) (only in Swedish).

4 'Unter einer "Menge" verstehen wir jede Zusammenfassung M von bestimmten wohlunterschieden Objecten unserer Anschauung oder unseres Denkens (welche die "Elemente" von M genannten werden) zu einem Ganzen'. Georg Cantor, *Gesammelte Abhandlungen* (Springer-Verlag, Berlin, 1932; 1895, p. 282).

5 Hao Wang, *From Mathematics to Philosophy* (Humanities Press, New York, 1974), p. 182.

6 ibid, p. 186.

7 According to Wang (ibid., pp. 324–6), Gödel has explicitly expressed this opinion.

8 Michael Dummett, *Elements of Intuitionism* (Clarendon Press, Oxford, 1977), p. 55.

9 The criticism of various ideas about the foundations of mathematics presented in this book should not be confused with the intuitionistic and ultra-intuitionistic critiques, which involve extreme forms of revisionism *vis-à-vis* existing mathematics. There is no revisionism whatsoever in the views presented here. The results of our investigation can neither refute nor justify any *mathematical* result or method. The investigation deals with problems that cannot be settled by doing mathematics.

10 Cantor, *Gesammelte Abhandlungen*, (1883, pp. 181–2).

11 This is of course not contradicted by the fact that there are mathematical models of temporal phenomena or of processes of change. There is nothing temporal in the mathematical structure of the sequence of numbers by which we measure the hours of a day. When we say that the number 3 comes *immediately after* the number 2 in the natural number series, there is no temporal sense in this use of *'immediately after'*. It would not make sense to ask: 'How soon after?'

12 Cantor, op. cit. (1886, pp. 410–11).

13 This idea about 'linguistic entities', as opposed to 'non-linguistic' ones, which is so generally accepted in philosophy and linguistic theory today, is due to a misconception of the (logical) form of mathematical expressions as a physical, pre-mathematical structure. The idea originates in Hilbert's meta-mathematics and will be dealt with later in this essay.

14 L. Wittgenstein, *Tractatus Logico-Philosophicus*, D.F. Pears and B.F. McGuinness (trans.) (Routledge & Kegan Paul, London, 1961), §6.03.

15 Someone infatuated by the extensional picture may want to object that I am confusing 'use and mention', 'names and things named'. But the idea of 'numerals' as names standing in an external relation of 'denotation' to numbers as 'abstract objects' is an example of a misuse of the ontological interpretation arising from the confusion of a form as a function. It is based on the view of 'denotations' as the extension of a (propositional) function or a predicate. But this view would give rise to the questions 'How are the arguments of *this* function given or determined?', 'What is their logical form?' It may be possible to *represent* the form of the natural numbers as a function, but then, this is not the way natural numbers are conceived in ordinary propositions of elementary arithmetic.

16 In *Principia Mathematica*, vol. 1 (2nd edn, Cambridge, 1950, p. 37), Russell states this principle as follows: 'Whatever involves *all* of a collection must not be one of the collection' and: 'If, provided that a certain collection had a total, it would have members only definable in terms of that total, then the said collection has no total.'

17 It might perhaps be said that something of this comes out in the 'non-constructive' character of an impredicative definition, namely in the feature of such 'definitions' that what is being defined must somehow already be in existence. If a mathematical object can only be defined in terms of the totality of which it is a member, it must already be there. What really must be in existence is a form of use of expressions, because a *new* form of use of expressions can only come into existence as a new practice, and not by defining it within an old form of use.

18 It is within the same perspective that Gödel is said to have constructed a sentence that 'says about itself that it is unprovable'. The problems with the syntactical view of language will be further discussed in section 9.

19 For this logical difference between an operation and a function, see Wittgenstein's *Tractatus*, §5.2ff.

20 B. Russell, *Introduction to Mathematical Philosophy* (Allen & Unwin, London, 1919), p. 77.

21 ibid., p. 131.

22 In order not to become confused here, we must carefully distinguish between 'a class of actual things' and 'a picture of a class of things'. Russell is presumably using the word 'world' in such a way that the things in his scientific picture of the world are also 'things in the world'.

23 An earlier version of the theory of types of Per Martin-Löf (*Intuitionistic Type Theory*, Bibliopolis, Napoli, 1984) contained the axiom V ∈ V, with the reading: 'The type of all types V is an object of type V', which was shown to lead to a contradiction.

24 D. Hilbert, 'On the infinite', in J. van Heijenoort, *From Frege to Gödel: A Source Book in Mathematical Logic* (Harvard University Press, Cambridge, Mass., 1967), 369–92.

25 Brouwer, *Collected Works*, 72–97. H. Poincaré, 'Les mathématiques et la logique', *Revue de métaphysique et de morale*, vol. 13, 1905, 815–35, vol. 14 (1906), 17–34, 294–317.

Brouwer and Poincaré were, it seems to me, correct *in their criticism* on this point, but the intuitionistic justification of induction which they proposed and which refers to our 'intuition' or our 'mind' was perhaps even worse than Hilbert's finitistic proposal. Despite their disagreement with Hilbert, they shared his belief in mathematics as a kind of natural science whose first principles must be epistemologically justified.

26 Brouwer, *Collected Works*, p. 93.

27 'Cette récurrence qui s'arrête dans le fini', J. Herbrand, *Recherches sur la théorie de la démonstration*, Travaux de la Société des Sciences et des Lettres de Varsovie, Classe III sciences mathématiques et physiques, no. 33, 1930, p. 4.

28 This is a mistake which is still waiting to be generally recognized. And it is important that it be recognized because a wealth of confusions and conceptual problems in modern philosophy and linguistic theory are rooted in it.

29 Hilbert, 'The foundations of mathematics', in van Heijenoort, *From Frege to Gödel*, p. 473.

30 Hermann Weyl, 'Comments on Hilbert's second lecture on the foundations of mathematics', in van Heijenoort, ibid., 482–3.

31 Herbrand, On the consistency of arithmetic, in van Heijenoort, ibid., p. 622.

32 In D. Hilbert and P. Bernays, *Grundlagen der Mathematik I*, 2nd edn (Springer-Verlag, Berlin, 1968), p. 21.

33 This comes out also in Hilbert's statement that 'from the finitist point of view an existential proposition of the form "There exists a number having this or that property" has meaning only as a *partial proposition*, that is, as a part of a proposition that is more precisely determined but whose exact content is unessential for many applications' ('On the infinite', p. 378). It is clear that Hilbert thinks of the existential proposition as an 'infinite disjunction' which extends finite disjunctions.

34 In Hilbert and Bernays, *Grundlagen der Mathematik.*, p. 21, it is said: 'Was die genaue figürliche Beschaffenheit der Ziffern betrifft, so denken

wir uns . . . für diese einen gewissen Spielraum gelassen'. This 'Spielraum' is of course delimited by the requirement that the signs must be capable of signifying the natural numbers.

35 S.C. Kleene, *Introduction to Metamathematics* (North-Holland, Amsterdam, 1967), p. 195.

36 Hilbert, 'On the infinite', p. 377.

37 But there are of course *mathematical representations* of objects and structures in physical space.

38 Kleene, *Introduction to Metamathematics* p. 62.

39 There are of course non-technical uses of words such as 'reference', 'denote', etc., which are *not* based upon this referential picture – a fact which philosophers tend to forget.

40 Cf. Carnap's explanation: 'Whereas Hilbert intended his metamathematics only for the special purpose of proving the consistency of a mathematical system formulated in the object language, I aimed at the construction of a general theory of linguistic forms.' (Carnap, *Autobiography*).

41 J.R. Shoenfield, *Mathematical Logic* (Addison-Wesley, London, 1967), p. 6.

42 W.v.O. Quine, *Mathematical Logic*, revised edn (Harper & Row, New York, 1951), p. 23.

43 ibid., p. 23.

44 This is connected with the problem of the possibility of mechanizing 'symbol recognition'. Cf. K.M. Sayre, *Recognition: A Study in the Philosophy of Artificial Intelligence* (University of Notre Dame Press, Notre Dame, Indiana, 1965).

45 What may make it difficult to understand this notion of form is the common naturalistic employment of the words 'form' and 'formal' as signifying an external, physical structure of expressions or constructions, an employment of the words that has been very influential. The type/token distinction, for instance, is obviously based on this naturalistic notion of form. The type of an expression is conceived as a spatial, 'extra-linguistic' shape.

What I am calling 'logical form' and which is the structure of expressions that is essential in their use in mathematics would, on Hilbert's way of thinking, have been an 'ideal object' to be replaced by something 'real', viz. a physical structure. However, the fundamental mistake here is to think as though a logical form is a kind of thing or object externally related to the expression or construction having it, as though mathematical expressions such as numerals refer to their logical form. They *express* or *show* their logical form. The numeral SS0 shows, for instance, its place in the series of numerals, it does not state it or refer to it. And if it were asked:'How can the numeral SS0 "show" this?', the answer would be: 'By the way in which it is *used* in arithmetic.'

46 This fact has of course been successfully exploited by modern computer science. But that these applications of meta-matematical methods are possible does not justify the ideas connected with the notion of an object-language in mathematical logic.

47 That the idea of the existence of an object-language of a formal system

is unnecessary and misleading seems to have been pointed out for the first time by H.B. Curry ('Language, metalanguage and formal system', *The Philosophical Review*, vol. 59, 1950). However, Curry could not free himself from the view that the expressions used in mathematical logic stand in an external relation of reference or denotation to some kind of objects. He called them 'unspecified objects'.

48 Shoenfield, *Mathematical Logic*, p. 7.

49 Kleene uses this term. Another established term is 'syntactical object'. However, we must remember that this employment of 'formal' does not signify concrete, physical form and 'syntactical' has nothing to do with actual languages

50 In the theory of Turing-machines, finite automata, generative grammars, etc., these kinds of *mathematical calculi* are investigated.

51 Cf. Carnap's statement quoted in footnote 40.

52 Shoenfield *Mathematical Logic*, p. 126.

53 In the popular, mythological employments of Gödel's theorem, as in Douglas R. Hofstadter, *Gödel, Escher, Bach: An Eternal Golden Braid* (Harmondsworth, Penguin Books, 1982), the strategy is to assimilate the technical sense of 'expresses', which occurs in the reading of Gödel's theorem, with the ordinary senses of this word. The issue is discussed by Stuart Shanker in 'Wittgenstein's remarks on the significance of Gödel's theorem', in S.G. Shanker (ed.), *Gödel's Theorem in Focus* (Croom Helm, London, 1988).

54 Hilbert, 'On the infinite', p. 379.

55 Cf. the discussion of these ideas in part 1 of this book.

56 Shoenfield, *Mathematical Logic*, p. 107.

57 Hilary Putnam, *Mathematics, Matter and Method, Philosophical Papers, vol. I*, second edn. (Cambridge University Press, Cambridge, 1979), pp. 54–5.

58 For the sake of argument I am accepting Putnam's example with the naturalistic presupposition about the 'finiteness of the physical universe', although it is not necessary for the conceptual points I wish to make.

59 For this general concept of function (which was a basic notion for the logical systems developed by Frege, Russell and others), the existence of a method for finding the value of a function for a given argument was not essential. A function in this sense can even depend on an unsolved problem, while nevertheless being a well-defined function on the basis of the laws of classical formal logic. The importance of the problem of delimiting the 'computable functions' within this general class of functions was of course connected with Hilbert's finitism and with the (mistaken) idea that this general concept of function is a basic part of the logical foundations of ordinary mathematics.

60 As already remarked, the misconceptions here about the notion of function are parallel to ones about the notion of a set discussed earlier. The problem is a consequence of the extensional view of a numerical function as an 'ideal or infinite object', consisting of an 'infinite list' of correlated numbers which cannot be 'physically realized' as an actual list, but which is somehow an extension of actual lists.

61 Shoenfield, *Mathematical Logic*, p. 120.

62 In 1936 Church presented the thesis as a *definition* of the notion of 'an effectively calculable function'. But then he goes on to speculate about its justification as though it were a hypothesis. (A. Church, 'An unsolvable problem of elementary number theory', in M. Davis, *The Undecidable*, Raven Press, New York, 1965, p. 100.)

63 Hao Wang, *A Survey of Mathematical Logic* (North-Holland, Amsterdam, 1963), p. 87.

64 Shoenfield, *Mathematical Logic*, p. 119.

65 Kleene, *Introduction to Metamathematics*, p. 301.

66 It is in a sense correct to say that 'Turing machines cannot get broken' or that 'they do not consume electric energy' or that 'their life is unlimited', etc., but not as factual statements about 'abstract machines'. It is correct if it means that it *does not make sense* to apply these forms of description to mathematical notions, as though they were some kind of extraordinary physical and temporal phenomena.

67 Cf. the works of Dennett and Nelson quoted in section 11 of the first part of this book.

68 Kurt Gödel, 'On undecidable propositions of formal mathematical systems' (1934), in M. Davis (ed.), *The Undecidable* (Raven Press, New York) 1965, pp. 43–4.

69 See the beginning of Hilbert's paper 'On the infinite'.

70 G. Frege, *Die Grundlagen der Arithmetik* (Verlag von Wilhelm Koebner, Breslau, 1884), p. 8.

71 This is pointed out by Judson C. Webb, *Mechanism, Mentalism, and Metamathematics. An Essay on Finitism* (D. Reidel, Dordrecht, 1980), p. 45.

72 What has been misleading here have been the ideas about 'the arithmetization of mathematics', i.e. the picture of mathematics as one conceptual hierarchy built up 'from below'.

BIBLIOGRAPHY

Baker, G.P. and Hacker, P.M.S., *Scepticism, Rules and Language*, Basil Blackwell, Oxford, 1984.

Baker, G.P. and Hacker, P.M.S., *Language, Sense, and Nonsense*, Basil Blackwell, Oxford, 1984.

Bar-Hillel, Y., *Aspects of Language, Essays and Lectures on Philosophy of Language, Linguistic Philosophy and Methodology of Linguistics*, North-Holland, Amsterdam, 1970.

Beardsley, M.C., *Aesthetics, Problems in The Philosophy of Criticism*, Hackett, Indianapolis, 1981.

Boden, M., *Artificial Intelligence and Natural Man*, Harvester Press, Hassocks, 1977.

Born, R. (ed.), *Artificial Intelligence, The Case Against*, Croom Helm, London, 1987.

Brouwer, L.E.J., *Collected Works*, vol. 1, ed. A. Heyting, North-Holland, Amsterdam, 1974.

Buchanan, B.G., 'Artificial intelligence as an experimental science', in J.H. Fetzer (ed.), *Aspects of Artificial Intelligence*, Kluwer Academic Publishers, Dordrecht, 1988.

Cantor, G. *Gesammelte Abhandlungen*, Springer-Verlag, Berlin, 1932.

Carnap, R., 'Autobiography', in *The Philosophy of Rudolf Carnap*, P.A. Schilpp (ed.), Open Court, Illinois, 1964.

Chomsky, N., *Syntactic Structures*, Mouton, The Hague, 1976.

Church, A., 'An unsolvable problem of elementary number theory', in M. Davis, *The Undecidable*, Raven Press, New York, 1965.

Curry, H.B., 'Language, metalanguage and formal system', *The Philosophical Review*, vol. 59, 1950, 346–53.

Davidson, D., *Inquiries into Truth and Interpretation*, Clarendon Press, Oxford, 1984.

Davidson, D., 'Truth and meaning', in J. Kulas *et al.* (eds), *Philosophy, Language and Artificial Intelligence*, Kluwer Academic Publishers, Dordrecht, 1988.

Dennett, D.C., *Brainstorms*, Harvester Press, Hassocks, 1979.

Dretske, F., 'Machines and the mental', *Proc. and Addresses of the American Philosophical Assoc.*, 59, 23–33.

Dummett, M., 'What is a theory of meaning?', in *Mind and Language*, ed. Samuel Guttenplan, Clarendon Press, Oxford, 1975, 97–138.

Dummett, M., *Elements of Intuitionism*, Clarendon Press, Oxford, 1977.

Dummett, M., 'What do I know when I know a language?' Lecture held at the Centenary Celebrations of the Stockholm University, 1978.

Dummett, M., 'Reply to Dag Prawitz', in Taylor, B.M. (ed.), *Michael Dummett. Contributions to Philosophy*, Martinus Nijhoff, Dordrecht, 1987.

Evans, G. and McDowell, J. (eds), *Truth and Meaning. Essays in Semantics*. Clarendon Press, Oxford, 1976.

Fetzer, J.H. (ed.), *Aspects of Artificial Intelligence*, Kluwer Academic Publishers, Dordrecht, 1988.

Fodor, J.F., *The Language of Thought*, Thomas Y. Crowell Co., New York, 1975.

Frege, G., *Die Grundlagen der Arithmetik*, Verlag von Wilhelm Koebner, Breslau, 1884.

Gödel, K., 'On undecidable propositions of formal mathematical systems' (1934), in M. Davis (ed.), *The Undecidable*, Raven Press, New York, 1965.

Grassmann, H., *Die Ausdehnungslehre von 1844 oder Die lineale Ausdehnungslehre*, Leipzig, 1878.

Haaparanta, L., 'Analysis as the method of logical discovery: some remarks on Frege and Husserl', *Synthese*, vol. 77, 1988, 73–97.

Harris, R., *The Language Machine*, Cornell University Press, New York, 1987.

Herbrand, J., *Recherches sur la théorie de la démonstration*, Travaux de la Société des Sciences et des Lettres de Varsovie, Classe III sciences mathématiques et physiques, no. 33, 1930.

Herbrand, J., 'On the consistency of arithmetic', in J. van Heijenoort, (ed.), *From Frege to Gödel*, Harvard University Press, Cambridge, Mass., 1977, 618–28.

Heyting, A., *Intuitionism: An Introduction*, North-Holland, Amsterdam, 1956.

Hilbert, D., 'Axiomatisches Denken', *Mathematische Annalen* 78, 1918, 405–15.

Hilbert, D., 'On the infinite', in J. van Heijenoort (ed.), *From Frege to Gödel*, 367–92.

Hilbert, D., 'The foundations of mathematics', in van Heijenoort, *From Frege to Gödel*, 466–79.

Hilbert, D. and Bernays, P., *Grundlagen der Mathematik I*, 2nd edn, Springer-Verlag, Berlin, 1968.

Hintikka, J., 'On the development of the model-theoretic viewpoint in logical theory', *Synthese*, 77, 1988, 1–36.

Hintikka, M.B. and Hintikka, J., *Investigating Wittgenstein*, Basil Blackwell, Oxford, 1986.

Hofstadter, D.R., *Gödel, Escher, Bach: An Eternal Golden Braid*, Harmondsworth, Penguin Books, 1982.

Husserl, E., 'Philosophie als strenge Wissenschaft', *Logos*, vol. I, 1910–11, 289–341. Translated as 'Philosophy as Rigorous Science' in E. Husserl, *Phenomenology and the Crisis of Philosophy*, Lauer, Q. (trans.), Harper & Row, New York, 1965, 71–147.

BIBLIOGRAPHY

Husserl, E., *Logische Untersuchungen*, vol. II, part 1, ch. 4, rev. second edn, 1913.

Katz, J.J. and Fodor J.A., 'The structure of a semantic theory', *Language*, vol. 38, 1962, 170–210.

Kelly, K.T., 'Artificial intelligence and effective epistemology', in Fetzer, *Aspects of Artificial Intelligence*, 309–22.

Kleene, S.C., *Introduction to Metamathematics*, North-Holland, Amsterdam, 1967.

Kripke, S., *Wittgenstein on Rules and Private Language*, Basil Blackwell, Oxford, 1982.

Levinson, S.C., *Pragmatics*, Cambridge University Press, Cambridge, 1983.

Lyotard, J.-F., *The Differend, Phrases in Dispute*, G. Van Den Abbeele (trans.), Manchester University Press, Manchester, 1988.

Martin-Löf, P., *Intuitionistic Type Theory*, Bibliopolis, Napoli, 1984.

Martin-Löf, P., 'Truth of a proposition, evidence of a judgement, validity of a proof', *Synthese*, vol. 73, 1987, 407–20.

Montague, R., 'Universal grammar', *Theoria*, 36, 1970, 373–98.

Moor, J.H., 'The pseudorealization fallacy and the Chinese room argument' in Fetzer, *Aspects of Artificial Intelligence* 35–53.

Nelson, R.J., 'Church's thesis and cognitive science', *Notre Dame Journal of Formal Logic*, vol. 28, no. 4, October 1987, 581–614.

Pap, A., *An Introduction to the Philosophy of Science*, The Free Press, New York, 1962.

Poincaré, H., 'Les Mathématiques et la logique', *Revue de métaphysique et de morale*, vol. 13, 1905, 815–35, vol. 14, 1906, 17–34, 294–317.

Prawitz, D., 'Dummett on a theory of meaning and its impact on logic', in B.M. Taylor, (ed.), *Michael Dummett. Contributions to Philosophy*, Martinus Nijhoff, Dordrecht, 1987.

Putnam, H., *Mathematics, Matter and Method, Philosophical Papers*, volume I, second edn, Cambridge University Press, Cambridge, 1979.

Quine, W.v.O., *Mathematical Logic*, revised edn., Harper & Row, New York, 1951.

Quine, W.v.O., *Word and Object*, MIT Press, Cambridge, Mass.,1960.

Rapaport, W.J., 'Syntactic semantics: foundations of computational natural-language understanding', in Fetzer, *Aspects of Artificial Intelligence*, 81–131.

Russell, B. *Introduction to Mathematical Philosophy*, Allen & Unwin, London, 1919.

Russell, B. and Whitehead, A.N., *Principia Mathematica*, vol. 1, 2nd edn., Cambridge University Press, Cambridge, 1950.

Sayre, K.M., *Recognition: A Study in the Philosophy of Artificial Intelligence*, University of Notre Dame Press, Notre Dame, Indiana, 1965.

Searle, J.R., 'Minds, brains, and programs', *The Behavioral and Brain Sciences*, vol. 3, 1980, 417–24, 450–7.

Searle, J.R., *Intentionality, An Essay in the Philosophy of Mind*, Cambridge University Press, Cambridge, 1983.

Searle, J.R., *Minds, Brains and Science*, Harvard University Press, Cambridge, Mass., 1984.

BIBLIOGRAPHY

Segerdahl, P., *En kritik av den logiska ordningen i pragmatiken*, Department of Linguistics, Uppsala University, Uppsala, 1988.

Shanker, S., *Wittgenstein and the Turning-Point in the Philosophy of Mathematics*, Croom Helm, London, 1987.

Shanker, S., 'The decline and fall of the mechanist metaphor' in Born, *Artificial Intelligence, the Case Against*, 72–131.

Shanker, S., 'Wittgenstein versus Turing on the nature of Church's thesis', *Notre Dame Journal of Formal Logic*, vol. 28, no. 4, October 1987, 615–49.

Shanker. S., 'Wittgenstein's remarks on the significance of Gödel's theorem', in S.G. Shanker (ed.), *Gödel's Theorem in Focus*, Croom Helm, London, 1988.

Shapiro, S.C., 'Representing numbers in semantic networks: Prolegomena', *Proc. 5th Internat. Joint Conference on AI (IJCAI-77MIT)*, Morgan Kaufmann, Los Altos, 1977.

Shoenfield, J.R., *Mathematical Logic*, Addison-Wesley, London, 1967.

Stenlund, S., 'On the concept of language in some recent theories of meaning', *Synthese*, 79, 1989, 51–98.

Stenlund. S., *Undersökningar i Matematikens Filosofi*, Bokförlaget Thales, Stockholm, 1988.

Tarski, A., 'The semantic conception of truth', *Philosophy and Phenomenological Research* 4, 341–75.

Tarski, A., 'The concept of truth in formalized languages', in *Logic, Semantics, Metamathematics*, Clarendon Press, Oxford, 1956, 152–278.

Turing, A.M., 'Computing machinery and intelligence', *Mind*, vol. 59, no. 236, 1950, 433–60.

van Heijenoort, J. (ed.), *From Frege to Gödel: A Source Book in Mathematical Logic, 1879–1931, Harvard University Press*, Cambridge, Mass., 1977.

Wang, H., *A Survey of Mathematical Logic*, North-Holland, Amsterdam, 1963.

Wang, H., *From Mathematics to Philosophy*, Humanities Press, New York, 1974.

Webb, J.C., *Mechanism, Mentalism, and Metamathematics. An Essay on Finitism*, Reidel, Dordrecht, 1980.

Weyl, H., 'Comments on Hilbert's second lecture on the foundations of mathematics', in van Heijenoort, *From Frege to Gödel*, 482–3.

Winograd, T. 'Is realism for real? – A response to John Perry's seminar', *CSLI Monthly*, vol. 2, no. 5, 1987.

Wittgenstein, L., *Tractatus Logico-Philosophicus*, D.F. Pears and B.F. McGuinness (trans.), Routledge & Kegan Paul, London, 1961.

Wittgenstein, L., *Philosophical Investigations*, G.E.M. Anscombe (trans.), Basil Blackwell, Oxford, 1974.

Wittgenstein, L., *Remarks on the Foundations of Mathematics*, G.H. von Wright, R. Rhees and G.E.M. Anscombe (eds), G.E.M. Anscombe (trans.), 2nd edn, Basil Blackwell, Oxford, 1989.

INDEX

227

For Product Safety Concerns and Information please contact our EU
representative GPSR@taylorandfrancis.com Taylor & Francis Verlag GmbH,
Kaufingerstraße 24, 80331 München, Germany

Printed and bound by CPI Group (UK) Ltd, Croydon, CR0 4YY
08/06/2025
01897003-0006